Sixty-Five Years of British Childhood

ALSO AVAILABLE FROM BLOOMSBURY

Historical Perspectives on Infant Care and Development, Amanda Norman

Early Childhood and Neuroscience, 2nd edition, Mine Conkbayir

Early Childhood Theories and Contemporary Issues, Mine Conkbayir and Christine Pascal

Children's Transitions in Everyday Life and Institutions, edited by Mariane Hedegaard and Marilyn Fleer

Reimagining Childhood Studies, edited by Spyros Spyrou, Rachel Rosen and Daniel Thomas Cook

Research Methods for Early Childhood Education, Rosie Flewitt and Lynn Ang

Researching Everyday Childhoods, Rachel Thomson, Liam Berriman and Sara Bragg

Sixty-Five Years of British Childhood

1959–2024 Unequal Change

Philip Graham

BLOOMSBURY ACADEMIC
LONDON • NEW YORK • OXFORD • NEW DELHI • SYDNEY

BLOOMSBURY ACADEMIC
Bloomsbury Publishing Plc, 50 Bedford Square, London, WC1B 3DP, UK
Bloomsbury Publishing Inc, 1359 Broadway, New York, NY 10018, USA
Bloomsbury Publishing Ireland, 29 Earlsfort Terrace, Dublin 2, D02 AY28, Ireland

BLOOMSBURY, BLOOMSBURY ACADEMIC and the Diana logo
are trademarks of Bloomsbury Publishing Plc

First published in Great Britain 2026

Cover design by Paul Smith
Cover image: FPG and Oliver Rossi via Getty Images

A catalogue record for this book is available from the British Library.

A catalog record for this book is available from the Library of Congress.

ISBN: HB: 978-1-350-57373-4
PB: 978-1-350-57372-7
ePDF: 978-1-350-57374-1
eBook: 978-1-350-57375-8

Typeset by Integra Software Services Pvt. Ltd.
Printed and bound in Great Britain

For product safety-related questions contact productsafety@bloomsbury.com.

To find out more about our authors and books visit www.bloomsbury.com
and sign up for our newsletters.

To my own children and grandchildren, Anna, Daniel, David, Esther, Sophie, Sam, Harry and George.

BY THE SAME AUTHOR

Non-fiction

Child Psychiatry: A Developmental Approach, 2nd Ed

Neuropsychiatric Disorders of Childhood, (with Michael Rutter and William Yule)

Preschool to School: A Behavioural Study, (with Naomi Richman and Jim Stevenson)

So Young, So Sad, So Listen, 3rd Ed, (with Nick Midgley)

The End of Adolescence

Where There Is No Child Psychiatrist, (with Valsa Eapen and Shoba Srinath)

Susan Isaacs: Freeing the Minds of Children, 2nd Ed

Men and Sex: A Sexual Script Approach

Mary Warnock: Ethics, Education and Public Policy in Post-war Britain

Going Gentle: A Guide to a Better Terminal Illness

Fiction

The Ages of Desire

Edited

Epidemiological Approaches in Child Psychiatry

Cognitive Behaviour Therapy for Children and Families, 2nd Ed

CONTENTS

PREFACE

This book is an account of the way children's lives changed in the sixty-five years from 1959 to 2024 when I began to write it. It is specifically aimed at people taking master's courses in psychology, teaching, social work, nursing and child health, but I hope it will also be of interest to a general readership. It is intended to help explain why children's lives came to be as they are today.

All books have a story, and the story behind this book is a very personal one. The reader may reasonably ask why my history of childhood begins in 1959. On 1 July 1959, shortly after qualifying as a medical doctor, I began my first job as a very junior house physician on the Children's Department of University College Hospital, London. At that time, the Department was staffed by a small medical team. There were two consultant paediatricians, my 'bosses'. Between them and me were two doctors-in-training, a senior registrar and a registrar, both very supportive. They needed to be. I really didn't have a clue what I was supposed to be doing. There were about twenty paediatric beds, and a neonatal ward with six very premature babies, nursed in incubators. Some of my time was spent in Casualty, when children were brought in as emergencies.

As well as taking the stories from mothers of new admissions, examining the patients and ordering relevant investigations, my main responsibility was to ensure that, when the consultants did their rounds, once or twice a week, I could give a coherent account of the history, physical examination and investigations of the inpatients so that the consultants could make a diagnosis and decide on the future management of the child. The registrar told me to be thorough but not too thorough. One of my consultants was disappointed and unhappy if he could not point out an investigation that had not been ordered but should have been. So, if I wanted to be in his good books, I should always omit an investigation so that he could suggest it. I had to be good, but not perfect.

Most of my time was spent tramping between my children's ward on the fourth floor of the hospital, other wards on which sick children were being nursed, the outpatients department, the various pathology laboratories and the X-ray department to make sure that the consultants had the very latest results on their patients when they did their rounds. I spent some time in Casualty, which was in another part of the hospital. The soles of my feet were so sore with walking, that, at night, I would put surgical spirit on them to harden the skin. I was on call all the time, twenty-four hours a day. Over the six months in this post, I had three evenings and two weekends off. This wasn't quite as exhausting as it sounds as, most of the time, my nights were uninterrupted. Most of my night-time calls were from the neonatal unit. A Nigerian nurse would wake me up about once a week in the early hours with a message I could not understand, so I would dress and race to the unit, nearly always to be told that some extremely low-weight baby had died, and I needed to certify the death.

But it was extremely tiring. On one of my two weekends off, I went home, arriving on the Saturday morning, and my mother cooked me a splendid lunch. While she was fetching it from the kitchen, I fell asleep, my head and shoulders sprawled over the kitchen table. She woke me, I ate my lunch and then went to sleep from mid-afternoon until the following morning. These extremely long working hours were par for the course for junior doctors until 1988 when the European directive on doctors' working hours came into force. Even so, it was not until the early 2000s that working hours were properly limited. The limitation of these working hours has had mixed effects. No longer are patients looked after by dog-tired doctors, but the fact that young hospital doctors have only limited contact with patients means they lose out on learning as much as they did about the course of illness and children and families lose out because of the lack of continuity of care.

After my six months' stint as a junior paediatrician, I spent three years working with adults, first in general medicine and surgery and then in general psychiatry, training at the Maudsley Hospital in south London. But it had always been my aim to work as a child psychiatrist; that was why I had studied medicine. So, in January 1963, I began to train in child and adolescent psychiatry. Since that time, until mid-2024, for sixty-five years, I worked almost continuously with children. After completing my psychiatric and child psychiatric training, I had the good fortune to be selected by Michael Rutter, a colleague a little senior to me, to work as his research assistant. He was obviously destined for a stellar career, and indeed, later in 1987, he was the first psychiatrist since Sigmund Freud to be elected a Fellow of the Royal Society.

I worked with him for four years from 1964 to 1968 on two major projects. The Isle of Wight Study was a groundbreaking population survey of the behaviour and educational achievement of nine- to fourteen-year-old children (Rutter, Tizard and Whitmore 1970, Rutter, Graham and Yule 1970). The Family Illness study, led jointly by Michael Rutter and George Brown, a pioneering social psychologist, was a study of the impact on children of mental illness in one or both parents. This research experience was invaluable. It gave me the unusual opportunity of administering psychiatric interviews to 'normal' children.

While working on these projects, I was appointed medical director of the Brixton Child Guidance Unit, which served a large West Indian migrant population. I began to carry out and publish my own research (Graham and Meadows 1967). Then, in 1968, I was appointed head of the Department of Psychological Medicine at the Hospital for Sick Children, Great Ormond Street, London (GOS). This gave me the opportunity to appoint some highly gifted colleagues, including Arnon Bentovim, Richard Lansdown, Bryan Lask, Jim Stevenson and Naomi Richman, who developed new services and greatly expanded the research programme of the Department. Naomi Richman and Jim Stevenson carried out the first population survey of behaviour and emotional problems in pre-school children (Richman, Stevenson and Graham 1982).

In 1974, I was appointed to a personal chair of Child Psychiatry at the Institute of Child Health (ICH), the postgraduate medical school linked to GOS. This led to involvement in a number of other organizations which greatly enlarged my experience. I acted as a psychiatrist to a school for autistic children for over twenty years in the 1970s and 1980s. From 1974 to 1978, I was a member of the Department of Education Committee on Special Education, chaired by Mary Warnock, who became a good friend. In 1976, I was appointed specialist adviser in Child Psychiatry to the chief medical officer. In 1977, I became consultant to the WHO Child Mental Health programme. This led to numerous consultancies in economically underdeveloped countries overseas, especially in Southeast Asia. From 1987 to 1991, I was president of the European Society for Child and Adolescent Psychiatry (ESCAP). In 1993, I was appointed to the Video Appeals Committee of the British Board of Film Classification.

I had always worked closely with paediatricians at GOS and had been the founding convenor of the Psychology and Psychiatry Special Interest Group of the British Paediatric Association. In 1985, I was appointed dean (director) of ICH, then, as now, the largest paediatric research institution in Europe. This was a major responsibility, and I was able to make some key senior appointments. In 1990, I resigned from this position and left GOS altogether in 1994.

In the thirty years after my leaving GOS and ICH, I have remained involved in work with and around children. From 1994 to 2000, I was chair of the National Children's Bureau, an organization providing advice on child policy to successive governments. Over the same period, I worked as a part-time professor in child psychiatry at the University of Oslo, Norway. I was chair of the organization Child and Adolescent Mental Health in 2001–3. I have acted as school governor to two schools, one secondary academy and one for children with special needs situated in the socially deprived area of Tottenham, north London.

I have continued to write and edit books relating to children. Over recent years, I've edited and co-edited three editions of *Cognitive Behaviour Therapy for Children and Families* (Graham and Reynolds 2013), jointly written a manual on child mental health for primary care workers in developing countries (Eapen, Graham and Srinath, 2012) and a guide for parents with a depressed child (Graham and Midgley 2020), as well as two biographies of influential twentieth-century educationists, Mary Warnock (Graham 2021) and Susan Isaacs (Graham 2023). This account of British childhood from 1959 seems a natural extension and probably a natural conclusion to my work with children over the years.

Acknowledgements

I am most grateful to the following who have made valuable comments on draft chapters.

Arnon Bentovim, Robert Boyd, Robert Cassen, Cyril Chantler, Stephan Collishaw, Bernard Donoughue, Derek Gillard, Danya Glaser, Anna Graham, David Graham, Nori Graham, Annie Hudson, Tara Midgen, Peter Mortimore, Jane Shallice, Sufian Sadiq and Dan Weisselberg. During the whole of the writing of this book, Sophie Wheeler has been a most helpful research assistant.

1

The Adult World

For a whole variety of reasons, 1959 is an excellent year to begin an account of modern childhood: it was a key moment in the lives of British children. In this chapter, I shall describe the main changes in British society over sixty-five years, insofar as they affected the lives of children. I shall not attempt to cover those events, such as the Suez crisis and the Falklands War which, although of great significance politically, did not directly impinge on the lives of children. Thus, this chapter describes the social context provided by the adult world that formed the background to the world in which children grew up.

Emergence from the Second World War

In 1959, the brooding aftermath of the Second World War that had ended fourteen years earlier was only just coming to an end. The parents of the children who were ten years old in 1959 had mostly been born between the beginning of the First World War in 1914 and the beginning of the Second World War in 1939. These had been traumatic years. After the horrors of the First World War with its slaughter of so many young men came a short period of slow growth and then the deep economic depression of the 1930s with very high rates of unemployment and searing poverty. The experience of those parents who had lived through the wartime years between 1939 and 1945 would remain with them often as the most memorable part of their lives. Many of their lives had been directly and sometimes tragically affected by the war. A sizeable number had been separated from their own parents during their childhood, either because their fathers had been called up to serve in one of the armed forces or because they had been evacuated from one of the large cities or perhaps for both of these reasons. A sizeable minority of their parents had been killed either on active service or as a result of bombing raids. Many others had had friends their own age who had lost a parent in this way. Nor were wartime experiences the only traumatic events this parental generation had undergone.

The numerous forms of deprivation resulting from the Second World War were only now coming to an end. Food rationing had only stopped in the mid-1950s. Now all sorts of vegetables and fruits, such as oranges, pineapples and bananas, that had been in short supply or, for some years, completely unattainable, were easily available. Though the menu was likely to be unexciting, if you could afford it, you could go out to eat in a restaurant. National Service, another aftermath of the Second World War, did not end until 1960, with the last conscript being discharged in 1963. This meant that up to that date, all young men, except the small number who were exempt, had to spend eighteen months or two years in the armed forces learning initially how to march on parade and then, as far as many were concerned, how to kill an enemy. Parents knew that also meant they had to get used to the idea their sons might themselves be killed. In the 1950s, national servicemen had been killed in the Korean War, dealing with the uprising in Malaya and in the action to quell the Mau Mau rebellion in Kenya. Gradually, as the years went on and no further major wars occurred, parents became less anxious they would lose their children through death in wartime.

But very shortly after the end of the Second World War came the launch of the 'Cold War', the unarmed conflict between the Soviet Union and the Western powers. The existence of the atomic bomb meant that there was always a fear that this would be used. This occurred especially in 1963 with the Cuban missile crisis. Children's drawings and the essays they wrote at this time revealed very clearly that they had been affected by the fears of their parents. The 'Cold War' lasted until 1991, when the Soviet Union collapsed only to arise in threatening form in the 2020s with the Russian invasion of Ukraine. The global angst of the 1950s and 1960s was not to recur until the twenty-first century when fears of global warming were also transmitted from parent to child and continued to do so at least until the mid-2020s.

The economic climate

The social climate in which children grow up is greatly influenced by the economic conditions of their time. Rates of adult unemployment, the ease or difficulty with which their parents can provide adequate housing and put food on the table, all these make real differences to the quality of life of their children.

In the late 1950s through most of the 1960s, the UK was in a state of relative, if precarious prosperity. In 1957, Harold Macmillan, campaigning to be prime minister, claimed: 'Go around the country, go to the industrial towns, go to the farms and you will see a state of prosperity such as we have never had in my lifetime, nor indeed in the history of this country.' 'You have', he proclaimed, 'Never had it so good.' In the 1960s, first under a Conservative administration and then, with Harold Wilson as Labour prime minister, the UK continued to be at least superficially economically successful. GDP growth averaged around 3.5 per cent, unemployment was at a low level and inflation was maintained at the low level of 2.5–3 per cent. Real disposable income was 25 per cent higher at the end of the 1960s than it had been at the end of the 1950s. Private car ownership became much more common, with the number of licensed cars increasing from 4 million in 1950 to 10 million in 1967. Unfortunately, the mobility of the car-less was significantly reduced in the 1960s as a result of the publication of the government-inspired Beeching Report, which resulted in drastic cuts in train services, especially on routes serving rural areas.

During the 1950s and 1960s, more and more families went away on holiday, though it was not until the 1990s that budget air travel underwent its great expansion, making holidays abroad accessible to many more. Nevertheless, in the 1950s and 1960s, the relatively cheap holidays offered at holiday camps such as Butlins and Pontins which catered particularly for families with children, made it possible for holidays in the UK to be affordable to many more (see Chapter 6).

Towards the end of the 1960s, the period of post-war stability and prosperity came to an end. In 1967, it was necessary to devalue the pound. Inflation and unemployment began to rise. Economic growth started to falter. During the mid-1970s, rising inflation led to increases in the cost of living and demands from the powerful trade unions for increased wages for their members. Strike action became much more frequent, culminating in the 1978–9 'winter of discontent' when rubbish piled high in the streets with strikes by refuse collectors and even grave diggers. Income inequality greatly increased, especially as the trade unions, while succeeding in maintaining the wages of their skilled manual workers, neglected to insist on increases in the incomes of the low-paid and single parents, at the bottom of the economic pile.

Margaret Thatcher became prime minister in May 1979 with a very different political philosophy from her predecessors. She espoused the idea of a free market, with a largely uncontrolled economy through tight control of the money supply, privatization and refusal to give in to the demands of the unions. Taxes were markedly reduced with the top rate of tax reduced from 88 per cent to 60 per cent benefitting the well-off. A simultaneous rise in value-added tax (VAT) was imposed which disproportionately hit people on lower incomes. The immediate effects of these policies were highly negative for the poor, though much more positive for the better-off sections of the population. The rate of unemployment more than doubled over the first five years of Thatcher's premiership with a similar doubling of the relative poverty rate, though by the end of the 1990s it had returned to pre-Thatcher levels. Measured by the Gini coefficient, income inequality, which had been relatively stable during the 1950s and 1960s, rose sharply during the 1980s, returning to relative stability with only slight increases during the 1990s and 2000s.

In 1984–5, the industrial unrest in the Midlands, the northeast and northwest of England, Scotland and Northern Ireland led to the closure of much of the industrial heartlands of the country with very high levels of unemployment, especially in the regions affected by government policies (Payne 2021). Little attempt was made to find alternative work for those who lost their jobs. In contrast, the 'big bang' of 1986, which deregulated the London financial market, resulted in a massive increase in the prosperity of bankers of all types, lawyers and accountants in London and the southeast of England.

The 1990s under the premiership of John Major saw a gradual return to economic stability so that Tony Blair inherited a very reasonable financial position when he was elected prime minister in 1997. There was a major increase in spending on health and education with general improvements in these and other public services. A minimum wage was introduced which made a very significant impact on levels of child poverty with half a million children being lifted out of poverty between 1989 and 2007. The achievement of an almost complete peace between the factions in Northern Ireland in 1999 brought an end to many decades of conflict which had seriously impaired the lives of many children.

However, in 2008, the recession in the United States triggered by over-reliance on unsupported lending led to severe economic repercussions throughout the banking world. The UK plunged into a serious debt crisis. The Coalition government elected in 2010, inaccurately blaming the Labour government for the dire financial situation, opted to deal with this by an 'austerity' programme, basically cutting all public services and financial benefits to the poor and disadvantaged. The resultant increases in income inequality, exacerbated by COVID-19 and the war in Ukraine, persisted over the following fourteen years until the end of the period covered by this book. These financial measures together with a significant rise in the cost of living selectively hit families with poor children, so that the rate of child poverty increased from 3.6 million in 2010/11 to a record 4.3 million in 2022/3. In 2017, the situation of a number of these families was exacerbated by the imposition of a two-child cap on those receiving child benefit and tax credits.

Social class

For a variety of reasons, at the beginning of our period, in the late 1950s, the rigid social class structure which had always characterized British society had begun to weaken. Social class, then as throughout, was measured mainly by income and occupation. The correlation between these two criteria gradually diminished, so that many of those in manual occupations such as plumbers and electricians earned more than, for example, white-collar workers such as nurses and teachers. The number of people regarding themselves as middle class slowly increased. While it is not possible to calculate changes in the size of the different social classes from the national census data, in 1951, 28 per cent of the population regarded themselves as middle class (Kynaston 2009, p.144) compared to 36 per cent in the 2021 national census (Office for National Statistics 2022).

The deference from those lower down in the hierarchy to the so-called 'upper' classes markedly reduced in the early years of this period. In 1961, the popular, iconoclastic West End and Broadway review *Beyond the Fringe* openly mocked the Eton and Oxford-educated prime minister, Harold Macmillan, who attended one of their performances, in a manner that would hitherto have been considered unthinkable. Popular television programmes such as *Not the Nine-o-Clock News* (1979–82) and *Spitting Image* (1984–96) made fun of leading politicians, showing little or no respect for them. There was much criticism of the hereditary peerage system which determined the membership of the House of Lords; life peerages based on public service had been introduced in 1958. In 1999, shortly after the election of the New Labour government in 1997, the House of Lords Act removed all but a hundred of the hereditary peers.

However, the hereditary nature of the Royal Family remained relatively unquestioned. Prince Charles's marriage to Diana in 1981 brought a highly popular, indeed adored new member into the Royal Family. Diana's work with worthy charitable causes such as the treatment of HIV and landmines and the way she was treated by her husband brought her massive support so that when she died as a result of a traffic accident in August 1997, many members of the general public felt personally bereaved. The hesitant way the queen acknowledged her death led to a decline in support for the Royal Family, but this was fairly rapidly reversed, so that by the time the queen died in 2022, her funeral was an occasion for great national mourning. A very modest amount of republican feeling was occasionally expressed, but the organization representing those who wished to see the monarchy abolished, Republic UK, which was founded in 1983, only had 9,000 members in 2023.

Reduction of deference occurred at all levels of society. Perhaps the most pervasive reduction in deference in British society was gender deference. Gradually, over the years, women's voices became more assertive until by the 2020s, in most spheres of life, they were equally vocal. An illuminating example is with driving licences. In 2024, about 80 per cent of men held driving licences, compared to 70 per cent of women. In the 1950s, 35 per cent of men had held driving licences and only 10 per cent of women. As another example, as time went on, doctors were no longer put on a pedestal and found their opinions more frequently questioned. The sharing between the social classes of taste in popular music, such as reggae, helped break down class barriers. Many of the originally working-class children who put British pop at the top of the musical charts had attended grammar schools in the 1940s and 1950s where they had been taught to play musical instruments. Throughout the period in question, but particularly from the 1970s onwards, comprehensive schools provided the opportunity for children from very different backgrounds to form important friendships. Before the 1970s, the separation of children at 11 years into those attending grammar and those attending secondary modern schools had further entrenched class differences (see Chapter 5). Further, the socially privileged remained dominant in politics and the professions. Independent or private schools right up to the 2020s continued to supply far more than their fair share of cabinet ministers, top doctors and high court judges. Despite efforts to redress the balance, Oxbridge colleges still admitted far more young people from independent schools than their size warranted. Right up to the end of our period, social class had far from disappeared as a determinant of occupational and financial success. It was only after the 2024 General Election in which Labour won a massive majority that there was a significant reduction in both members of parliament and cabinet members who had been educated at independent schools.

Immigration and racism

While from Roman times and probably beforehand, there have always been immigrants to Britain, the levels of inward migration increased considerably from the 1890s until the end of our period. The successive waves of migration are described in Chapter 8. Each migrant group included children and young people who usually came with one or both parents but occasionally alone. The groups always brought their own cultural beliefs and practices. They integrated and retained their own lifestyles to very varying degrees. In reaction to such migration, racist attitudes and sometimes violent racist behaviour developed in the 1950s and 1960s in response to the presence of newcomers, especially those of the Windrush generation from the West Indies. In reaction to such racism, in 1965 the Race Relations Act banned racial discrimination in public places and made the promotion of hatred on the grounds of 'colour, race, or ethnic or national origins' an offence. This Bill improved the situation but by no means brought racism to an end, a blight on the lives of many children from ethnic minority families. The Race Relations Amendment Act 2000 imposed a statutory duty on public bodies to promote racial equality and demonstrate that procedures to prevent race discrimination were effective. Nevertheless, major race riots occurred in Toxteth and Brixton in 1981, on Broadwater Farm in Tottenham in 1985 and as late as 2024, following the killing of three little girls, in Southport. Such negative discrimination as well as progress towards assimilation is described further in Chapter 8.

In contrast, however, there was a very considerable improvement over the decades in the numbers of members of ethnic minorities entering and rising in the ranks of the liberal professions of law and medicine. In 2024, 14 per cent of members of parliament were from ethnic minorities, a proportion roughly equivalent to their representation in the UK.

Welfare state

Article 25 of the UN Declaration of Human Rights (1945) to which the UK was a signatory states:

> Everyone has the right to a standard of living adequate for the health and wellbeing of himself and his family, including food, clothing, housing and medical care and necessary social services and the right to security in the event of unemployment, sickness, disability, widowhood, old age or other lack of livelihood in circumstances beyond his control.

This right to a basic standard of living was reinforced by the leading political philosopher of the second half of the twentieth century, John Rawls, who declared that when national resources are redistributed, this should be done in a way that is 'to be of the greatest benefit of the least advantaged members of society' (Chandler 2023, p.21).

By the late 1950s, though this process had begun in the first decade of the twentieth century under Liberal governments, the structure of a 'welfare state' had been further put in place by the 1945 Labour government and maintained by subsequent Conservative administrations. The Beveridge Report (1942) had recommended that the 'five giants' (want, disease, ignorance, squalor and idleness) that damaged individual well-being should be vanquished by state intervention (Timmins 1995). In particular, sufficient state benefits should be made available to ensure that individuals, including parents, at risk of hardship particularly because of illness, disability or unemployment, should be given financial benefits to enable them to achieve a reasonable standard of living compared to the rest of the population. The 1940s saw major changes to the welfare state in the UK. Within two or three years, the National Insurance Act (1946) and the National Assistance Act (1948) were put into effect. For many people, the Beveridge Report which foreshadowed most of these reforms had iconic status. The implications for the effects of this legislation on inequality were not as clear-cut as those who framed it had hoped and are still not entirely clear (Crafts 2024). In retrospect, however, the 1960s have been regarded as the golden age of welfare. At this time, Family Allowances were paid to all families with more than one child. This was a universal benefit and was not taxed. It was expanded to include the first child in 1975 and replaced by child benefits in 1977. The benefit was, however, subject to taxation from 2013, after which the number of child benefit claimants declined. In 2017, as part of the austerity programme, a two-child cap was placed on the number of children eligible for child benefit, putting more families with larger numbers of children into poverty.

During the second half of the twentieth century, the welfare bill gradually increased to levels not previously envisaged, and the welfare system became more complicated. A controversial attempt was made to simplify the system in 2013 with the introduction of Universal Credit. This replaced six means tested benefits, including housing benefit, income support, child tax credits and working tax credits. There were significant cuts in the level of benefits paid to poor people during the austerity years of 2010–20 (see above).

That there was rising affluence, an increase in the ownership of material goods (see below) and a significant benefit system should, however, not hide the fact that poverty remained widespread during the whole of the period in question. Indeed, the COVID-19 epidemic, the rise in the cost of living as a result of the war in Ukraine and the negative effect of Brexit meant that the period from 2020 to 2024 also saw a significant rise in the number of poor families. Food banks were used by tiny numbers of people in the early years of the twenty-first century. Fewer than a million people were using them in 2013, but over three million by 2023 (Trussell Trust 2024).

The NHS

By 1959, the population had become used to the idea that, following the 1948 establishment of the National Health Service, one did not have to pay to see a doctor either in general practice or in a hospital. In fact, the principle of free health care was rapidly breached. In 1951, charges were made for dentures, and in 1952, a charge was made for all dental treatment though there was no charge for children's medical or dental care. A very high proportion of health care remained free, and relatively few people took out insurance to pay privately for health care. For most of our period, around 10 per cent of the population had private health insurance but the number climbed to 19 per cent in 2019, increasing to 22 per cent in 2023.

The cost of the NHS to the Treasury increased very sharply during the last half of the twentieth century for a variety of reasons. Health care costs increase with age, and the ageing of the population was a major factor. In addition, patients were more intensively investigated by more expensive methods, often requiring skilled and time-consuming imaging techniques. Finally, many terminally ill patients who would previously have been transferred to non-hospital beds in the residential sector had to stay in expensive hospital beds because there were no beds available in social care.

One of the innovations introduced in 1991 to reduce costs was the so-called 'purchaser-provider divide', which dictated that those commissioning care, especially family doctors, should be given a limited budget. The cost of care they commissioned (investigations, days in hospital, etc.) should be calculated to ensure they did not go 'over budget'. The problem was that calculating and recording costs turned out to be in themselves expensive procedures which reduced the efficiency with which nursing time was spent, so the advantages of the new system were limited.

In its early years, the NHS had the reputation for being one of the most, if not the most, efficient health care systems in the world, but as time went on, the number of doctors and nurses, now mostly recruited from abroad, became insufficient to meet the demand. Waiting lists grew in size so that by 2024, the waiting list for hospital treatment had grown to 7.5 million, with increasing difficulty in meeting the standard 18-week referral to treatment target. (The growth in demand for child mental health services was particularly acute for the reasons described further in Chapter 4.) The quality of primary care became difficult to maintain as a result of recruitment problems. A reduction in continuity of care arose partly from increasing numbers of part-time doctors and partly from the 1988 European Directive on the number of working hours junior doctors were permitted to work. The Labour government made it even more difficult for family doctors to provide continuity of care when, as part of the 2000 NHS plan, they prioritized continuity over an insistence that everyone should be able to see their GP within 48 hours of requesting a consultation.

Housing

Much of the housing in large British cities had been destroyed by bombing, and much that remained was of very poor quality. Bombing during the Second World War was estimated to have destroyed 500,000 homes and many were left badly damaged, especially in cities like London and Coventry. Many houses needed modernization, for example, 500,000 homes did not have an indoor toilet in 1950.

The Attlee government, elected in 1945, in its 'Homes for All' policy attempted to solve this problem by building 1.2 million new homes, all social housing for rent by councils, between 1946 and 1951. A substantial proportion of these, about one in ten, were so-called prefabricated houses or homes built for only temporary accommodation, though many lasted much longer than was originally intended. There was then a lull in house building but the shortfall of supply of affordable homes became obvious. In 1957, Harold Macmillan was elected prime minister partly on the basis of his promise to build 100,000 houses a year. A major house building programme was put in place so that the number of available council houses increased and their quality improved. Many families now had an inside toilet for the first time. Much of the new housing was achieved by knocking down slum areas in large cities and replacing them with tower blocks. The flats had no gardens, and the large concrete spaces below the blocks were intended as play areas. The politically progressive nature of housing policy in this period, embedded as it was in the establishment of the Welfare State, was based on the principles of equality of opportunity, equitable distribution of wealth and public responsibility for those unable to avail themselves of the minimal provisions for a good life.

Architecturally, the modernist desire expressed by Le Corbusier, the Swiss architect on whose ideas these tower blocks were constructed, was to provide an environment that was spiritually fulfilling, creating harmony between people and their surroundings and freeing communities from the misery of poor housing. This was consistent with the prevailing political commitment to break away from insanitary, overcrowded slums. It was not, however, as we shall see in Chapter 6, necessarily conducive to a better life for children with the disruption of long-established working-class communities and the increase in the number of cars making it too dangerous for them to play outside their homes in the streets.

After the 1970s, housing construction slowed again and, as we have seen, after the election of Margaret Thatcher as prime minister in 1979, an entirely different political philosophy prevailed. The desire was to give individuals much greater autonomy and to free them from the constraints of local government. The aim was to create a property-owning democracy. Council tenants were given the right to buy their own homes at a sharply discounted rate. The money raised by these sales went largely to central government, and local authorities were restricted in their ability to use their share to build more social housing. The result was a sharp decline in the building of social housing and a reduction in available homes.

By the end of the 1980s, it had become clear that, as a result of these policies, there were nowhere near sufficient homes to meet demand. The 1988 Housing Act tackled this problem by controlling rents and the right of landlords to evict tenants, and by providing support for the establishment of housing associations. From that time, housing associations, often backed by private finance but also by central subsidies, delivered most of the new social homes. Housing associations were not-for-profit organizations that provided affordable housing and support to local communities, often focusing on those with lower incomes or specific needs and were a key provider of social housing. However, social housing providers of all kinds lacked access to the resources and powers needed to come close to meeting housing demand. As a result, council homes were sold off faster than they were replaced, and local authorities were left with just a fraction of the social housing they once had to offer. The situation did not change with the election of the Labour government led by Tony Blair in 1997. Indeed, at the end of New Labour's thirteen years in government, there were 655,000 fewer 'social homes' than when it was first elected.

The second half of the twentieth century saw massive inflation in house prices, especially in London and the southeast of England. This occurred as a result of the establishment of London as an international financial centre, with many of the people who worked in its institutions earning very high incomes. The situation was worsened by an influx of wealthy people from abroad who bought properties in London and the southeast for investment purposes rather than to live in them. The housing affordability situation was aggravated by the large rises in the size of the UK population without any commensurate rise in available housing. The UK population rose by approximately one million each decade during the second half of the twentieth century but by two million during each decade in the twenty-first century (Office for National Statistics 2022). This meant that, from the 1980s onwards, but especially in the twenty-first century, young families could not get their feet onto the bottom rung of the property ladder unless they had substantial help from their parents through what came to be called 'the bank of Mum and Dad'.

The election of the Cameron government in 2010 was followed by the extension of the legal definition of social housing and by legislation intending to increase the number of homes available at affordable rent. But this did nothing to alleviate the housing shortages. Indeed, the deregulation of consumer standards and a lack of investment in good-quality social homes meant that an increasing number of tenants faced health and safety risks in their homes. This became painfully evident in the catastrophic fire at Grenfell Tower in North Kensington, London, in June 2017, in which seventy-two people (including eighteen children) died.

In July 2024, Keir Starmer was elected UK prime minister with a commitment to build 1.5 million new homes over the next five years. In order to achieve this objective, he promised to remove planning restrictions that had previously defeated attempts to increase the UK's supply of affordable housing.

Improvements in the home

The end of the 1950s marked a period of slowly increasing material well-being. By this time, but only by this time, nearly half of all British households either owned or rented a television set. All programmes were shown in black and white, and there were only two channels, the BBC and one ITV channel. Single-tub washing machines became more widely owned by households in the 1950s and twin-tub machines in the 1960s. There were still, however, large numbers of households where washing was done by hand. Dishwashing machines remained costly, and only a minority of households owned one until the 1980s. It was not until the 1970s that the majority of households owned a refrigerator and the late 1990s before most had a fridge freezer. At the beginning of this period, homes were still largely heated by coal fires, with central heating only becoming more common in the 1970s and 1980s.

Before central heating, mothers would spend a significant amount of time before going to bed or first thing in the morning, raking out the ashes and setting the coal fire for relighting. Further, prior to the mid-1950s, mothers had spent much of their week washing and ironing clothes and doing the washing up after meals. The introduction of all these labour-saving devices freed mothers to spend more time with their children and to go out to work, at least part-time.

Between the 1980s and the 2020s, very considerable advances were made in the speed and methods of communication. Early in this period, the first computers for use in the home were made. In 1983, the internet was launched which allowed people to communicate between computer networks and enhanced the availability of information well beyond that which had previously been available. In the late 1990s, mobile phones became available and soon after were linked to the internet. It became possible to 'stream' television programmes, music and then a vast range of programmes produced by streaming companies. Facebook, with its capacity for linking friends and those sharing interests, was followed by the multiple forms of social media platforms. A smaller, more portable form of computer, the iPad, came out in 2010. The numerous ways these developments changed children's lives and how they spent their free time are discussed in Chapter 6.

Employment of mothers of young children

Over this period, a number of women remained childless as a result of their desire to lead an independent life. The majority of women, however, helped by the introduction of labour-saving devices and encouraged by the increasing availability of full- and part-time work, managed to combine motherhood with employment though this was still problematic while their youngest child was under five. All the same, in London, for example, even in 1950, 42 per cent of women with children under the age of five did go out to work (Wilson 2006).

The main reason why mothers of young children went to work was financial: the wish to earn money and enable the family to reach a level of affluence in terms of material possessions that would otherwise not be possible with a single wage-earner. But there were other reasons. Women wanted to have money of their own to spend so that they did not have to ask their partners every time they wanted to buy something. Many found life at home with a young child tedious and boring and so were attracted to the social life in the workplace (Hakim 2004, Table 3.3). Because of the frequent criticism of mothers of young children who worked (see below), the reasons women gave for working were often phrased in terms of their wish to give their children a better life and indeed this often did represent an important motivation. In fact, from the 1950s to the 1970s, there was full employment which meant that women made an important contribution to the gradual expansion of the UK economy.

As the years went on, the opportunities for part-time employment became greater. Understandably, many women preferred part-time to full-time work to fit in with the needs of their children. But initially, opportunities for part-time work were limited. In 1951, only 9 per cent of women were working part-time, while even by 1971, this had increased only to 38 per cent (Wilson 2006). The decision a mother made to go to work affected the life of her child. In terms of the quality of life of the child, this depended on her capacity to find and pay for good substitute care. For those who did, the opportunity to develop independence away from the mother, often in a stimulating environment in a nursery, day nursery, infant school or with a loving relative or child-minder, was a positive experience for the child. For others, substitute care, for example, with a neglectful child-minder or relative, the reverse was the case.

In the 1960s and 1970s, there was a very low level of childcare provided by the state available to mothers who, for one reason or another (usually their wish for employment), wished to have their child looked after outside the family for part of the day. There were three reasons why this was the case (Davis and King 2018). First was the widespread view that children, especially under-fives, were best looked after by their mothers. Second (see below) was the view that children were harmed by separation from their mothers, and thirdly, there was the reluctance of governments, especially in times of economic recession, to make funds available for substitute care. In the twentieth century (until childcare very gradually became more widely available), mothers therefore looked to members of their families, to friends and neighbours and to informal arrangements with professional or unofficial carers to provide substitute care.

In the 1960s, at the time of their birth, a relatively small number of babies had grandmothers who were still alive and fit enough to care for them. The expectation of life of women born in 1900, about the average age that a grandmother would be at this time, was 52, so many would have already died. The average expectation of life of women born in 1960 (about the average year of birth that a grandmother would have at this time) was 74, so many more of them were alive and healthy. Being alive and healthy by no means necessarily meant they were available to look after their grandchildren. Many were still at work, though often working part-time. In the early twenty-first century, one-in-three working mothers relied on grandparents for childcare, and one-in-four of all working families. Forty-three per cent of children under five whose mothers were employed were looked after by grandparents, and 42 per cent aged 5–10, after school, when sick and in school holidays. In 2011, the value of this childcare contribution was estimated at £3.9 billion per year. Grandparental care was most common in poorer families but not exclusive to them. A substantial amount (40 per cent) of grandparental care was provided by grandfathers. Whether grandparental care is more or less common than in the past we do not know because there are no reliable, long-term statistics (Thane 2011). One of the problems with grandparental care was that once their grandchildren reached five years, the need for such care rapidly diminished and this left a hole in the older person's life. All the same, many grandparents continued to help in less demanding ways, and the rich contact in the early years of the child's life meant that a strong grandparent/grandchild relationship often continued throughout the former's life.

For very young children before they became eligible at the age of three to four to enter the tiny numbers of nursery schools that existed, there were, apart from grandparents, various options available as far as substitute childcare was concerned. For better-off parents a nanny, trained or untrained, could be employed in the home. Nannies could be resident or work as au pairs who were often university students from abroad. The child could be placed with a professional child-minder who usually looked after a total of three to six other children, often including their own. Children's centres under local authority control began as part of the SureStart programme in 1998 and usually provided some early years education, advice on child rearing and finding employment as well as counselling for a variety of problems. Day nurseries might be run by the local authority or be private or run by a workplace. They provided care and, for older children, significant education. Pre-school playgroups were usually run by parents on a voluntary basis and offered part-time, often very part-time care. Crèches might be provided in the workplace for young children of employees. For relatively short periods, to enable mothers to go shopping, for example, neighbours or friends might be called upon.

None of the alternatives for substitute childcare while a mother was at work was cheap. In the early 2000s, there was considerable pressure for the state to provide subsidies, and in September 2010, the Department for Education introduced an entitlement to 15 hours of free childcare per week for all three- and four-year-olds in England. In 2025, this was extended to thirty free childcare hours per week for working women who had a child living with them.

The level of employment open to mothers also changed. In the 1950s and 1960s, women were disproportionately employed in relatively unskilled jobs, for example, as cleaners or cooks or on the factory floor. If they were in middle-class occupations, they tended to work in the less well-paid and sometimes less responsible areas of their fields, for example, as secretaries or in lower-level administrative jobs. By the 1980s, many were in more responsible employment. The proportion of women working as solicitors or barristers in the legal profession or as doctors in general practice or as hospital consultants increased significantly. The numbers of women elected to become members of the House of Parliament remained low, but at the 2024 election, it had risen to 41 per cent (Wilson 2006). This meant a considerable change in the role models available to girls as they moved through the education system.

This increase in mothers of young children going out to work occurred in the face of much resistance from 'experts'. Early on, John Bowlby (1958), an eminent psychoanalyst, produced a pamphlet titled 'Can I leave my baby?' In it he claimed that to leave a baby with anyone but a father or close relatives (even in an emergency) imperilled the child, putting it at increased risk of becoming a juvenile delinquent. He based this view quite inappropriately on studies of delinquents separated from their mothers and brought up in institutions. Psychoanalysts were not alone in thinking maternal employment damaged children. Broadly speaking, they were supported by the general public who believed it was appropriate for women to work but not if they had young children (Wilson 2006). It was not until Michael Rutter pointed out that Bowlby had confused separation with neglect and that it was perfectly possible for young children to be separated from their mothers without being neglected, and, if they were, they were in no way at increased risk of developing mental health problems (Rutter 1972). It still took many years for this view to prevail among the general public. As the century progressed, fathers, whether or not their wives went out to work, gradually took on more childcare and domestic responsibilities. While the general belief remained that mothers were the 'experts' in the family and should retain the main responsibility for childcare throughout the whole of childhood but especially in the first five years of a child's life, men's share of the childcare tasks increased though, except in unusual circumstances, remaining smaller than that of mothers (Davis and King 2018, Henz 2019). House or home fathers taking the greater share of childcare remained very much the exception and generally existed when the mother earned significantly more than her partner.

Fertility control

The late 1950s and 1960s were turning points in many aspects of pregnancy and childbirth. In particular, these early decades were important in making it more likely that, when babies were born, they were positively wanted. 1959 was the year in which it was established by Jérome Lejeune, a French geneticist, that Down syndrome, the most common cause of mild and moderate learning difficulties (mental retardation, see Chapter 4), was caused by a chromosomal abnormality (trisomy 21, the presence of three rather than two chromosomes at position 21). This opened the way for pregnant women to have a scan between 10 and 14 weeks to help them decide whether to keep a Down syndrome baby or to have their pregnancy terminated (see below).

Contraception before the 1960s, though widely practised, had been largely dependent on mechanical methods such as the condom and intra-uterine devices. These required planning before intercourse (not always easy) and were, in any case, by no means fully efficient. In the early 1960s, the pill (oral contraception) became available and was soon very widely adopted. Not only was the pill more likely to be taken regularly but it was also a much more efficient method of contraception with fewer failures (Wellings and Mills 1984).

The passing in 1967 of the Abortion Act was also a significant advance. Up to that date, doctors who performed abortions were liable to prosecution even if they were highly competent and carried out the procedure in safe circumstances. Many women, however, who could not afford proper medical care, went to 'abortionists' who were poorly qualified and working in unhygienic conditions. The Act made it possible for a woman who was less than 28 weeks pregnant (reduced in 1990 to 24 weeks) to have a termination in a safe and regulated manner if the continuation of pregnancy involved a serious risk to her physical or mental health or if there was a substantial risk that if the baby was born it would be seriously handicapped.

There was evidence that, when a mother wanted a termination, but the pregnancy was allowed to continue, the child had a higher likelihood of developing mental health problems. Further, many pregnant women who wanted a termination were motivated by the wish to give better care to the children they already had. Thus, the Abortion Act was a significant advance both in the prevention of mental health problems and in improving the care of existing children (Lee, Sheldon and Macvarish 2018). Since its passing, the Act was criticized for making it possible for women to have a termination virtually 'on demand' but, in general, its provisions proved popular among women.

Various attempts to reform the Act were made and, through the Human Fertilisation and Embryology Act 1990, the time limits were lowered from 28 to 24 weeks for most cases on the grounds that medical technology had advanced sufficiently to justify the change. However, largely the Act has stood the test of time. A particular issue arose in relation to babies diagnosed to have Down syndrome between 10 and 14 weeks of pregnancy. Some pregnant women chose not to have chromosomal tests carried out on their foetus but among those who did so choose, where the condition was found to be present, well over 90 per cent chose to have an abortion. Subsequently, an abortion to prevent a Down syndrome birth could be carried out at any time during pregnancy.

These two changes, the oral contraceptive and the Abortion Act 1967, meant that unwanted pregnancies were less frequently carried to term in the UK. When babies were born, they were more likely to be wanted. The fact that women were more able to limit and plan their pregnancies meant that they could more easily take up full-time or part-time employment or spend time in education for longer periods of their lives. Though there is no systematic evidence to support this view, it seems highly likely that infants benefitted from being more often warmly welcomed into the world because fewer of them arrived as a result of unintended pregnancies.

Another scientific advance soon brought benefits to hitherto infertile couples. In 1978, the first so-called test-tube baby was born as a result of the introduction of an egg that had been fertilized in a test tube into the receptive womb of the mother. The procedure, in vitro fertilization (IVF), then became widely used in the UK, albeit with a modest success rate. Again, the resulting pregnancies were widely welcomed and produced babies with no undue risk of abnormalities or subsequent problems. A more controversial form of assisted pregnancy was pioneered nearly a decade later in 1986, when an egg fertilized in a test-tube was transferred into the 'guest' womb of a volunteer in which it was carried to term. Despite various risks, such as the 'host' mother changing her mind and deciding she wanted to keep the baby, surrogacy continued to be practised in the UK under strictly controlled legal conditions.

Now that women had so much greater choice in whether to have children, it became clearer as the twentieth century progressed that there was a conflict between their biological urge to procreate and a number of reasons why they might wish to remain childless. The birth rate (number of births per 1,000 women in the population) boomed after the Second World War, so that in 1950 it was 18.42. From then on, it gradually declined to about 12.0, after which it remained flat until the end of our period. This meant that there were many more women who remained childless, many more only children and the mean number of children was less than two, the number needed for the population numbers to remain steady. By the end of our period, the total fertility rate per woman was only 1.43 (Office of National Statistics 2022). This was well below the fertility rate of 2.0 that was required to keep the size of the population steady. The fact that there was a significant growth in the size of the population (see below) was due to the influx of immigrants with much smaller number of emigrants, as well as an increase in the expectation of life.

The sexual 'revolution' and women's liberation

The 1960s saw a 'sexual revolution' during which there was a shift towards more liberal attitudes towards sex and increased acceptance of premarital sex, homosexuality and the use of contraception. The first step in this direction may be seen in the verdict of the trial of the publishers of *Lady Chatterley's Lover*, the novel by DH Lawrence in which a gamekeeper has an affair with his affluent employer (Rolph and Robertson 1990). Though this novel is in no way pornographic, the verdict in favour of the publishers may be seen as opening the way to the publication of the vast amount of porn characterizing the last decades of the twentieth century, turning into a billion-dollar business. This development raised concerns for the safety and corruption of children (see Chapter 6).

The 1960s also saw the beginning of second-wave feminism. The first wave of the feminist movement, occurring in the late Victorian and Edwardian eras from the 1880s to the outbreak of the First World War, had focused particularly on the campaign to obtain votes for women. Partial victory in this respect had been won in 1918 and in 1930, with the granting of the vote to all women over 18, complete victory. The feminist movement then went into relative quiescence until the early 1960s when, with strong winds blowing from the United States, a second wave with Germaine Greer's *The Female Eunuch* (1970) at its crest, broke into the UK. This was characterized by a demand for equality in the workplace and in the home, free childcare, the re-writing of history to give women their rightful place in descriptions of past events and a claim for women to be able to be assertive without being regarded as unfeminine. A somewhat less well-defined third wave emerged in the early 1990s with a movement critical of what were perceived to be the limitations of second-wave feminism, which was seen to fail to champion sufficiently gender autonomy and improvements in the status of women from ethnic minorities and other minority groups.

Accompanying the second sexual revolution was an increasing awareness of the objectivization of women's bodies, together with strong feelings this should no longer be acceptable. Page 3, which contained the photographs of nearly naked young women in tabloid newspapers, was gradually dropped. There was increasing anger at the unsolved cases of women by male rapists. The 2003 Sexual Offences Act tightened up the law against rape.

Sexual orientation

Over the historical period covered by this account, there was no change in the legal position in relation to sexual behaviour in children and young people. The age of sexual consent was 16 years for both men and women. This was despite the fact that there were very considerable changes in such behaviour. Information collected between 2010 and 2012 suggests that 31 per cent of British males and 29 per cent of British females had full sexual intercourse before the age of 16 years. Fifty years previously, this had been the case for 15 per cent of males and 4 per cent of females (Mercer et al. 2013). Clearly, the lack of change in the legal position did not mean that adult attitudes to sexual behaviour in the young remained the same. It is clear that there was much greater tolerance of sexual behaviour of young people in their mid-teens, providing that it was consensual.

Attitudes to homosexuality were also transformed (see Chapter 8). At the beginning of our period, same-sex attraction was heavily stigmatized and indeed criminalized. It was not until the passage of the Sexual Offences Act in 1967 that private, consensual homosexual acts between men were decriminalized in England and Wales and then only if the men were over the age of 21. The law was only changed in Scotland in 1980 and in Northern Ireland in 1982. In 2000, the Sexual Amendment Act was passed, bringing the age of consent to homosexual activity down to 16.

Gay and lesbian sexual attraction continued to be stigmatized after the passage of the Sexual Offences Act but to a more limited degree. A major controversy arose in 1988 when, under the premiership of Margaret Thatcher, the Local Government Act 1988 was passed. This stated that local authorities in England, Scotland and Wales 'shall not intentionally promote homosexuality or publish material with the intention of promoting homosexuality' or 'promote the teaching in any maintained school of the acceptability of homosexuality as a pretended family relationship' (Section 28). This section of the Act was only repealed in England and Wales in 2003. Changes in attitudes to children sexually attracted to others of the same sex are discussed further in Chapter 8.

Religion

One of the most marked changes over the years 1959–2024 was in the pattern of religious belief in the UK population. The 2021 National Census revealed that for the first time, less than half the population (46.2 per cent) described themselves as 'Christian'. The second highest number was those describing themselves as having 'no religion' (37.2). Religious affiliation was collected for the first time in a national Census in 2001, when the number describing themselves as Christian was 71.6 per cent. This decline in religious belief was also reflected in regular church attendance which declined from about 12 per cent in the 1960s to less than 2 per cent in the 2020s. The impact on children's lives as a result of their parents' decline in religious belief is revealed by attendance at Sunday school, tiny today and indeed only 4.1 per cent of the child population in 1961 (Brierley 1993). This decline in Christian church attendance was not mirrored in migrant populations, especially those from Eastern Europe and West Africa (see Chapter 8) who often worshipped in Catholic churches or those of charismatic sects. It should be added that this decline in Christian church affiliation was probably not accompanied by a reduction in attachment to so-called 'Christian values', though such values were generally shared by those of other religions and, indeed, by those describing themselves as having 'no religion'.

Conclusions

The adult world in which children grew up remained relatively stable and consistent from the late 1950s to the early 1970s when first economic instability and then a strong move towards a free market resulted in rising inflation, increased unemployment and income inequality. The period of austerity between 2010 and 2020 saw significant cuts in public services which adversely affected the lives of children and young people, especially those from poorer families. Beginning in the 1960s, with the advent of a so-called 'permissive society', the period was also marked by a liberalization of attitudes towards sexual behaviour and marriage, as well as legislation reflecting this change.

2

Children and the Family

Changing ideas about children

The second half of the twentieth century saw a number of major changes in the way children and their families were viewed. In his pioneering book, *Centuries of Childhood* (1960), Philippe Ariès proposed that there had been major shifts over the centuries in the way childhood had been constructed and that, indeed, children had really not been seen as different from adults until the eighteenth century. However accurate this view might be (and it is controversial), there were a number of significant changes in the concept of childhood (the way childhood was viewed) from the late 1950s onwards, particularly as far as infancy and the teen years were concerned.

Before the 1950s, there had been psychoanalytic speculations published between the 1920s and 1940s by Melanie Klein (1998) about the fantasies of young infants, but generally, infants in their first six months of life were seen as passive receptacles of experience with little agency or effect on their own fate. Now, neuroscientific work, particularly the pioneering developments in neurolinguistics and observational psychological studies, gradually made it clear this was far from the case (Gopnik et al. 2000). For example, it was realized that the infant cry was not just an involuntary expression of distress, but a communication, differing in its sound depending on whether the infant was telling its parents it was hungry or in pain or needed its nappies changing or was in need of attention because it felt bewildered. Infants, even from the very first few days of life, did not just look around pointlessly, but fixated on people's faces, especially their parents if they were present. They attended particularly to speech-like sounds and, from a few days old, would engage in conversational turn-taking. As they matured, they rapidly became active agents in developing attachments to their mothers. They started to draw on their limited experiences to use ways of attracting their mothers' attention. Their behaviour became explicable on the basis of an interaction between their genetically influenced personalities and their previous experiences. These discoveries about the early learning capacities of infants made it possible for child-rearing advice to parents to become more informed and appropriate.

As far as even young children, those between the ages of three and ten years, there were changes in the degree to which they were consulted about matters concerning them, for example, their food preferences, the decoration of their bedrooms and where they would like to go for a walk. Advice to parents as time went on increasingly urged them to give their children a voice and to listen to them as they became capable of making decisions for themselves. For example, Penelope Leach (1977, p.536), a leading authority on the upbringing of children, writing about four- and five-year-old children, counselled: 'Encourage your child to join in decision-making processes that affect him. It's very important he should have his say even when he cannot have his way.' Similarly, by the twenty-first century, government advice to divorcing or separating parents pointed out:

> Listening to your child might be key to helping both them and you understand what is best for them. It is important to listen carefully but not to put any pressure on them to give their views, and not to ask them to choose between their parents. Listening to your child's needs, wishes and feelings will help you and the other parent to make better decisions about your child's future.
>
> (HM Courts and Tribunals Service 2024)

From the early 2000s, primary schools increasingly established school councils, usually formed by children electing two representatives from each classroom to sit on a committee that provided an opinion on matters affecting the pupil body. This contributed to the aims set out in the 'Every Child Matters' agenda, formulated by the government in 2003 to ensure that, as far as possible, children's views were taken into account (Department for Education and Skills 2003). By 2015, the government had laid down a 'Children's Views, Wishes, and Feelings Standard', which was a regulation in the Children's Homes (England) (Home Office 2015) that required staff to consider children's views, wishes and feelings when making decisions about their care and welfare. The idea that it was important to take into account the views of children and young people was naturally increasingly reflected in the degree to which secondary age young people (11 to 18) were consulted through school councils.

Throughout recorded time there had been a marked contrast between both public ideas and those of authorities about the way teenagers (those aged thirteen to nineteen years) behaved and the way the great majority of them *actually* behaved in real life. From Socrates onwards, through G. Stanley Hall (the originator of the idea of adolescence), to Erik Erikson, the eminent psychoanalyst writing in the late 1950s and early 1960s (Erikson 1950), there had been a view that those of teenage were 'naturally' moody, aggressive, irritable, quarrelsome, impulsive and confused about themselves and their identities. Yet from the 1960s, surveys of teenage behaviour regularly found them to be very similar in their behaviour to both younger children and young adults. The title of a paper describing a population study of fourteen years olds asked the question 'Adolescent Turmoil: Fact or Fiction?' (Rutter et al. 1976) and come down firmly in favour of the latter.

After the publication of my book *The End of Adolescence* (Graham 2004), I frequently gave talks to both lay and professional audiences on this topic. At the beginning of my talk, I would put up on the board a list of twelve adjectives, six positive (e.g. kind, thoughtful, generous, calm, hard-working and focused) and six negative (such as moody, aggressive, irritable, quarrelsome, impulsive and confused). I would ask the audience to choose which adjectives best described the behaviour of teenagers as portrayed by journalists in the Press. They would unfailingly choose all the negative ones. I would then ask them to think of four or five teenagers whom they knew personally, as children of, for example, relatives or friends. Which were the adjectives that best described them? They would equally unfailingly choose the positive ones. Now, of course, there are teenagers who are well described by the negative adjectives. The survey evidence suggests that these are confined to the roughly one in ten who have mental health problems (see Chapter 4). They are not typical of their cohort.

Further impetus has been given, however, to the idea of adolescence as a special and distinctive phase of life by neuroscientists reporting on their findings from the late 1970s onwards. By examining post-mortem slices of the brain, it was possible to show that early in brain development, there was an over-production of neuronal synapses, the connections between nerves, which was corrected during childhood and adolescence in a process called 'synaptic pruning' (Huttenlocher 1979). This process enabled the brain to function more efficiently in adult life by ignoring irrelevant stimuli. Then, in the late 1990s, it was found using paediatric imaging that grey matter was pruned at a different rate from white matter depending on the part of the brain involved (Giedd et al. 1999). Later, in the twenty-first century, using a combination of brain imaging and psychological testing, it was found that there was a correlation between changes in brain structure and cognitive functioning. These studies led Sarah-Jayne Blakemore to claim that adolescents' brains are physically different from younger children's brains and from adults' brains. 'In terms of brain development, adolescence is a distinct stage' (Blakemore 2018, p.73). This claim has been contested, particularly on the grounds that the brain changes described continue well into the late twenties and beyond (Graham 2019).

The implications of these neuroscientific findings were considerable. For example, on their basis, it was claimed that adolescence was a well-defined phase of life that can be defined biologically and that there are maturational developments in the brain that are specific to adolescence. Further, there were clear-cut changes in behaviour and cognitive development that characterized adolescence and distinguished it from other phases of life and that each of the behaviours regarded as characteristic of adolescents, such as moodiness, risk-taking and impulsive decision-making, could be traced to changes in those parts of the brain responsible for their control. Adolescence therefore presented a window of opportunity, a sensitive or even a critical period for learning and personality development. It was even suggested that it would be inappropriate to give the vote to sixteen to eighteen-year-olds on the grounds that the brain is not fully developed at this age. This view that the teens are unique, both neurobiologically and behaviourally, was, however, controversial and contested (ibid.).

In the twenty-first century, a number of social changes, especially the extension of the school-leaving age (see Chapter 5), led some psychologists to propose another developmental phase they termed 'emerging adulthood'. The term was first coined by Arnett and Mitra (2020), who saw it as lasting from ages 18 to 25, forming a period of transition from the teenage years to adulthood, as people experience more independence and responsibilities. As such it was only found in industrial and post-industrial societies in which emotional and financial independence was often not achieved until well after the teens.

Changes in family structure and function

The second half of the twentieth century was a time of significant change in both family structure (the way families were made up) and family function (the way family members related to each other and performed their roles). Both had a large impact on children's lives.

Family structure

As outlined in Chapter 1, in the 1950s and 1960s, overwhelmingly the most common family structure was the nuclear family with two parents married and living together with one to three children. Of the children born in 1958 who formed part of the National Child Development Study (Connelly et al. 2014), nearly 90 per cent were living with their two natural parents at age 11, with only 6 per cent in lone-parent families. Only one in 100 was not living with either of their natural parents. As the century progressed, particularly after the passage of the Matrimonial Causes Act 1973 which made divorce easier and provided only that a marriage had to have lasted for three years (shortly afterwards, it was only one year) before a divorce could be granted. In 1970, 21 per cent of children were not in a nuclear family with their two biological parents for the whole of their childhood (Children's Commissioner for England 2023), but by 2022, as many as 44 per cent were not in their original nuclear family for the whole of their childhood. Further, an increasing number of single women began to have babies and look after them without living with the father of the baby and an even larger number cohabited (lived with the fathers on an enduring or long-lasting basis without marrying them). In the Millennium Cohort born in 2000, by the age of 11, nearly four in ten children had experienced some form of disruption. The number of families that included both natural parents decreased from 85 per cent at 9 months to 61 per cent at age 11. More than one in four (26 per cent) children were living with a lone parent at age 11 (ibid.). By the end of our period, in 2024, only about 70 per cent of children were living in classical nuclear families, with many living with single parents or reconstituted families. In 1970, only 8 per cent of the families were headed by a single parent, whereas by 2024, it was 24 per cent. That still meant that 76 per cent were headed by two parents, some married and some cohabiting. There was an important difference, however, between the partnerships of cohabiting and married parents in their risks of breaking up. The chance of a child of 12 with cohabiting parents having their parents break up was nearly twice as high than if they were married.

Size of family

The size of families reduced markedly over our period. In the late 1950s, about 12 per cent of women had only one child. Although the figures are not strictly comparable, in 2022, as many as 42 per cent of families had just one child, 42 per cent had two children and 15 per cent three or more children (Children's Commissioner for England 2023). This reduction in family size took place gradually over the sixty-five years of our period. For much of this period, there was a widespread belief that there was a disadvantage to being an only child because of the risk of the child being 'spoiled' or over-indulged. There was little evidence this occurred but clearly only children were at a disadvantage during the COVID-19 epidemic when they were more isolated than those in larger families (see Chapter 9).

Family structure and income

Single parents were more commonly to be found among those with low income, so there were only 10 per cent of single parents in the highest socio-economic group, while there were 28 per cent of single parents in the lowest socio-economic group. Over the years, there were fewer married couples with children and more cohabiting couples. Single parents were, of course, less well-off. In 2020, 49 per cent of children living in lone-parent families were in relative poverty after housing costs, compared with 25 per cent of children living in married or cohabiting families (Children's Commissioner for England 2021). Children in larger families (with three or more children) were, however, also disproportionately affected by child poverty, with 44 per cent living in poverty compared to 21 per cent in families with one child.

Family function

There were even greater differences in changes in the way families functioned than in their structure, especially in their gender roles (Davis and King 2018). At the beginning of our period, parents were living largely gender-determined lives with fathers going out to work and mothers staying at home to do the housework, shopping and other domestic tasks. Gradually, it became more acceptable, even desirable, for married women with children to go out to work (Wilson 2006). In the UK, among fathers of children under 5 years of age, fathers' childcare time increased from 15 minutes a day in the mid-1970s to around two hours a day in 1999. Fathers' involvement in child-related activities with children aged between five and fifteen years rose from about 15 minutes per day to 50 minutes per day in the same period. Fathers' share of all childcare time increased from around 12 per cent to 15 per cent in 1961 to about a third in 1999. These trends confirm that fathers in the late twentieth century assumed more of a caring and nurturing role, prioritizing the quality of their emotional relationship with their children more than had been the case thirty and forty years earlier (Henz 2019). However, mothers retained the main responsibility for childcare, especially in emergencies, such as when children were ill.

Those were the role models to which children were largely exposed in the 1950s and 1960s. Further, boys tended to form closer relationships with their fathers, sharing common (especially sporting) interests and girls with their mothers, more often focused together on appearance and clothes. Then in their later teens children formed more into mixed-sex groups and then, in later teens and early twenties, into couple formation. As more and more women entered higher education and employment, and more and more girls continued into higher education, this gender difference in roles became much less marked. Towards the end of the twentieth century, boys gradually began to do more housework and showed greater interest in appearance and clothes; girls took a greater interest in current affairs and often began to support the same football teams as their fathers.

So, differences over time occurred in the roles filled by fathers and mothers. But there were large regional variations. In the industrial heartlands of the Midlands, northern England, Scotland and Wales, in the 1960s and 1970s, the traditional pattern of men going out to work and women staying at home had largely prevailed, but the destruction of the steel and coal-mining and other heavy manufacturing industries in the 1980s resulted in high rates of male unemployment with women going out to secretarial, administrative and service jobs, for example, as checkout clerks (Payne 2021). As these examples reveal, women were still being employed in relatively low-status jobs compared to men, although increasingly they took on managerial roles.

Dependence and independence

There is a biological necessity for dependence on parents, especially mothers, driven by the need for helpless babies to survive the early years when they cannot feed themselves or keep themselves clean and warm. The nature of dependency and the speed with which independence develops are, however, much influenced by the way parents behave and the social circumstances in which families live. So, it is not surprising that a number of aspects of childhood dependence changed over time in the second half of the twentieth and early twenty-first centuries. The marked decline in breastfeeding and thus time necessarily spent by mothers and babies in close proximity over the period covered by this book is discussed below.

There was also a marked change over the years in the age at which parents (nearly always the mother) started toilet training. In the 1960s, it was widely regarded as a reason for parental pride if a baby was toilet trained by eighteen months. In the early 1960s, only about one in five mothers had not yet started to toilet train their babies by the age of one year. Attitudes towards babies who 'failed' in this respect were mildly punitive. One cook's wife said, 'I can't say I'm going out of my way, you know, I put her on three times a day; and then I tell her she's a naughty girl and tap her bottom when she fills her nappy' but otherwise I'm not trying to force her or anything' (Newson and Newson 1963). Gradually, a more relaxed, and eventually a much more relaxed attitude was taken as to whether a young child was toilet-trained. By the early 2000s, only 83 per cent of three-year-olds were always dry and clean by day (Hansen and Joshi 2007). By 2024, infant schoolteachers were complaining that it was no longer at all unusual for children to arrive in school at the age of five years not yet toilet-trained.

It was thought there were a variety of reasons for this change in attitude. The widespread use of disposable nappies reduced the motivation of parents to start potty training earlier. There was a more widespread focus, encouraged by the most popular child-rearing manuals, such as that by Penelope Leach (1977), to depend on the child's emotional readiness to take responsibility for itself, and thirdly, parents largely preferred to 'leave it to the child'. Finally, the COVID-19 epidemic (see Chapter 9) meant that a number of children who, because their parents were in social difficulties, would have been placed in early child care facilities, were not able to do so. This meant they were not seen by childcare professionals who would have promoted toilet training.

There were various negative effects of this delay in toilet training. The increased use of disposable nappies led to the accumulation of more plastic waste. Infant schoolteachers found themselves spending time on helping children with toileting when they would rather have been engaged in teaching activities.

The effects on patterns of play among children of primary school age (5–11 years) of the gradual replacement of narrow back streets and bomb sites by tower blocks with little or no play space are described in Chapter 7. Instead of playing out by themselves, children of this age spent far more time in the 1970s and 1980s near their mothers, sitting on couches watching television, with consequent loss of independence.

The gradual raising of the school-leaving age from 15 to 18 had a similar effect, as did the marked increase in the shortage of housing for young couples. This meant that, at the time of the 2021 national census, young men and women in the early or even mid-twenties, who, ten years earlier would have left home, were forced because of lack of suitable, affordable housing, to carry on living with their parents. Those living at home, sometimes couples but more often unpartnered, provided models of continuing dependency for children in their mid-teens who became more and more relaxed about having their parents look after them.

Children in low-income families

Early in our period, Abel-Smith and Townsend (1965) found that in 1960 7.4 million people (about 12 per cent) of the population were living in relative poverty, including 3 million retired people and 2.25 million children – 41 per cent of them in households that included a full-time worker, despite the social security reforms and unprecedented full employment since 1945. The Child Poverty Action Group, founded in 1965, immediately started to campaign for the government to provide a significant level of child benefit (Thane and Davidson 2016), but it was not until 1977 that the then prime minister, James Callaghan, announced the phasing in of this benefit.

He was defeated by Margaret Thatcher in the 1979 General Election. Thatcher took a very different view of the problem and indeed banned the words 'poverty' and 'inequality' from official discourse. The first Conservative Budget in 1980 froze child benefit for a year, and was followed, in the same year, by two Social Security Acts. The first removed the obligation to link long-term benefits, including child benefit and pensions, to wage or price levels, whichever was higher, and linked them only to prices, which normally rose more slowly. As a result, child poverty doubled between 1979 and 1990, from about 15 per cent to almost 30 per cent and remained high during Thatcher's premiership. When John Major succeeded her in 1990, he announced his support for child benefit and increased payments to first children, followed in 1991 by further increases and index linking (ibid.).

Although Tony Blair, who became the New Labour prime minister in 1997, had not hitherto been at all positive about child benefit, in 1999 he made a wholly unexpected announcement. 'Our historic aim [is] that ours is the first generation to end child poverty forever … it is a 20-year mission, but I believe it can be done,' he declared. New Labour did more than any previous government to reduce child poverty significantly. Child poverty fell and incomes of the poorest families rose on average during Labour's time in government. Although higher incomes also rose unchecked and there was much regional inequality between the richest and poorest, poverty levels grew very much less than that in the 1980s. The fall in child poverty did not continue following the election of the Conservative/Liberal Democrat coalition government in 2010; instead, it grew. Child benefit was frozen for three years in the Budget of June 2010, and there was a cut of £22 billion to benefits and tax credits; VAT, a tax which affected the poorest most, was increased.

The use of food banks increased sharply from 2014 and remained high for the next ten years (Trussell Trust 2024). The main reason for this was an acute income crisis for the poorest sections of the population, most frequently due to cuts in benefits, including sanctions, delayed payment or missing tax credits. Users of food banks were generally unaware of crisis payments that might be available to them. Most were unable to work because of ill health or other reasons or had recently lost a job. Most found it 'embarrassing' or 'shameful' to use food banks, but felt they had no alternative. Generally, as research carried out by the London School of Economics showed, the poorest half of the population seriously lost out from austerity measures, while the richest half became better off.

Studies showed that low family income was associated with nearly all the adverse influences for child mental health problems, as described further in Chapter 4. The most common adverse influences affecting children were maltreatment of all types, disharmonious family relationships (especially parental conflict and breakdown), academic failure, parental mental illness, brain dysfunction and lack of community support arising from weak neighbourhood cohesion. These were more likely to produce disorders if they were present in combination. There was one common factor underlying all these stresses and therefore, indirectly, child and adolescent mental health problems, namely poverty (Graham and Maughan 2025).

Bonding, affection and love

Babies and children need loving care in order to thrive. Such care is ordinarily provided by both parents, but particularly the child's mother. Questions regarding how and when such loving care should be provided have, however, been more contentious, and this was the case in the 1950s and 1960s at the beginning of our period. There were two main sets of ideas expressed by so-called 'experts'. In practice, the parents of the day were largely untroubled by the disagreements between experts on childcare and gave their children the best loving care they could, drawing from their own experience of the care they had received when they themselves were children as well as from the advice given by other family members and friends. The advice given by the paediatrician and psychoanalyst, Donald Winnicott, in one of his popular radio programmes, to be a 'good enough' parent, was widely quoted and found helpful by many. This probably reassured parents, who, for example, lost their tempers with their children and smacked them when they wished they hadn't.

At that time, the most popular book for parents on how to bring up their children was Dr Benjamin Spock's *Baby and Child Care*, which, although its author was an American paediatrician, sold in many millions in the UK. The words 'love' and 'affection' do not appear in the index of its 1960 edition, but there is every indication that Spock wanted parents to love their children and show it. 'Don't be afraid to love him and enjoy him. Every baby needs to be smiled at, talked to, played with, fondled – gently and lovingly – just as much as he needs vitamins and calories' (Spock 1960, p.54). The UK childcare experts who endorsed Spock's views on this matter early on were largely drawn from the field of psychoanalysis. Later experts on child rearing, such as Penelope Leach, whose book *Your Baby and Child* (1977) went into many editions, were more eclectic. Of the psychoanalysts, probably the best known was John Bowlby (1958). This was partly based on work he had carried out with juvenile delinquents, many of whom had been brought up in institution, having been neglected by their parents and taken out of parental care. As we have seen, the book contained some unnecessarily alarmist opinions about the dangers of even brief separations of children from their parents. However, it also contains much information that parents found encouraging. What children need, he wrote, is 'a warm, intimate and continuous relationship with his mother' but to achieve this all mothers need to do is 'what comes naturally to them'.

Bowlby was greatly influenced in his views on the need for babies and young children to form attachments to their mothers by Robert Hinde, a Cambridge ethologist, whom he first met in 1954. They became close friends, and Bowlby always regarded ethology as one of the main influences on his ideas (Bowlby 2007). Ethology, the study of the behaviour of animals (including human animals), in their natural environment, has largely developed since the Second World War. It looked to the observation of non-human animals to provide keys to questions about the way human behaviour was adapted to ensure the survival of the species, thus linking current scientific observation to Darwin's theory of evolution. It was noted that ducks that do not stay close to their mothers were less likely to survive. Bowlby's own observations of lambs never roaming far from their mothers and what he learned from Hinde about the behaviour of baby ducks confirmed views he probably already had about the nature of attachment in human mothers and babies.

A new gloss was added to the psychoanalytic approach in the late 1970s by two American paediatricians, Marshall Klaus and John Kennell (1978), who suggested that the hospital practice of removing newborn babies from their mothers immediately after birth was harmful to their later mental health. In contrast, insisting that mother and baby remained in close skin contact after the birth ensured that babies 'bonded' with their mothers, thus increasing the chances of a mentally healthy future.

An alternative approach to the expression of affection and love was that espoused by the behaviourist school of psychology. As early as 1928, in his book, *The Psychological Care of the Infant and Child*, the psychologist J. B. Watson had told parents, 'Never hug and kiss your children, never let them sit in your lap. If you must, kiss them once on the forehead when they say goodnight.' Children should learn to behave well without affectionate physical contact. Another behaviourist approach, so-called 'operant conditioning' was that espoused by B. F. Skinner, who suggested that hugs and kisses should be reserved for occasions when children were obedient and helpful and withheld when they were naughty. Behaviourist approaches remained popular during the whole of the rest of the twentieth century and were revived in the twenty-first with the television series *Supernanny* (2004–8) fronted by the American psychologist, Jo Frost, who was filmed helping parents with extremely troublesome children using operant conditioning methods.

The twenty-first century saw an increase in studies examining the neuro-correlates of maternal love. For example, Bartels and Zeki (2004) showed that the brain activities stimulated by maternal love had common features with those activated by romantic love, although each had its own specific type of neuronal activity. Further, both types of love were accompanied by deactivation of a common set of regions associated with negative emotions, social judgement and mentalizing, thus reducing any tendencies to be critical of the child (in the case of maternal love) and lover (in the case of romantic love).

From before the 1950s, it was recognized that some parents were incapable or unwilling to love their children who were thus neglected. The 1948 Children Act (see Chapter 7) placed a duty on local authorities to provide alternative care for children suffering from parental neglect. Although many local authority children's homes, foster and adoptive parents did provide excellent alternative care, unfortunately throughout the rest of the century and beyond, there were frequent scandals regarding the inadequacy of children's homes. The privatization of the running of children's homes in the 1980s increased these concerns. In particular, the low pay earned by the staff in children's homes meant there was frequent staff turnover resulting in delayed language development and increased rates of mental health problems (Tizard and Hodges 1978). Later, it was pointed out that, not infrequently, there was a veritable taboo on the expression of love in children's homes (Evans 2020). It was further revealed that children brought up by cold, neglectful parents had an increased probability of developing into juvenile delinquents, who themselves showed cruel, callous traits in their behaviour (Frick et al. 1999).

Children, food and the family

The child's first experience of food in the family nearly always came from the mother. Lengthy breastfeeding was encouraged but, in the 1960s, it was uncommon. It is notable that 69 per cent of the 1958 birth cohort were breastfed for at least three months compared to 38 per cent of the 1970 cohort (Centre for Longitudinal Studies 2018), compared to 25 per cent of the ALSPAC cohort born 1991–2, and about 1 per cent of the Millennium cohort born in 2000. The reasons for this sharp decline in breastfeeding were varied. There was considerable commercial promotion of artificial milk. Uncovering the breast even in front of other family members had become something to be avoided. Artificial feeding freed the mother to get on with other things and particularly allowed the father to participate more in the preparation of food and in feeding the baby. Gradually, however, the prevalence of breastfeeding increased. By 2010, mothers in the UK were breastfeeding their babies for longer with one in three mothers still breastfeeding at six months compared with one in four mothers in 2005. However, the proportion of mothers following current UK government guidelines on exclusive breastfeeding remained very low and, in 2010, only one in every hundred mothers breastfed exclusively for the first six months of their baby's life. Throughout this whole period, the introduction of artificial milk at two or three weeks followed by solid foods before four months, or, after the 1990s, six months became the most usual pattern (McAndrew, Thompson and Fellows 2010). The gradual, though rather small, increase in the prevalence of breastfeeding in the first decade of the twenty-first century was at least partly due to demographic changes with, as time went on, a higher proportion of educated, better-informed, middle-class mothers.

For the first three or so years of life, children usually ate separately from the rest of the family at times suited to their sleep patterns. Then they gradually joined the rest of the family at table. During the 1960s and 1970s, the time of the evening meal was generally determined by the time the father came home from work. Gradually, however, as more mothers went out to work, the timing of family meals, including the children's evening meal, became much more varied to take account of the working hours of both parents. This meal remained, however, a family social event with much exchange of information about everyone's social activities. The amount of family conversation was influenced by whether the television was kept on, as it frequently was, during the family meals. This was less likely to occur during the Sunday lunch which, with a roast main course, remained a tradition in many families.

The introduction of mobile phones into the UK in the 1980s and then of texting in the 1990s made a difference to the family meals. Parents and then not long afterwards children began to take calls during the family meals, though some parents, especially if middle class, banned the use of phones by their children during mealtimes, even if they used them themselves.

In the early 1960s, lunch was provided at modest cost to all children attending school. However, the 1964 Labour government 1964–70 introduced a significant rise in cost to the parents, and in 1968 ended free school milk in secondary schools. The 1980 Education Act then removed the obligation to provide school meals except for pupils whose parents were in receipt of supplementary benefit or family income supplement. The content of school lunches became controversial during the last years of the twentieth century with health campaigners protesting at the high levels of salt and sugar provided. Most children were given something to eat when they returned home from school in mid-afternoon or helped themselves to snacks from the refrigerator.

A major change over the years was the variety of foods available in the shops. Avocados, garlic, peppers and aubergines were considered exotic foods in the 1960s and only gradually became widely available. This change was linked to increasing food choosiness by children. In the 1960s and 1970s, emerging from the days when food was rationed and in limited supply, children largely ate what their mothers provided or went hungry. All family members ate the same meal. By the 1980s, a combination of food faddiness, vegetarianism, veganism and gradually rising rates of food allergies (see Chapter 3) meant that this was no longer the case. By the 2000s, mothers or whoever cooked for the family often had to cater for at least two or three different palates and sometimes more.

Except for fish and chip shops, eating out was a luxury until the 1970s, when relatively cheap fast food and Indian and Chinese restaurants began to open. Before that, better-off families were able to eat in pubs, though more often, potato crisps were the only types of food available there. Later, in the 1970s and 1980s, American burger bars and then chains such as McDonald's and Kentucky Fried Chicken opened and, from their mid-teens, young people began to frequent these in groups or on their own, less often with their parents. In the early 2000s, the internet played a part in making home deliveries and takeaways more popular with young people. Family meals in French, Italian or up-market British restaurants were only affordable by well-off families, and then often only for celebrations such as birthdays.

From the 1990s, with greater attachment of older children and teenagers to their screens to play video games, talk with their friends or absorb information available on the internet or from one of the social media, it became much less common for the whole family to sit down to a meal together. Teenagers began to take their meals to their rooms and eat there with one or both eyes on their screens, away from the rest of the family. This became easier with the availability from supermarkets of prepared meals that could just be heated up at the last minute in a microwave oven. In contrast, in some families, teenagers began to take an interest in the preparation of meals, sometimes not just for themselves but for the whole family.

Young children and family activities

For the first two years or so of children's lives, over the whole of this historical period, their biological needs for nourishment, warmth, cleanliness and physical protection determined their social interactions with the members of their families, especially their mothers. Breast and bottle feeding are discussed above, as is the conversation and other things at mealtimes that happened later on. Face and hand washing with toothbrushing were occasions for further interaction. Until the 1980s, it was only considered necessary for children to have one bath a week, but this was also an occasion for much talk and laughter around splashing, especially if more than one child was involved.

Pregnant mothers have always sung to their babies in the womb. In the early 1960s, experimental scientists were able to show that by about twenty weeks of pregnancy, foetuses could discriminate sounds and react to their mothers singing to them. Expert advice changed so that mothers were encouraged to sing to their babies during their pregnancies and continue after they were born. Such advice, though unnecessary as mothers had always done this, was followed throughout the whole of our period. Mothers have sung to their babies and toddlers especially, for example, while they are playing games such as *Pat-a-cake* and *Eeny Meeny Miny Mo* with them.

For most people, the music they think of as *theirs* is the popular music they listened to and sang between about eighteen and twenty-five. This is likely to be the music they sing to their young children. This means that, for babies born in the 1960s and 1970s, music listened to on the radio, in the early years of television and on gramophones, was the most commonly sung. Rather than musical groups, the popular music of the 1940s and 1950s was American soloists such as Bing Crosby, Frank Sinatra, Ella Fitzgerald, Dean Martin, Nat King Cole and Judy Garland. For babies born in the 1970s, 1980s and 1990s, it was the music of the 1950s to 1970s to which they were exposed. So, they particularly heard the songs of the Beatles, the Supremes, the Rolling Stones and vocalists such as Elvis Presley. Once they were old enough to stand, their mothers would dance around the kitchen with them, perhaps with their mothers holding them up, to rock music. Babies born after the 1990s would be likely to listen to their mothers singing a wider variety of popular music, including Soul, Funk, country music, reggae, Madonna, David Bowie and the evergreen Beatles. Listening to such music meant that by the time children went to playgroups or infant schools (later in the period, when they began to exist, nursery schools), they usually had a sense of rhythm and knew the lyrics of some popular songs of an earlier era.

Much family interaction in the 1960s and 1970s took place in front of the television. For those families without a television, a small minority by the mid-1960s, there was always the radio. For young children, *Listen with Mother* was broadcast on the *BBC Light Programme* until 1982. It went out to over a million listeners in a fifteen-minute slot every weekday afternoon at 1.45 pm, just before *Woman's Hour* and consisted of stories, songs and nursery rhymes. It was succeeded in the 1950s by *Watch with Mother* which was aimed specifically at very young children aged 6 months to 5 years. In 1963, the timing of *Watch with Mother* was changed to 10.45 am with, shortly afterwards, an additional programme at 1.30 pm. The shows were timed for when older children were at school and the title was chosen to discourage mothers from letting very young children watch by themselves. A different show was broadcast each day. Over the years, a very large number of different shows were screened. Among the most durable were *Camberwick Green* and *Trumpton.* Television viewing by older children, largely on their own or with other children, is described in Chapter 7, as are other ways children and young people spent their free time.

Obedience and disobedience to parents

Children learn from their parents how to behave in two main ways: by modelling and by being told what to do and what not to do. Attitudes to obedience have changed over the years. In the 1960s, *Baby and Child Care* by Benjamin Spock was the most popular child-rearing manual in the UK (see above). In the section on discipline (Spock 1960), he begins by pointing to a number of ways in which ideas about discipline have changed in preceding years. We have learned, he writes (ibid., p.329), 'that many of the ones who get into the most trouble are suffering from lack of affection rather than from lack of punishment'. Ideas about obedience and disobedience continued to change over the years. The World Values Survey of parenting priorities (King's College, London 2023) reported: 'Over the last three decades, Britons' views have shifted on the key qualities that children should be encouraged to learn at home, with the main changes being a decline in the perceived importance of obedience and unselfishness and an increase in how much people value hard work and imagination.' This decline in the perceived importance of obedience since the 1990s was seen as having started well before that and, as Benjamin Spock's observations reveal, we probably need to go back into the first half of the twentieth century to establish when it began. Indeed, by the 2020s, obedience was seen as the enemy of imagination, with over-compliant children being less likely to think imaginatively for themselves.

Although the perception of obedience clearly changed, this does not necessarily mean that parents were, in reality, less insistent on obedience. Indeed, as discussed in Chapter 7, there was rather little change in the amount parents smacked their children for disobedience from the 1960s onwards. There is little other evidence on the amount parents changed in demanding obedience from their children. Nevertheless, it is significant that less emphasis was placed on obedience as time went on, and little information as to what effect, if any, this had on child behaviour. We know that every generation of parents thinks that their children 'get away with blue murder' compared with what they themselves were allowed to do as children.

Gender fluidity and transgender

Sexual orientation, whether young people are sexually attracted to their own or the opposite or to both sexes, is discussed in Chapter 1. Gender identity and children identified as trans are discussed in Chapter 8.

Conclusion

This period saw major changes in a variety of ways in which children interacted with their parents. Babies and young children were seen as more active participants. The popular stereotype of teenage behaviour was questioned. Family structure changed with fewer families fitting the 'norm' of two parents and two or three children. Fathers gradually played more part in household tasks, including childcare, though their contribution remained relatively minor. Attitudes to obedience to parents became less rigid.

3

Physical Health

The sixty-five years from 1959 saw great improvements in the quality of the health care of children, the prevention of most physical illness and disability, as well as major advances in treatment. While in most areas of children's lives, it is arguable whether there was improvement or deterioration, with one or two notable exceptions, this stands out as a beacon of unarguable progress.

Advances in the quality of care

Welfare of children in hospital

Children had been admitted to children's wards in hospitals in Britain since the mid-nineteenth century, the number of them gradually increased. However, even in the 1950s, a large number of children who needed hospital admission were admitted to adult wards. Even on children's wards, visiting by parents was often restricted to a couple of hours a day. Occasionally parents were not allowed to visit at all, except at weekends. The reasoning behind such restrictive practices lay in the belief that young children were upset by their parents and that when parents left, prolonged crying often followed which nurses found difficult to deal with. For many years there had been pressure from parents to allow unrestricted visiting. A voluntary organization, the National Association for the Welfare of Children in Hospital, had campaigned for such a change. In 1952, the release of a film made by James Robertson, a researcher at the Tavistock Clinic, London, titled 'A Two Year Old Goes to Hospital', showing the confused, highly distressing reaction of a child of this age to hospital admission provided further impetus. The Platt Committee was set up to consider the matter and to make recommendations, and this was reported in 1959. It recommended that there should be unrestricted visiting of all children in hospital (Ministry of Health 1959). This recommendation was gradually implemented over the next twenty years. Fewer and fewer children and by the 1990s, hardly any children were admitted to adult wards. Although the film by James Robertson is usually credited with stimulating the improvements in the welfare of children in hospital, there were many other influences pointing in the same direction (van der Horst and van der Veer 2009).

Over the years, various other improvements were made to the care of children in hospital to make it more humane (Vernon, et al. 1965). By the 1970s, most hospitals admitting children had facilities for parents to stay overnight, either in the same room as the child or in an adjoining suite. Much greater attention was paid to the need to prepare children for hospital by explaining what was going to happen to them, for example, in procedures or operations. Toys and other play material were provided for them. From the 1970s, more and more children's wards employed trained play leaders to engage children in play when they were well enough to do so. By the 1990s, with a few exceptions, the attitude of hospital nurses to parents had changed to such a degree that instead of seeing parents as a pernicious interference to the care of children, they had increasingly come to be seen as partners in the care of their children. This is therefore an area in which there would be very widespread agreement that the lives of children improved over the years.

Prevention

Childhood immunization

This has been a major success. Before the 1960s, the only diseases for which children could be immunized were diphtheria and tuberculosis. In 1956 immunization with inactive polio vaccine was introduced and in 1962 an oral polio vaccine became available. This led to the establishment of the Joint Committee on Vaccination and Immunisation in 1963 (Lang et al. 2019). This was rapidly followed by vaccination for measles (1968), rubella (1970), the triple MMR vaccine for measles, mumps and rubella (1988) and meningococcus (1999). The immunization rate has generally been around 90 per cent of all children, but between the 1990s and 2003/4 it fell well below this after the publication of a later-discredited paper linking MMR to autism (Wakefield 1998). Immunization has saved millions of lives worldwide and probably hundreds of thousands in the UK. Before the introduction of the polio vaccine in the UK, there were about 7,000 cases of paralytic polio and around 700 deaths from polio annually. But perhaps the most spectacular success for immunization came with the incredibly rapid development of vaccines during the COVID-19 epidemic (Callaway and Naddaf 2023) (see Chapter 9).

Spina bifida

The incidence of spina bifida and other neural tube defects prevalent until the early 1970s has been reduced by the encouragement to women of childbearing age to take a small dose of folic acid once they decide to become pregnant (Oakley 2019).

In addition, foetal surgery (see below) in the last trimester of pregnancy has improved the outcome of spina bifida, especially limb paralysis. It has also been practised to prevent congenital diaphragmatic hernia.

Prevention of injuries

Injuries

Over this entire period, injuries sustained in the home were a common cause of disability and death. Children aged under five were at greatest risk. Infants who were able to crawl but not yet walk falling down unprotected staircases were commonly the victims. Burns from open fires in poor households and scalding from upturned saucepans also frequently occurred. The risk of poisoning from tablets prescribed for parents was recognized in the mid-1970s when child-resistant packaging was introduced. Peanuts and small toys on which children could choke to death were other hazards. From the 1980s onwards when many families could afford holidays abroad, drowning in unprotected swimming pools occurred in rented villas overseas. However, in general, UK children were less exposed to water environments than those in most other countries and deaths from drowning were less common in the UK than elsewhere. Generally, as with road traffic accidents (see below) there is a strong association between social class and injuries sustained in the home (Raine and Diplock 2001).

Over the years, various organizations were set up to provide information about ways of preventing injuries to children. In 1962, the Medical Commission on Accident Prevention was established, and this was followed by the Joint Committee on Child Accident Prevention which changed its name to the Child Accident Prevention Trust in 1982 (Jackson 1995).

Road traffic accidents (RTAs)

In the late 1950s and 1960s, RTAs were among the three most common causes of death both in the 1–4 and in the 5–9 age groups. There was a steady decline in KSI (killed and seriously injured) for the whole of this period for zero- to fifteen-year-olds, with 12,458 serious injuries in 1979 and 1,980 in 2013 (Department of Transport 2015). The number killed went down from 700 in 1979 to around 50 a year in 2013, a massive reduction. Fatalities and serious injuries are heavily concentrated among disadvantaged groups.

Children 4–10 years old and 11–15 years old residing in the most deprived areas were nearly three times more likely to be killed or seriously injured as pedestrians than their peers in the least deprived areas (ibid.). The use of seat belts in cars (compulsory in the UK since 1983) and the requirement for small children to be placed in car seats in the back of cars have made a significant impact on the number of children killed and injured passengers travelling in cars. The encouragement to cyclists of all ages to wear helmets (though this is not mandatory) has also reduced child deaths and head injuries.

The decline in deaths and serious injury came at a price. On any day without rain, immediately after returning home from school, or in holidays after breakfast, boys living in the cities would pour out of their houses to play on bomb sites, or in local parks or, just as likely, out on the streets. There they would usually play football with improvised goalposts. As well as football, and (more often played by girls in the street), there were skipping games, hopscotch and variations of run-outs. There were doorstep games like lolly sticks, five stones, jacks and marbles. As, during the 1960s, more and more families owned a television set, street play was partly abandoned in favour of popular television programmes. Further, in many large cities, streets disappeared as large tower blocks with bleak downstairs courtyards for play were built in their stead. But even where, as in many places, there continued to be streets, the motor car made these increasingly unsafe. The occurrence of accidents as well as fears of 'stranger danger' made parents unwilling to let their children play outside unsupervised. Describing his childhood in the 1960s, Paul Feeny (2010, pp.56–7) fifty years later, reports:

> Most people felt comfortable with the comings and goings in their local streets and believed themselves to be reasonably safe in their own environment. However, as the years went by, growing numbers of motor vehicles were causing more and more traffic congestion on the main roads, resulting in more and more use of side roads as shortcuts or rat runs as they were commonly called. By the mid-1960s, previously quiet residential streets were becoming congested with large numbers of vehicles passing through and cars and vans competed for roadside parking spaces outside homes ... kids were finding that they could no longer play safely in their local streets. Instead, they had to play in each other's back gardens or to go to the park to play their games and find adventure.

The authorities were slow to recognize the importance of children's play and, throughout this period, gave the motor car priority. Towards the early 2000s, speed controls were lowered on some streets and a few streets were pedestrianized but these were the exceptions. The car industry or at least the car trade continued to dominate the thinking of city planners. Playing in the street as part of childhood lifestyle is described in Chapter 6.

Dental health

After the Second World War, the UK Department of Health became interested in work being carried out in the United States on the prevention of dental caries in children by fluoridation of the water supply (Mullen 2005). In 1955, three sites were selected for the initial fluoridation schemes: Watford, Kilmarnock and part of Anglesey. The areas selected as controls were Sutton, Ayr and the remaining part of Anglesey. Studies carried out after five years of fluoridation demonstrated much lower caries levels in the fluoridated areas in five-year-old children (Marinho et al. 2025). However, despite the strong evidence for the beneficial effects of fluoridation of public supplies of water, legal challenges have meant that by 2024, only about 10 per cent of UK drinking water was fluoridated.

Studies of the teeth of English five-year-olds in the twenty-first century revealed that about a fifth are showing at least some dental caries. There is a strong social class gradient with those children in the wealthiest areas having a risk of dental caries of around 10 per cent while those living in the most deprived areas have a risk of 35–40 per cent (Public Health England 2023). However, caries prevalence reduced from 1973 to 2013 from 72 per cent to 41 per cent in five-year-olds and from 97 per cent to 46 per cent in fifteen-year-olds (Murray, Vernazza and Holmes 2015). There was a reduction in the prevalence of caries in the first decade of the twenty-first century, but this did not continue.

The shortage of NHS dentists in the UK in the twenty-first century meant that most dental caries went untreated. Whereas in the 1960s over 90 per cent of children had an annual check-up of their teeth by an NHS dentist this was the case for only about 60 per cent of children in the 2020s (Clark 2024).

Advances in medical and surgical treatment

Over these sixty-five years, there have been advances in the treatment of all the diseases affecting children.

Congenital heart disease

In the 1950s and early 1960s, most forms of congenital heart disease, the most common congenital condition, were not amenable to surgery and affected children usually died within the first five years of life. However, over the next two decades, with the development of open-heart surgery, major advances were made (Alvarez-Díaz F, Brito JM, et al. 1973) and by 1980 most, though not the most severe congenital malformations could be corrected surgically. From the 1990s, advances in interventional treatment meant that many conditions could be corrected without the need for open heart surgery. By 2024, with regular monitoring for congenital anomalies at 19 weeks of pregnancy, most patients with congenital heart disease were surviving at least into middle adult life, though some had needed further operations in early adult life.

Cancer in childhood

Childhood cancer is rare but is nevertheless the most common disease-related cause of death in childhood. In the 1950s and early 1960s, most forms of cancer were untreatable. For example, acute lymphoblastic leukaemia, a form of cancer of the blood, had a virtually 100 per cent mortality five years after diagnosis, whereas by the 2000s, over 80 per cent were still alive five years after diagnosis (Bartram, Veys and Vora 2020). The improvement occurred as a result of careful research, monitoring outcomes after a combination of radiotherapy and chemotherapy. Harmful side effects of treatment were also much reduced. Largely as a result of randomized controlled trials, there are now considerable numbers of adult survivors of all forms of childhood cancer, though often these are at risk for the development of new cancers and other serious conditions.

Diabetes mellitus

Major advances were made in the treatment of both types of diabetes. The management of type 1 diabetes, caused by a failure of insulin secretion, gradually improved over the years, particularly in the last thirty years of the twentieth century with a move away from overly didactic and prescriptive care to a much more patient-centred approach. Monitoring by urine testing was replaced by continuous glucose monitoring; new insulins were introduced as well as new delivery devices (Shaw 2022).

The explosion in the number of children and adults with type 2 diabetes (arising from the increased prevalence of obesity [see below] and insulin resistance) meant there was a need for better management. This also improved greatly with the introduction of metformin in 1958, which was superseded by the sulphonylureas, themselves to be displaced by a reintroduction of metformin at the beginning of the twenty-first century (Bailey 2022). Advances in the treatment of childhood obesity (see below) also had an effect on the rate of type 2 diabetes.

End-stage renal failure

From the 1940s, the institution of renal dialysis has prolonged the lives of large numbers of children. Combined with renal transplantation, the five-year survival rate increased to 83 per cent (Shroff et al. 2006). Until the use of medication to counter immune rejection, renal transplantation was not possible; but in the 1960s, kidney transplantation between genetically non-related individuals became a routine treatment for end-stage renal failure (Hatzinger et al. 2016). In 2023, it became possible to have a kidney transplant in a specialist centre without the need for long-term drugs to prevent rejection. Improved medication for the nephrotic syndrome also radically improved the prognosis of this condition from the 1960s.

Cystic fibrosis

One of the most remarkable transformations of prognosis over this period was that of cystic fibrosis. This is a genetically determined condition transmitted by recessive inheritance. It particularly affects the lungs and intestinal tract. Many children with this condition died at birth of meconium ileus, a condition causing intestinal obstruction and chronic respiratory infections, resistant to antibiotics. Few children survived until their teens. Then, in the late 1950s, American clinicians focused heavily on accurate diagnosis at birth and immediate treatment. Based on effective clinical management, the prognosis slowly improved until the 1990s when the results of controlled clinical trials guided interventions. With new generation antibiotics, the prognosis continued to improve so that life expectancy increased to sixty years by the mid-2020s, with an optimistic attitude being a positive factor leading to longer survival (Abbott et al. 2023). In the 2020s, the introduction of molecules correcting genetic failure of ion and water transport into the lungs and gut transformed prognosis for some variants.

Paediatric surgery

Prior to 1953 when the British Association of Paediatric Surgery (BAPS) was founded (see below), surgery in the newborn was mostly carried out by general surgeons with an interest in paediatrics (Spitz 2012). From 1953 neonatal surgery was exclusively carried out by paediatric surgeons, either in children's hospitals or from children's wards in general hospitals. In the 1980s, the advent of neonatal surgical units staffed by paediatric trained nurses and dedicated paediatric anaesthetists resulted in greatly improved outcomes. Advances in surgical technique gradually enabled surgery to be performed on the foetus (see below). From the 1980s, the advent of keyhole surgery meant it was no longer necessary to open up the child's abdomen even to perform quite extensive surgery. This resulted in improved pain control and again better outcomes.

Foetal medicine

Prior to the 1960s, although amniocentesis had been introduced in 1952, the condition of a foetus could only be determined by checking the heart rate and listening to the mother's report of the activity of the unborn child. During the 1960s and subsequently, the speciality of maternal-foetal medicine emerged as a discipline with rapidly expanding approaches to prevention and intra-uterine treatment. In 1961, the first needle-based blood transfusion for rhesus disease was made into the uterus. During the 1970s diagnostic foetoscopy was pioneered. In the 1980s, a foetal shunt for hydrocephalus was inserted and open foetal surgery for congenital heart disease was performed. The twenty-first century saw further pioneering foetal heart surgery, though this remained of very limited application. In 2017, a trial of in utero stem cell treatment of thalassaemia was instituted (Evans and Harrison 2021).

Plastic surgery

This period saw major improvements in surgery aiming to improve appearance and function arising from congenital conditions associated with visible deformities and scarring following burns. In the 1950s and 1960s, it was easy to identify those who had been born with hare lip and cleft palate after operation by the visible scarring around the mouth and the characteristic articulation defect. By the end of the century, surgical techniques had improved to the extent that there was no longer any visible deformity and speech sounded normal. Treatment for those children who had sustained severe burns had also dramatically improved the outcomes (Fell, Davies and Wren 2022).

Short stature

The use of human growth hormone to increase the height of children with very short stature was pioneered in the United States but employed in the UK from the mid-1960s (Tanner and Whitehouse 1967). The treatment used in children with no known cause for their short stature had modest success, though not all children benefitted.

Harms caused by medical interventions

Drugs taken in pregnancy

1959 was a significant year in the recognition of the harmful effects of certain types of medication in pregnancy. It became apparent that taking thalidomide as a hypnotic in pregnancy sometimes caused serious limb deformities in the baby (Kim and Scialli 2011). Subsequently pregnant women were advised not to take any form of medication unless it was essential for health reasons. This was particularly the case for drugs taken for epilepsy.

Infected blood products

From the early 1970s to the early 1990s, about 380 children with haemophilia were given human blood plasma infected with HIV (see below). A similar number of adults with haemophilia were infected (Desposito et al. 2013). A much larger number, nearly 30,000 adults were similarly given infected blood transfusions. A high proportion of those given infected blood products developed AIDS and either died or suffered from long-term illnesses.

New challenges to the physical health of children

Obesity

During the Second World War, food was rationed and made available in quantities that provided a healthy diet in sufficient quantities to satisfy hungry children. Rationing continued until the mid-1950s when food became available to anyone who could afford it. The fact that the rates of overweight and obesity remained steady through the 1970s until the end of the 1980s suggests that parents at that time were feeding their children healthy diets.

Until the early 1980s, it was unusual for children to drink large quantities of sweet drinks or to eat outside the home. The first McDonald's restaurant opened in London in 1974 but there was rapid expansion to other cities. McDonald's opened in Liverpool in 1985. Meanwhile, other chains of fast-food restaurants such as Burger King and Kentucky Fried Chicken (KFC) opened in all British towns and cities. They gave children a taste for unhealthy foods, high in fat and sugar and children then looked to their mothers to provide the same sorts of food. Deep-fried chips, often heavily salted, became favourites for most children and were a quick way to fill them up. Children developed a taste for sugary drinks, fizzy fruit drinks and Coca-Cola being favourites. Snacking between meals became much more common.

As a result of these changes in diet towards increased consumption of energy-dense, high-calorie foods, as well as a variety of other factors in the lives of children, such as a reduction in exercise, more time watching television and on screens, more mothers going out to work resulting in less supervision of the content of meals (Anderson and Butcher 2006), childhood overweight and obesity rapidly increased from the 1970s onwards. National surveys found no increases in weight from 1946 to 1970. Then, overweight, as assessed by a body mass index of 30–39.9 went up from 1984 onwards and continued to increase. Obesity, as assessed by a body mass index of 40+, similarly increased from 1.2 per cent in 1984 to 6.0 per cent in 2002 in five- to ten-year-old boys and from 1.8 per cent in 2002 in girls of this age to 6.6 per cent in 2012–13. These trends continued well into the twenty-first century. Further, children from manual social classes developed higher rates of obesity than those in higher income households (Stamatakis et al. 2005; Stamatakis et al. 2010). In the child population generally, the rate of overweight and obesity combined went up from 26 per cent in 1995 to 31.7 per cent in 2019 and, in eleven- to fifteen-year-olds, from 29.7 per cent to 38.0 per cent. There were markedly higher rates in socially disadvantaged children (Broadbent et al. 2024).

Obesity in childhood is almost always a prelude to overweight in adulthood. This means that, as a result of their childhood diets, an increasing number of adults will have an increased risk of heart disease, high blood pressure, type 2 diabetes, arthritis, liver disease and certain cancers. Obesity in childhood is extremely difficult to treat successfully, which makes it doubly important for children to eat healthy diets from early infancy. It has to be added that, throughout the whole of the historical period in question, eating in a fast-food restaurant has been one of the treats that children have greatly appreciated. Teenagers often met and hung out in them. These aspects of lifestyle are described further in Chapter 6.

Human immunodeficiency virus (HIV)

HIV infection was first identified in the early 1980s, and it soon became apparent that the infection led on to acquired immunodeficiency disease syndrome (AIDS) which had a fatal outcome. The virus was identified in 1983. During the 1980s, the number of deaths from AIDS rapidly increased. Although initially thought to be confined to homosexual men, it rapidly became clear that HIV could be transmitted to female sexual partners and then that infected women could transmit the virus to their newborn babies via so-called vertical transmission. Most affected babies were infected not during the pregnancy but during delivery or from infected maternal milk (Siberry 2014). A number of babies infected in this way were identified in the UK in the late 1980s. By the early 1990s about seventy diagnoses were made per year, rising to a peak of 164 in 2003. From then on, the number declined so that there were only three vertical transmissions in 2017 and 2018 (NHS England 2024a). As soon as it became apparent that HIV infection could be successfully treated with antiretroviral medication such as zidovudine, this was routinely administered to pregnant women found to be infected as well as to infants immediately after their birth. Infected women were discouraged from breastfeeding their babies who were given milk substitutes.

Allergic illness

Allergic disease was not recognized until the second half of the nineteenth century when hay fever was realized to be a reaction to pollen and increased attention to hygiene. Soon after the beginning of the period covered by this book, there was a rise in the prevalence of asthma and, by 1990, it had reached epidemic numbers in all countries where children had adopted an indoor lifestyle. The link to an indoor lifestyle was probably mediated by increased sensitization to indoor allergens, diet, prolonged periods of shallow breathing and decreased physical activity (Platt-Mills 2015). Since 1990, there has been a remarkable increase in food allergy which has now also reached epidemic proportions (ibid.). Ingestion of peanuts is the most important cause, but there may have been other changes in lifestyle affecting the permeability of the skin.

Trans medical interventions

In the last decade of the twentieth century and the beginning of the twenty-first, a group in Amsterdam pioneered a psychiatric and medical approach to enable that very small number of children who felt they had been born into the wrong sex to change gender. After careful assessment, this group was put on puberty-blocking agents. Then, at the end of their teens, if they still wished to change gender they were given sex hormones, followed by reconstructive surgery. The results were favourable (Cohen-Kettenis et al. 2011).

A gender identity clinic was set up in 1989 at the Tavistock Clinic in London to provide a similar service but received very few referrals. However, around 2006–7, the demand increased and then became overwhelming and it became clear that a different population of trans young people had emerged, affected by more general identity confusion (Graham 2023). Unfortunately, because of the numbers involved, the Clinic was unable to offer a satisfactory service and, after a judicial review initiated by a dissatisfied client and adverse external reports, together with a review led by Hilary Cass (Department of Health 2024), the Clinic was closed down in 2022. It was replaced by a small number of regional centres operating on a research basis. These began to operate in 2024.

Sudden infant death syndrome (Cot death)

This is an uncommon cause of death in babies under the age of one year. The infant is put down to sleep at a normal time but is found dead in the morning. The death is nearly always unexplained, although a campaign to encourage parents never to put their babies to sleep face down but always on their backs resulted in a significant decline in prevalence in many countries. It had been recognized for many years that a small number of such deaths, perhaps 2–5 per cent were due to suffocation by parents. In the late 1990s, a woman who had had three cot deaths was found guilty of murdering them, on the basis of expert evidence that it was a statistical impossibility they could have died of natural causes. The verdict was hotly contested on statistical grounds and reversed. Following this case, there has been considerable controversy about the diagnosis and, although it still occurs, especially in the first four months of life, the diagnosis is less frequently made (Garstang and Pease 2018).

COVID

The COVID-19 epidemic (2020–2) presented such a massive challenge to child health services, mental health professionals and the education services that it is dealt with separately in Chapter 9.

Drugs, alcohol and smoking

Alcohol

As discussed in Chapter 6, drinking alcohol is part of the lifestyle of teenagers. Alcohol consumption is, however, also discussed in this chapter as, for a minority of teenagers, it is a health hazard and the first sign of a pattern of drinking leading to chronic alcoholism. There are no accurate figures for the consumption of alcohol by teenagers in the 1960s and 1970, but it is likely that they mirrored adult intake at this time. There was a slow rise to the 1980s when it became steady with about 60 per cent of eleven- to fifteen-year-olds having already had an alcoholic drink. This remained the case until around 2005 when teenage drinking went into decline. This decline continued until at least the early 2020s by which time it had once again stabilized. Thus, in 1990, 8 per cent of twelve-year-olds, 32 per cent of fourteen-year-olds and 40 per cent of fifteen-year-olds had consumed an alcoholic drink, by 2005, the figures for these ages were 8 per cent, 32 per cent and 46 per cent, but by 2021, the figures were 2 per cent, 10 per cent and 20 per cent. However, there is evidence that the heaviest drinkers and some socially disadvantaged subgroups have not followed this pattern of declining consumption. The reasons for this very significant decline are unknown (Pape, Rossow and Brunborg 2019), but it is most likely that the increased cost of alcohol and closer parental supervision, particularly the former, were responsible.

Smoking

Cigarette smoking is the most preventable cause of disease and death in the UK. People who die of smoking-related lung cancer and heart disease have nearly always begun to smoke in childhood. Smoking by children and teenagers has been a major cause for concern since before the Second World

War, but it was the evidence linking smoking to lung cancer by Doll and Hill (1950) that first triggered calls for public health action. By the early 1960s, taxation on cigarettes had already begun to rise above the rate of inflation, and in 1965 advertising of tobacco on the television was banned. But, despite the continuing high rates of cigarette smoking among children, it was not until 1991 that the Children and Young Persons Act introducing penalties for those who sold tobacco to under-16s was passed. (This was extended to under-18s in 2007.)

Meanwhile the number of teenagers who smoked regularly remained remarkably steady during the second half of the twentieth century and the beginning of the twenty-first (Charlton 2001). For example, 16 per cent of fourteen-year-olds and 26 per cent of fifteen-year-olds were regular smokers in 1982 and the rates were almost the same in 2005. However, in 2021, only 1 per cent of fourteen-year-olds and 3 per cent of fifteen-year-olds were regular smokers, with those spending more time on social media smoking the most (Purba et al. 2025). It is notable that during the whole of the period when the rate of regular smoking among teenagers was high, despite the cost, the rates were always highest in those of lower social class. The reasons for the decline in teenage smoking after the first few years of the twenty first century are unclear. A few gave up smoking, but mostly there was a sharp decline in those starting to smoke.

Electronic cigarettes (vaping) entered the market in 2007 as an alternative to cigarette smoking and were immediately taken up by teenagers. Whereas it was established that vaping was safer than cigarette smoking, it was also clear that vaping was not without its own dangers. By 2024 it was recommended that vaping should only be practised as an alternative to smoking cigarettes. In the same year, the Conservative government made a commitment to create a smoke-free nation and that, from that time onwards, children who turned fifteen in that year should never for the rest of their lives be able to buy cigarettes legally. It is unclear how the 2024 Labour government will tackle this issue. Smoking as part of teenage lifestyle is discussed further in Chapter 6.

Illegal drugs

While it is every parent's nightmare that their child will develop addiction to a so-called 'hard' drug, in fact, over the period in question, the risk of this happening has been very low. Cannabis was the illegal drug most often consumed by teenagers. Although about a third of teenagers tried it at some point, during most of the period in question, only about one in twenty-five teenagers was using it as often as once a month. It was the drug for which help was requested most frequently from drug addiction specialists but fortunately, although adverse effects such as lack of concentration were common, addiction was most unusual. However, psychotic episodes were not infrequently recorded when high-potency strains of cannabis were used.

Cannabis, although present in the UK beforehand, only became part of UK culture with the 1950s 'Windrush' immigration from the West Indies. Its consumption began to rise sharply in the 1960s as part of the so-called 'permissive society'. Together with reggae music, this culture captured the affections of middle-class white youth with ganja, grass or less direct references often entering into the lyrics of popular music. Throughout, it was illegal to possess or sell the drug which was variably rated as a Class B or a Class C drug following the Misuse of Drugs Act 1971. In 2018, it became medically prescribable and could be grown and sold legally under strictly controlled conditions.

Over the whole of this period, especially in older teenagers, the most widely used 'hard' drugs were cocaine, used in powder form, and ecstasy. About one in ten teenagers has tried these on a small number of occasions but the number of regular users is very small. Among younger children, there were sporadic epidemics of glue-sniffing, often in socially deprived sections of the population.

Changes in child health services

Community care

From the beginning of the twentieth century, there had been a realization that there was a need for children's health services that provided more than diagnosis and treatment for acute and chronic diseases. There was a need for services that would check on the developmental progress of young children and provide advice if this was faltering. Infant welfare and school health clinics had been set up and funded by local authorities for this purpose. These were largely staffed by part-time nurses and doctors without formal training, who nevertheless provided valuable checks on development both after birth and during the school years, immunization programmes and the care of disability.

In 1976, the Court Report (Department of Health 1976) called for improved, community-based, integrated care led by consultant community paediatricians and those working in local authority clinics to be gradually absorbed into the NHS. Over the next twenty years there was a gradual development of a large community paediatric service under the umbrella of the British Association of Community Child Health focusing on vulnerable and disabled children, with surveillance, immunization and health promotion reverting to primary health care (Lenton 2016).

Throughout the whole of the period covered by this account, the community child welfare service provided essential care after the birth of a baby. A community midwife carried out a home visit shortly after the mother returned home. After discharge from the midwifery service, a community district nurse then visited to check that feeding was established, the baby was gaining weight and developing normally. The mother and baby were then followed up at community child development or infant welfare clinics at regular intervals.

Primary health care

The advent of the NHS in 1948 meant that, by the end of the 1950s, all children had a family doctor and, initially, most children saw the same doctor every time they attended their practice. Before the age of five years, most children were taken to the GP more than once, often several times a year, usually for relatively minor illnesses but sometimes for conditions that required referral to hospital. With increasing age, the rate of GP consultation declined rapidly so that most teenagers were not seen by a GP even as often as once a year. The great majority of young children therefore had the experience of being taken to the doctor with an ear infection or a sore throat or perhaps abdominal pain. The effectiveness of antibiotics for acute infections, their generally excellent short-term prognosis and the effectiveness of antibiotic treatment for those that did not improve spontaneously, meant that only a small minority needed to be referred to hospital to be seen in outpatients and a smaller number were admitted for a few days to a children's ward. A small minority had recurrent admissions perhaps with wheezy bronchitis and got to know the nurses on the ward quite well.

The Court Report (Department of Health 1976) recommended closer integration between community, hospital and primary care services for children but no action along these lines was taken. Similarly, the Report recommended the creation of general practitioner paediatricians who would have the sole responsibility for looking after children in primary care. This did not find favour with the profession and again was not implemented.

This situation with considerable continuity of care continued until the introduction in 2005 of incentives to GPs to provide 48-hour access. The COVID-19 epidemic further increased demand for urgent medical advice and a shortage of doctors, most of whom were now working part-time, meant that much continuity of care was lost. Waiting lists built up and more children were directly seen in Accident and Emergency Departments who would previously have been dealt with in primary care. In 2024, the new Labour government pledged to restore continuity of care in general practice, but, given the number of part-time doctors, it was uncertain how possible this would be.

Hospital care

This was largely carried out in outpatients departments and paediatric wards in general hospitals. However (see above), some children were admitted to adult wards. There were a small number of children's hospitals in London and other major cities. In the late 1950s and 1960s, the great majority of doctors working in hospitals looking after children were general paediatricians. There were a small number of medical specialists working as paediatric cardiologists and neurologists. Paediatric surgery was the first speciality to establish itself in a significant way as working exclusively with children. The British Association of Paediatric Surgeons had already been established in 1953, and the speciality thrived over the next fifty years at first with centres mainly in London but soon all over England and the rest of the UK (Spitz 2012). From the 1970s onwards the number of sub-specialities gradually increased so that by the 2020s there were eighteen paediatric sub-specialities with proportionately fewer general paediatricians. However, all paediatricians underwent training in general paediatrics before entering their chosen sub-speciality (Royal College of Paediatrics and Child Health 2024).

The day-to-day and most of the essential care of sick children was, however, carried out by nurses. Before the 1960s, although large numbers of nurses worked exclusively with children in children's hospital or on paediatric wards, they had very low status and were not allowed to join the Royal College of Nursing until 1960. Most training continued to be 'on the job', and there were few opportunities to train specifically in children's nursing. In 1986, however, schools of nursing were transformed into higher education establishments and children's nursing became one of four key branches in which all student nurses were expected to train. By the twentieth century, there were numerous specialities in paediatric nursing, including neonatal intensive care, paediatric oncology, diabetes, child protection and counselling (Royal College of Nursing 2023).

Mortality, illness and disability

Although, fortunately, only a tiny minority of infants, children and adolescents suffer fatal illnesses, trends in mortality give some indication of improvements in child health. In previous sections, advances in the care and treatment of children have been described as well as changes in the pattern of delivery of child health services. The impact of these changes and advances is seen most clearly in the infant mortality rate (death under the age of one year). This was around 25 per thousand births in 1960 and fell to around four per thousand births in the period 2015 to 2020 (Office of National Statistics 2022). This dramatic fall occurred for a variety of reasons. Childbirth itself became less dangerous for the newborn child as a result of advances in obstetric technique. Attention given to the nutrition of the pregnant mother meant that both mother and newborn child were in better shape to face the trauma of childbirth. After the 1980s, fewer mothers smoked and drank alcohol in the first three months of pregnancy. Medical and surgical care of the premature, especially the very premature newborn baby, improved greatly so that more very tiny babies survived. Survival rates greatly improved in the last decades of the twentieth century (Saigal and Doyle 2008) for infants of borderline viability; however, these infants remained at risk of developing a wide array of complications, not only in the neonatal unit, but also in the long term. Morbidity was inversely related to gestational age. However, there was no gestational age, including term, that was wholly exempt. Neurodevelopmental disabilities and recurrent health problems took a toll in early childhood. Subsequently hidden disabilities such as school difficulties and behavioural problems became apparent and persisted into adolescence. Reassuringly, however, most children born very preterm adjusted remarkably well during their transition into adulthood. Unfortunately, a significant number of the premature babies who survived suffered from disabilities later on. These might be relatively minor or more severe learning difficulties or more major problems involving the lungs, the eyes or paralysis of one or more limbs. However, prevention and treatment of such disabilities improved so that overall, the rate of disability in children hardly changed over the years.

There were changes in mortality and disability throughout the age range of 1–19 years. There was a slow but steady decline in mortality of children of this age over the years (Office of National Statistics 2021). The most common causes of death in the 1–4 age group were cancer, accidents and congenital conditions. In the 5–9 age group, respiratory disease replaced congenital conditions as a leading cause of death. In the adolescent age group, while cancer and accidental injury remained leading causes of death, self-harm or suicide now became one of the three most common reasons for a fatal outcome (see Chapter 4 for further discussion of self-harm).

Management of terminal illness

In the 1960s and 1970s, terminally ill children remained under the care of the paediatricians who had looked after them during the course of their chronic illness until they died. Sometime before their death, paediatricians sat down with the parents to tell them their child only had a limited prognosis and to discuss how the final weeks or months were to be managed. Often parents had realized before they were told that this would be the case. There was usually an assumption, implicit between the doctors, nurses and the parents, that children under the age of fifteen or sixteen would not be told their death was imminent and that they would not realize this was the case (Bluebond-Langner 2024, personal communication). This belief that the child was in ignorance of the prognosis was often unfounded, especially if the child had been nursed alongside other terminally ill children with the same condition as their own and had witnessed their fate. Children expressed their awareness of their prognosis as well as their parents' reluctance to speak about it in a number of ways; often choosing to protect their parents from what they knew.

The parents and/or staff were often aware that children knew of their prognosis and wanted to protect them.

> Jeffrey was an 8-year-old boy with leukaemia who often yelled at his mother. When asked why he did this, he simply replied, 'Then she won't miss me when I'm gone.' When I asked Jeffrey's mother 'Why does Jeffrey yell at you so much?' she replied, 'He knows when I can't take it in that room any more. He knows that if he yells at me I'll leave. He also knows I'll come back.'

> One morning when the home care/hospice nurse asked Stephen, a 6-year-old with multiple relapsed diseases what makes him feel better he said: 'Pushing the button,' referring to the morphine pump. He also told her, 'Don't tell my mother.' When the nurse asked him why he told her, 'So she doesn't get worried.'

Some parents, while acknowledging that their children knew the prognosis, chose not to speak about it with them when decisions about further disease-directed treatment were made For Jeremy, a fourteen-year-old boy who was treated 14 months earlier with radiation and chemotherapy for a then partially resected anaplastic astrocytoma that now how had recurred, the only disease-directed option available was a phase 1 clinical trial. His father did not want him told that it was a trial or anything much else about it. His mother, on the other hand, was willing to tell him about the drug, but not that it was a trial. She explained, 'We felt like telling him it's a clinical trial, but that sounds so harsh. We never did use the word trial. We didn't want him to think that it was some kind of experiment. You know, sometimes experiments don't work. He is only 13, 14 in 3 weeks. We just felt like this was something that he didn't have to know.' 'Jeremy knows he has cancer. He knows people have died from cancer, but we try to have him rely on faith. You have people praying for you, you pray for yourself. It doesn't necessarily have to mean that you know, but that he knows.'

Until the mid-1980s, paediatricians had not followed the lead of their adult colleagues (in particular, Cicely Saunders), who had founded the modern hospice movement for terminally ill adults in the 1960s. Then in 1982, Helen House, the first hospice for children in the world, was established in Oxford by Sister Frances Dominica. Several other children's hospices were subsequently founded in the UK. In 1986, Ann Goldman established the Symptom Care Team at Great Ormond Street Children's

Hospital, London, the first multi-disciplinary paediatric hospital palliative care team in the UK, and this served as a model for other such services in major centres throughout the country. This meant that paediatricians, when caring for a terminally ill child, could call on the services of a group of professionals (paediatricians, nurses, social workers) who would, in collaboration with them, care for the child and the family up to the time of the patient's death and then provide care for the bereaved members of the family. Both hospital and hospice palliative services began to provide care for terminally ill children living at home in the 2000s and such domiciliary care became more widely available. In 2009, paediatric palliative care was recognized as a sub-speciality of paediatrics.

Although paediatric palliative care in the UK initially developed out of oncology services, cancer being the most common cause of death in children after the first three or four years of life, the service rapidly became more comprehensive. In particular, in the 1990s, it became available to premature babies with a short expectation of life.

Social disadvantage and child health

It had been realized throughout the period in question that social disadvantage plays a large part in determining the risk of ill health. For example, the Court Report (Department of Health 1976) pointed to the importance of social factors in the prevalence of infectious disease (Department of Health 1976, p.40). Bronchitis and pneumonia were found most commonly in families in Social Classes IV and V. The Black Report (Department of Health and Social Security 1980) also found major differences in the health of children according to occupational social class. It revealed that, at birth and during the first month of life, the risk of death in Social Class V (unskilled manual workers) was double the risk in Social Class I (professional workers). From the end of the first month to the end of the first year, class differentials in infant mortality reached a peak of disadvantage. For the death of every one male infant in Class I, one could expect almost two deaths in Social Class IIIM and four deaths in Class V. The steepest gradients in childhood were found for accidents (33 per cent of total causes). For deaths caused by fires, falls and drowning, the risk for boys in Class V was ten times the risk for their peers in Class I.

From pregnancy onwards, there was a marked association between social disadvantage and child health. Financially disadvantaged mothers were more likely to have children of low birth weight and low birth weight was associated with poorer long-term health outcomes (Marmot 2010, p. 60). It has been estimated that one quarter of all deaths under the age of one could be avoided if all births had the same level of risk as those to women with the lowest level of deprivation. Information about social causes for ill health is not always found acceptable by governments. When the Black Report was presented to the recently elected Thatcher government ministers in 1980, the printing of only a limited number of copies was authorized. The secretary of state for social services, Patrick Jenkin, wrote in his Introduction that, for financial reasons, he 'could not endorse the Group's recommendations'. While subsequent governments have been less blatant in their unwillingness to face up to the major links between health and poverty and what to do about them, children from the poorest families continued throughout to suffer poorer health in virtually every respect.

Conclusion

Over the sixty-five years covered by this book, there were remarkable improvements in the welfare of children in hospital, in the prevention of illness and accidents, in the treatment and outcome of disorders (other than overweight and obesity in which there was marked deterioration) suffered by children, in childhood mortality, in all aspects of child health services and in palliative care. In the twenty-first century, inadequate funding of health care and staff shortages led to increasing waiting lists. Throughout, although socially disadvantaged children benefitted from the improvements, they remained less healthy than their better-off contemporaries.

4

Mental Health

Introduction

In this chapter, I shall start by describing the major national and local surveys of disorders of child mental health, beginning with those in the 1960s and continuing through to those carried out in the twenty-first century. This will lead to an account of the changing approaches to understanding and treating such disorders before descriptions of the ways specific disorders changed in prevalence and in how they were viewed over the decades. This will be followed by an account of the response of mental health and other services with different service models and management strategies to the challenges posed by these problems.

Population surveys of child mental health problems

The Isle of Wight: 1960s to 1970s

From 1964 to 1970, under the direction of Michael Rutter, a survey of the mental health problems of all the nine- to eleven-year-old children living on the Isle of Wight was carried out. This study is described in some detail as it turned out to be a template for many other epidemiological investigations carried out both in the UK and abroad. As a preliminary to this survey, extensive studies were carried out to ensure the reliability and validity of the methods that were used to define whether or not a child had a mental health problem. Great care was taken to ensure that the research workers used the same criteria to define a 'case' and that these criteria identified children who suffered from a behaviour or emotional problem that caused impairment of their social lives and/or learning. Similar methodological studies established the reliability of judgement of mental health problems in parents and the quality of the parental marital relationship.

The entire population of nine- to eleven-year-old children was then screened using reliable and valid behavioural questionnaires to identify those most at risk for having a behavioural or emotional disorder. These, together with a randomly selected group of low-scoring children, were then given individual psychiatric interviews and tested for their general intelligence and reading ability; one or both of their parents was interviewed about their own mental health and the behaviour of their children. In addition, teachers were asked to complete behavioural questionnaires about the intensively investigated children and were similarly interviewed. Thus, for each child, a comprehensive amount of information was available to determine whether or not the child had a significant psychiatric disorder, the probable diagnosis, the academic level the child had achieved and the situation in the child's family, in particular whether a parent had a mental health problem and the social circumstances of the family.

The study provided the first scientifically sound estimate of the prevalence of behaviour and emotional disorders in children of this age. A disorder was regarded as present when 'abnormalities of behaviour, emotions or relationships were sufficiently marked and sufficiently prolonged to be causing persistent suffering or handicap in the child himself or disturbance in the family or community'. According to this definition, about 6 per cent of ten- and eleven-year-old children on the semi-rural Isle of Wight were regarded as showing disorders (Rutter, Tizard and Whitmore 1970).

After the completion of the study of nine- to eleven-year-olds, a follow-up study was carried out in the late 1960s when the children were fourteen years old. The results showed very considerable continuity in behaviour and emotional disorders over the three to four years. The rate of disturbance was slightly but not greatly higher than it had been previously. The study also provided valuable insights into the controversy over the existence of so-called 'adolescent turmoil', the notion that the teenage years were a time of 'normal' disturbance, with increased rates of moodiness, irritability, difficulties in relationships with parents and aggressive behaviour. The findings from this study revealed that such behaviour was largely confined to that relatively small minority of teenagers who were showing a range of behaviour and emotional problems (Graham and Rutter 1973).

The Isle of Wight study was further extended by full investigation of all the school-age children who suffered from neurological disorders. This revealed that if the neurological disorder affected the structure or functioning of the brain, such as a congenital malformation of the brain or epilepsy, these children were highly significantly more likely to show a behaviour or emotional disorder (Graham and Rutter 1968). Psychiatric disorders in children with neuro-epileptic conditions were five times as common as in the general population and three times as common as in children with chronic physical handicaps not involving the brain. It was concluded, on the basis of a study of factors associated with psychiatric disorder, that the high rate of psychiatric disorder in the neuro-epileptic children was due to the presence of organic brain dysfunction rather than just the existence of a physical handicap (though this also played a part). However, organic brain dysfunction was not associated with any specific type of disorder. Within the neuro-epileptic group the neurological features and the type of fit, intellectual/educational factors, and socio-familial factors all interacted in the development of psychiatric disorder.

The Camberwell Study: 1970s

After the Isle of Wight studies were completed, in the early 1970s, Michael Rutter and his team embarked on a study of the nine- to eleven-year-old children in Camberwell, an inner London Borough, using virtually identical methods, except that only a teacher's questionnaire was used for screening. This made possible comparisons in the health, behaviour and educational ability of children living in a semi-rural environment with those living in an inner city. Briefly, it was found that the rate of deviance (as assessed by questionnaire) and of psychiatric disorder (as assessed from parental interview) was twice as high in the Camberwell (Inner London Borough, ILB) children as in the Isle of Wight (IOW) children. The higher rate applied to both boys and girls and extended to both emotional disorders and disturbances of conduct (Rutter et al. 1975).

Because the investigations in both places had been so comprehensive, it was possible to examine the reasons for the very large differences between the two areas in the rates of psychiatric disorder. The comparisons related to three sets of variables: the quality of family relationships, the social circumstances in which the children lived and the quality of the schools the children attended. It was found that many more of the ILB children were not living with their two biological parents as a result of the breakdown of family care. There were, however, interesting differences both in the reasons for family breakdown and in the fate of the parents after the marital breakdown. First, most of the breakdown of the marriages of the ILB children had occurred as a result of divorce due to incompatibility while the IOW marriages had largely broken down because of one of the parents having died. Second, after the marital breakdown, many of the IOW mothers had remarried, while most of the ILB children remained in single-parent families. Basically, a higher proportion of the marriages of the parents of the ILB children had been characterized by tension, mutual dislike and arguments than was the case in the IOW parental marriages which more often showed mutual affection and love.

The social circumstances of the two groups of children were also different. A higher proportion of the ILB children's' mothers were suffering from a psychiatric disorder (usually depression) and their fathers were more often in prison or had served prison sentences. Moreover, the ILB children came from larger families and consequently they were more often living in overcrowded homes. More IOW children were living in homes owned by their parents and not in social housing.

Finally, there was evidence that the quality of the school experience of the IOW children was better than the school experience of the ILB children. The ILB schools had higher rates of teacher turnover, higher rates of pupil turnover and higher rates of children receiving free school meals because more of their families were in receipt of social benefits. It seemed highly likely therefore that the ILB children showed distinctly higher rates of psychological disturbances for a whole variety of reasons, but particularly because they had more interpersonal conflict in the home, they were more often living in unsatisfactory accommodation, their parents more often showed psychological problems and the schools they attended were of poorer quality (Rutter et al. 1976).

There may, of course, have been other underlying problems stressing parents of children with psychological problems. Although, at the time, this was not a particular focus of the population surveys, in fact they all showed a concentration of mental health problems in the poorer sections of the population. This is not surprising in that the major stresses associated with nearly all the common types of mental health problem are all experienced disproportionately by those in situations of financial hardship. Family relationships are inevitably more likely to be strained when there is worry about having enough money for food, housing and heating. Irritation with children, a forerunner to abuse, is more likely when parents are at the end of their tether for other reasons. School attendance and performance are more likely to suffer when there is no money to buy books or laptops. It is certainly not the case that mental health problems do not occur in the affluent; they certainly do, but they are less likely to emerge than among the poor.

Waltham Forest Study of pre-school children: 1970s to 1980s

The possibility that mental health problems could occur in pre-school children was not considered seriously until the late 1970s when Naomi Richman and Jim Stevenson embarked on a population survey of behaviour problems in three-year-old children who were followed up to eight years. They identified the 705 non-immigrant three-year-old children living in the London Borough of Waltham Forest. One parent, usually the mother, was personally interviewed about the behaviour of their child, using a reliable and valid questionnaire. The interviewer assessed the child's health and development and the family's housing, recent stresses, parental occupation and education. The child's level of language development was also assessed. On the basis of the interview, it was calculated that 7 per cent of the children showed moderate or severe disturbance and 15 per cent mild problems. The disturbed children and a randomly selected group of non-disturbed children matched for sex and social class were more intensively interviewed. It was found that the disturbed group was characterized by disharmonious parental marriages and negative attitudes of parents towards the child. When the children were followed up five years later at the age of eight years, there was considerable continuity in the presence of behaviour problems. Nearly two-thirds of the problem group remained with some degree of disturbance compared to only one of five of those who had been rated as without problems five years earlier (Richman, Stevenson and Graham 1982). To give the reader some idea of the nature of the problems shown by these young children, two examples are provided here.

> Peter is the elder of two boys. He is very over-active and is said to 'run around like a madman'. He is reported to be very wild and totally out of control, having a tantrum whenever he is frustrated. He torments his nine-month-old brother so that he cannot be left with him. He will not play with other children and will only fight with them. It is impossible to take him out. He follows his mother around all day. He has a poor appetite, is faddy, and he occasionally eats paint. It takes a very long time to settle him at night, and he often gets into his parents' bed. He shows facial grimacing at times. He can amuse himself but is disinclined to do this. He cannot be left for long with others and is irritable if he doesn't get his own way. He worries that his mother might die and is also frightened of monsters and of noises at night. He has many other fears as well as nightmares. He frequently shouts and screams and the neighbours and other children will not have anything to do with him.
>
> (ibid., p.20)

This boy was rated as showing a 'marked' problem, the most severe category.

> Moira C was the younger of two girls. She was said by her mother never to do what she was told, but to run around the room, never still, climbing on the table at mealtimes. She has a smallish appetite and eats inappropriate materials such as tissues. She takes about half an hour to get to bed and then sleeps through the night. She is a very active girl with poor concentration and is always playing with things that she shouldn't. She seems to annoy her mother deliberately. She is uncontrollable at times, for example, when her mother takes her out shopping. She has infrequent tempers but is often grisly, whiny and moody and her moods may last up to one hour. She fights with her sister a good deal and is generally boisterous and gets into fights with other children from whom she has to be separated. She wears both her parents out. She has no fears. She tends to dominate the other members of her family.
>
> (ibid., p.19)

This girl was rated as showing a 'moderate' problem.

National Child Development Surveys: 1958–70

A national survey of health and development was carried out under the direction of James Douglas in 1946. It involved a representative sample of 5,362 babies born in one week in March of that year. This was the first national cohort to be studied in any country. Subsequently, similar surveys were carried out at roughly twelve-year intervals. In 1958, the National Child Development Study involved 17,415 children all born in one week in March of that year. The British Cohort Study then examined all children born in one week in April 1970. The initial aim of these surveys was to identify the causes of neonatal mortality and morbidity, but all the cohorts were continuing to be followed up until 2024, when the oldest participant was seventy-eight years old. The participants were all followed up using multiple methods, including behavioural questionnaires during their childhood and teen years. The data from these studies gradually became integrated, with the University College, London, Centre for Longitudinal Studies taking responsibility for the analysis and publication of the data from the 1958 and 1970 studies, as well as the Millennium Cohort study (see below).

Avon Longitudinal Study of Parents and Children (ALSPAC): 1991–2 onwards

In the meantime, under the direction of Jean Golding, a large local study centred on the Bristol area was launched. In this study, over 15,000 pregnant women were identified and investigated over a fifteen-month period and then followed up over the subsequent years. Numerous findings of the health and welfare of their children have emerged from this study.

The Millennium Cohort: 2000–2001

It is of interest that national surveys had been carried out at roughly twelve yearly intervals from 1947 until 1970, but it was not until thirty years later, in 2000, that another national study, the so-called Millennium Cohort was established. The reasons for this long gap probably lie in a relative decline in interest in social influences on behaviour following the election of the Thatcher government in 1979. It certainly did not occur because of lower rates of emotional and behavioural problems which increased over this period probably as a result of a rise in the rates of relative and absolute poverty, higher rates of unemployment and the reduction of availability of social housing. Successive Conservative administrations were not particularly supportive to child mental health services or to the study of the origins of behaviour and emotional disorder. Indeed, John Major, then prime minister, commenting on public attitudes to crime in 1993, opined, 'Society needs to condemn a little more and understand a little less', not a view likely to lead to useful research into the origins of antisocial behaviour in children. With the election of a Labour government in 1997, attitudes both to the provision of child mental health services and to the funding of relevant research improved. In the Millennium Cohort study, when another national survey was commissioned, over 18,000 British children born over a two-year period from 2000 to 2002 were studied at three, five, seven, eleven, fourteen and seventeen years. This was the first time that DNA samples were taken to illuminate the relative contributions and modes of interaction of genetic and environmental influences on cognitive and behavioural characteristics.

NHS England Digital Surveys: Twenty-first century

Major surveys of the mental health of children and young people in England were carried out in 1999, 2004 and 2017 (NHS Digital 2018). In contrast to the previous national surveys, this study did not rely on brief questionnaires, but used rigorous, detailed and consistent methods to assess for a range of different types of disorder according to International Classification of Disease (ICD-10) diagnostic criteria. All cases were reviewed by clinically trained raters. The stand-out finding was that one in eight of five- to nineteen-year-olds had at least one mental disorder when assessed in 2017. Rates of mental disorders increased with age with 5.5 per cent of two- to four-year-old children experiencing a mental disorder compared to 16.9 per cent of seventeen- to nineteen-year-olds. Time trends in specific mental disorders are described below.

Changing approaches to the understanding of the causes and treatment of disorders

The situation regarding the assessment and treatment of behavioural and emotional difficulties in the late 1950s had been set out in the Report of the Underwood Committee (Ministry of Education 1955). This revealed that such problems were most commonly seen as 'maladjustment', a failure of the child to adjust satisfactorily to his or her circumstances. Maladjustment was difficult to define, as the Report frankly acknowledged. But it went on to add 'yet even if it proves impossible to define maladjustment at all closely, nobody can doubt that maladjustment exists, and it should at least be possible to identify it with sufficient precision for our purpose'. The services available to help parents and children with emotional and behaviour problems, as well as in hospital outpatient departments and in-patient wards, were 'child guidance clinics', largely administered by local authorities, whose approach is discussed in more detail below. It is notable that the Underwood Committee was chaired by a doctor working in the Department of Education, not the Department of Health. In fact, within a few years, the term 'maladjusted' became confined to schools and educationists.

The psychiatrists and social workers serving in the child guidance clinics largely took a 'psychodynamic' approach to understanding and treatment with the Tavistock and Anna Freud Clinics seen as the authoritative sources of ideas and training. In the London area and southeast England, many clinics had psychoanalytic psychotherapists trained at one of these clinics attached to them. By the mid-1970s, significantly influenced by the research surveys, the language used to describe the problems shown by such children had become medicalized with a change from the use of the term 'maladjustment' to 'psychiatric disorder'. Those working in clinics, now more commonly situated in health facilities, were keen to make 'diagnoses' and talked about 'prognosis' or outcome.

In the 1970s, the child guidance approach with its emphasis on seeing emotional and behavioural problems as sited within the child was gradually replaced by a strong family therapy movement in which the role of fathers and other family members was emphasized. A variety of different types of family therapy emerged, most of which worked with family communications, boundaries, and alliances aiming to alter interactions between family members and thus improve the functioning of the child. This model was transmitted widely by videos of therapeutic work, as well as large-scale dramatic demonstrations for professional audiences and on public media (Bentovim 2021).

In the 1980s and 1990s, while family therapy approaches remained widely used, there was a strong incursion of cognitive behavioural therapy (CBT) techniques (Graham 1998). This approach, originally developed for adults, aimed to change negative thinking patterns, which, it was hypothesized, influenced the feelings of children. Psychodynamic theory had assumed the reverse was the case, with feelings affecting thought patterns, so this was a departure from previously accepted beliefs. CBT was subjected to numerous controlled trials and shown to be effective, though subsequent studies suggested psychotherapeutic approaches could work equally well. However, CBT remained widely used during the twenty-first century.

In the 1990s, a new influence entered the child mental health field. In 1989, George Bush had signed a presidential decree declaring the 1990s to be the 'decade of the brain' promoting the idea that major advances in understanding and treatment not only of neurological but also of psychiatric disorders would emerge from neuroscientific research. Research organizations in the UK followed suit and put vast resources into genetic and neuroscientific studies. Research into psychological approaches was relatively neglected. Much of the neuroscientific research was focused on brain imaging, especially (as far as children were concerned) of those showing autistic spectrum disorder and attention-deficit hyperactivity disorder (ADHD). The results are discussed below when these disorders are considered in more detail.

In addition to neuroscientific approaches, new interest was taken in the possible importance of genetic factors. After the Second World War, during the 1950s and 1960s, there was deep reluctance to engage in any sort of genetic research because of the way such research had been used to justify the killing of Jews and children with mental retardation or learning difficulties. Indeed, in some quarters, genetic research was regarded as repugnant and immoral. However, attitudes slowly changed, particularly as a result of the twin study of autism (see below), produced results of outstanding interest (Folstein and Rutter 1977). Genetic research using twin and family pattern methodology as well as biological methods involving the use of cytogenetic, biochemical and molecular techniques gradually expanded. The findings from twin studies stimulated a vast amount of biological research aimed at identifying a gene for autism, but basically all these showed was that the genetic influences on the development of this condition could not be explained on the basis of any simple pattern of inheritance. Genetic studies of other behaviour and emotional disorders revealed that, apart from ADHD, where clearly there were significant genetic influences, these were largely environmentally determined (Stevenson and Graham 1988).

As far as treatment was concerned, the findings from neuroscientific and genetic research were disappointing. For example, thirty years after the launch of the decade of the brain, Kingdon (2020) reported that 'it is still not possible to cite a single neuroscience or genetic finding that has been of use to the practicing psychiatrist in managing these (psychiatric) illnesses'. This is not to say that further genetic and neuroscientific research might not be more fruitful, but the results so far cannot be regarded as encouraging. Perhaps the brain mechanisms underlying the thoughts, feelings and behaviour of children and young people are just too complex to be amenable to the relatively crude biological research methods at our disposal. It has to be added that this negative evaluation of the contribution of neuroscience and genetic research is by no means universally shared, in particular especially by those who have dedicated their working lives to this field. It is indeed reasonable to anticipate a more positive contribution to emerge eventually, but, in the mid-2020s, this cannot honestly be claimed to be a likely outcome.

In the 1990s, a strong movement emerged to de-medicalize particular psychiatric disorders, initially childhood autism. People with the label 'autistic spectrum disorder' began to object to what they regarded as the unnecessary medicalization of their behaviour. They pointed to the wide range of personality differences, based ultimately on differences in brain function. Why should some of these differences be regarded as medical syndromes and stigmatized as pathological? The concept of neurodiversity, with its rejection of medical labelling, became increasingly popular. With its linguistic similarity to biodiversity, neurodiversity was a concept that championed difference. Just as the world benefitted from a vast variety of plants and animals, so, it was argued, did it gain from brains that are built differently. Further, the question was asked, why should so-called neurotypical people be privileged over the neurodivergent?

Insofar as the concept of neurodiversity 'normalized' people with autistic brains, it acted to their advantage, removing stigmatization. Where it might have been less useful was in discouraging those who were 'different' from consulting professionals who were expert in helping people who were knowledgeable in their particular type of difference. The neurodiversity movement also affected attitudes to ADHD. Rather than seeing those with ADHD as requiring a medical diagnosis and treatment, those (particularly adults who had been diagnosed with the condition) began to press for alternative ways of viewing their behaviour. It was claimed they too should no longer be seen as having a disorder but being examples of 'neurodiversity'.

Adverse childhood experiences and trauma-focused treatment

At least from the 1960s (Wolff 1969) mental health professionals had been aware of the importance of environmental stresses in creating vulnerability and triggering episodes of psychological disorders in childhood. It was not, however, until the late 1990s when the CDC Kaiser Permanente study identified the importance of adverse childhood experiences in the later onset of a whole range of adult mental disorders that attention became more strongly focused on the ways in which such adverse events (particularly physical, sexual and emotional abuse and neglect) played a major part in the mental health problems of children themselves. Such adverse child experiences (ACEs) could, it was clear, cause significant negative impacts and increase the risk of internalizing and externalizing disorders in children (Hagan et al. 2016). One study based in schools (Plumb et al. 2016) found, for example, that a child with four or more ACEs was thirty-two times more likely to be labelled with a behavioural or cognitive problem than a child with no ACEs. Greater awareness of the significances of ACEs resulted in so-called 'trauma-informed care' with much greater attention being given by mental health professionals to the prevention of such experiences and to the building of resilience (Piotrowski et al. 2020). This approach is discussed further in Chapter 7 where child protection is considered in more detail.

Changing views of specific mental disorders

Emotional disorders

Emotional disorders characterized by depression or anxiety or both of these made up about half the total number of mental health problems identified in the Isle of Wight and Inner London Borough studies (see above). In the late 1950s, there had been serious doubt arising partly on theoretical grounds, as to whether any children could become clinically depressed. The psychoanalytic view was that depression arose from inward-directed feelings of aggression which the child's psyche was too immature to experience. It was important therefore to provide convincing examples of children who were indeed depressed. To give some idea of the nature and severity of the disorders identified, this is the description of a child with a depressive disorder, seen in the Isle of Wight population survey and not seen in a clinic, when she was eleven years old.

> At about the age of five years she began to be really worried and unhappy. This state gradually worsened so that in the year before she was seen she felt very miserable, became quiet and withdrawn, thought she was shunned by other children and came home almost every day in tears. She was tense and frustrated and temper tantrums occurred about three times per week. Her teacher described her as 'the unhappiest I have ever seen', and the girl begged her mother to take her away from school. At psychiatric interview she became somewhat tearful when talking of being picked on by other children. She was preoccupied with worries about her relationships with others and said she sometimes didn't care whether she was alive or dead. She appeared markedly depressed and somewhat anxious.
>
> (Rutter et al. 1970, p.187)

This girl's symptoms were typical of those shown by depressed children and younger teenagers then and subsequently. As well as lowness of mood, such children were often tearful and unhappy, slept poorly, had a diminished appetite, thought that other children didn't like them and were picking on them. They may have had suicidal thoughts and in extreme cases made suicidal attempts or even tried to end their own lives (see below). Up to their early teens, girls and boys were about equally vulnerable to depressive states, but after puberty, girls were and remained more affected than boys.

The girl described above was unusual in that her depression was not triggered by any obvious stress or loss. In general, depressed children and teenagers were living in depressing circumstances with parents who had a disharmonious marriage, were on the breadline or who had depressive or other mental or physical illnesses themselves. Alternatively, or perhaps in addition, they had experienced significant losses, perhaps a much-loved grandparent or a pet that had been in the family for some years. Some form of abuse was commonly present in the background. The fact that depressive states were so often understandable in terms of the circumstances in which children were living or traumas that they had undergone meant that it was sometimes difficult or impossible to distinguish between what might be regarded as 'normal' depressive reactions and depressive disorders. On occasions, the presence of certain unusual symptoms made it clear that a depressive disorder was present. For example, depression lasting more than a few weeks or the presence of unrealistic feelings of self-blame or suicidal ideas or behaviour made it apparent that a depressive disorder was present and medical, psychological or psychiatric treatment was indicated.

The problems arising from the fact that it was difficult to decide whether a child's mood was understandable in terms of their circumstances were dealt with in the International Classification of Diseases, 10th version (World Health Organisation 1977) by focusing purely on mood and behaviour without taking circumstances into account when making diagnosis of depression. Using this classification, a diagnosis of depression was made if a child had persistent or low mood and/or loss of interest or pleasure, or fatigue or low energy, lasting at least two weeks. The presence of disturbed sleep, poor concentration or indecisiveness, low self-confidence, poor or increased appetite, suicidal thoughts or acts, guilt or self-blame or agitation or slowness of movements determined whether the depression was mild, moderate or severe. Thus, a sixteen-year-old girl who had been jilted by her boyfriend or lost a much-loved grandmother and then for two weeks was miserable and lacking in energy, had difficulty sleeping, couldn't concentrate on her schoolwork and lost her appetite was regarded as showing a depressive disorder of moderate severity. This probably involved a significant broadening of the criteria for depressive disorder, which may have had an effect on prevalence (see below).

Children suffering from depression usually showed anxiety symptoms as well, either general fearfulness or phobias of specific feared situations. Less commonly, refusal to go to school either because of fears of separation from one or both parents or because of some feared situation in school occurred. About three in a hundred children living in rural or semi-rural areas suffered from emotional disorders. In general, such emotional disorders had a good outcome, clearing up in a few weeks or months, but they had a strong tendency to recur when triggered by traumatic events.

A review of population studies by Costello et al. (2006) suggested that no increase in depressive disorder occurred over the previous thirty years, indicating that an increased use of services and antidepressants that occurred over this time was largely influenced by changes in attitudes, including decreased stigmatization, rather than increased prevalence. However, a review of more recent studies did indicate a rise in prevalence of emotional problems, especially in teenage girls in high-income countries (Collishaw 2015).

A rise in emotional problems, especially in older girls, was confirmed by a study comparing rates of such disorders in children born in 1991–2 in the ALSPAC survey (see above) and those born ten years later and studied in a national survey, the Millennium Cohort Study (Armitage et al. 2023). The later cohort had an earlier onset of problems than the previous cohort, and sustained higher average trajectories from around eleven years, with female adolescents showing the steepest trajectories of emotional problems. Differences between cohorts peaked overall at age fourteen years.

Further, according to epidemiological studies, the impact of the occurrence of an emotional disorder increased over this time (Armitage et al. 2025). The main effects were on friendships, with more difficulty in seeing other children and getting on with them, and on academic achievement. Home life and leisure activities were also more affected by the presence of an emotional disorder as time went on. Not only did impact increase but there were increasingly strong links with a number of variables, mainly reflecting social disadvantage, especially living in rented accommodation, being in the lowest income quintile or being from an ethnic minority background.

There were probably a number of reasons for the rise in prevalence of emotional disorders that took place in the twenty-first century, especially in older teenage girls (Armitage et al. 2025). These may have included an increase in parental emotional problems, especially emotional disorders in parents which was itself probably related to the increase in precariousness of income and employment. The concomitant rise in eating control problems in adolescent girls may also have been significant as preoccupation with diet and appearance led to emotional distress.

Such preoccupation was fuelled by social media to which older students became increasingly wedded from the 1990s onwards. Older children and adolescents spent large amounts of time on social media (see Chapter 6). Some websites actually portrayed young people self-harming, providing singularly unhelpful models as to how to go about this. On other sites, extremely attractive young people were put forward as the norm, making the viewers feel themselves to be doomed to be social failures. There was also evidence of increased pressure on schools to achieve improved academic performance with penalties for schools failing to deliver what were seen as satisfactory results (see Chapter 5). Such pressure was transmitted to students who responded with stress-related symptoms, including anxiety and mood disorders. Underlying all of these stresses was an increase during this period in income inequality and relative poverty.

Conduct or behaviour problems

These are discussed in Chapter 6.

Self-harm

During the 1960s to the 1980s, children and young people who took an overdose or injured themselves physically were referred to as having 'attempted suicide'. However, it became clear that in many cases of so-called 'attempted suicide' the motivation was not to end life but to express severe distress as well as to draw attention to a need for help to escape from an intolerable situation. From then on, such children and young people were referred to as self-harming or as showing deliberate self-poisoning or self-injuring.

Rates of self-harm have been high throughout this period. Over 10 per cent of adolescents reported having self-harmed on at least one occasion (Hawton 2012). Most have not reported to services. The rate is from three to five times higher in girls than in boys. Self-cutting, which was most unusual in the 1950s and 1960s, became the most common form of self-harm in the 1980s and 1990s so that by that time, it was not at all unusual to see scarring of the wrists, especially in girls. However, paracetamol was the most common mode of self-harm among those admitted to hospital, probably because of the need for stomach washouts in those who had poisoned themselves in this way. In 1998, legislation was passed, making it more difficult to obtain large amounts of tablets and this was modestly effective. The rate of self-harm increased in the 2020s around the COVID-19 epidemic (see Chapter 9). At this time, academic pressure grew in importance as a trigger for self-harm, with a reduction in episodes during the school holidays.

The rate of self-harm increased quite sharply at the age of thirteen years, probably in relation to the onset of puberty. Risk factors included the presence of depressive symptoms, the misuse of alcohol and illegal drugs and involvement in sexual activity (Hawton et al. 2012). Self-harm was also linked to low socio-economic status with young people who were LGBTQ also at high risk. The trigger for a self-harming episode often involved a loss of some sort, perhaps of a long-standing boyfriend or girlfriend, but any negative life event could act in this way.

Although the risk of a completed suicide after an episode of self-harm was not high, it certainly occurred and those young people who self-harmed needed careful assessment to determine their need for help and the risk of a more extreme attempt. In fact, throughout this period most episodes of self-harm did not come to professional attention but were dealt with by friends and family.

Suicide

Suicide in children under the age of fourteen was rare and under the age of twelve extremely rare. It was, however, the second most common form of death in the fifteen- to nineteen-year age group, second only to road traffic accidents (see Chapter 2). The rate of youth suicide increased slowly from the 1960s to the 1980s, but then declined for the rest of the century, with a further increase in the 2000s. By 2021, the rate was the highest it had been for thirty years. The rate then was about 7.5 per 100,000 in males and about a third of that in girls. However, because of concern about stigmatization, it was probably significantly under-reported with coroners not infrequently stating an uncertain cause when suicide was highly likely. Vehicle exhaust gas and hanging were the most common methods used. In young men, there was often a background of seriously aggressive behaviour.

There were many similarities in the background factors of suicide and self-harm, though the presence of psychiatric disorder was more frequently present with suicide, especially in males, with personality disorders especially prominent (Hawton et al. 2012). Other risk factors included restricted educational achievement, a family history of suicidal behaviour, parental separation, divorce or death and the presence of others in the social network who had self-harmed or taken their own lives, an example of so-called 'social contagion'. Twin studies with much greater concordance in monozygotic (identical) than in dizygotic (non-identical) twins strongly suggested genetic influences, but poor family relationships and drug usage were also of significance. It has been known for many years that portrayal of the self-harm or suicide of a young person on television is followed by an upturn in such behaviour, and, in the twenty-first century, the internet and social media were increasingly implicated. It is notable that in the later years, during the 2020s, about a quarter of suicide deaths in young people were related to negative online experiences (Rodway et al. 2023).

Eating disorders

Eating disorders over most of the sixty-five years covered by this book were largely classified as either anorexia nervosa or bulimia nervosa. The central feature of anorexia nervosa was a distorted body image with young people seeing themselves as fat or overweight, when, in fact, the reverse was the case. As a result of the fear of fatness, food intake was greatly reduced, and weight was lost. In affected girls and young women, periods did not start or, if they had begun, they stopped. Bulimia nervosa was characterized by recurrent severe over-eating. However later studies showed that eating disorders were far more diverse and, as well as anorexia nervosa and bulimia nervosa, included binge eating disorder, pica, rumination disorder, and other specified and non-specified eating disorders (Himmerich et al. 2024). Further, these studies showed that the long-accepted stereotype of a person with an eating disorder as that of a thin, young, white female, often from a financially privileged background was not strongly evidence-based. In fact, eating disorders may be even more common in people who are financially disadvantaged, are overweight or experience food insecurity and in communities with multiple marginalized identities (ibid.).

Before the 1960s, at the beginning of our period, severe weight loss among teenage girls and young women was regarded as arising from underlying medical pathology and was treated accordingly. It was only during the 1960s that it became widely accepted that anorexia nervosa was a psychiatric disorder and responded best to psychological approaches

(Court and Kaplan 2016). This belief persisted over time, although twin studies showed that individuals were more likely to be affected if they were genetically vulnerable (Holland et al. 1988).

When food is scarce, as in the poor countries of the world, eating disorders barely exist so it is not surprising that anecdotal evidence suggests that anorexia nervosa hardly occurred in the UK during the Second World War. As the food supply improved during the 1950s and 1960s, more and more teenagers came to attention with anorexia (self-starvation) or bulimia (compulsive over-eating). General practice and hospital studies of the prevalence of anorexia nervosa suggest that the rate of this condition has probably varied rather little over the sixty-five years in question until the very end of this period (Holland et al. 2016). There was a rapid rise in hospital admissions in the 1990s but this was probably because of changed admission policies. However, from about 2017, there was a significant rise in prevalence (Trafford et al. 2023) accelerated during COVID-19 (see Chapter 9) until the end of our period in 2024. The General Practice Research Database for the period 2017–23 suggested that one in forty 11–16-year olds and one in eight 17–19-year-old girls had an eating disorder of some sort. But only one in five hundred met criteria for anorexia nervosa and one in two hundred for bulimia nervosa; most were what one might call non-specific eating disorders that did not fit into either category.

The highest prevalence rate by far occurred in fifteen- to nineteen-year-old girls, although from the 1980s onwards, increasing numbers of girls in their early teens and increasing numbers of boys with the condition were reported. As women moved into their twenties and thirties, the onset of the condition became increasingly unusual and about half the girls who developed it in adolescence become symptom-free. About a third improved considerably but retained some symptoms often for the whole of their lives. Studies revealed that even among those women who appeared to recover completely from anorexia nervosa there was an increased risk of feeding difficulties in their own children. A minority remained chronically affected with a small minority dying of starvation or related illness. Mortality in anorexia nervosa was higher than that in any other mental illness but only a small percentage of those with the condition died from it.

The main symptom of bulimia was eating large amounts of food over a short period of time (bingeing) and then ridding the body of what had been eaten by inducing vomiting, purging (using laxatives) or exercising excessively or a combination of these. Bulimia, which tended to start in the late rather than the mid-teens, was often accompanied by anorexia nervosa, so fear of putting on weight and thinking about food a great deal were symptoms common to both. Most people with bulimia did not consult a health professional, and there were many fewer studies of the condition than was the case with anorexia nervosa.

Approaches to treatment changed over time with a gradual increase in emphasis away from individual psychotherapy towards cognitive behavioural techniques aimed at increasing food intake and weight, at first at home but, if this was unsuccessful, by admission to hospital. Influential studies in the late 1980s suggested that once some weight gain had been achieved, family approaches to treatment (family therapy or family counselling) produced better results in the younger age groups than did individual psychotherapy (Russell et al. 1987).

Autism and autism spectrum disorder

In 1943, Leo Kanner, an American child psychiatrist, described a number of children with disorders he named 'autism'. These were characterized by severe disturbances of inter-personal relationships, language delay and speech abnormalities such as echolalia, repetitive behaviours and mannerisms. A high proportion, about half, of the children he described, had mental retardation or learning difficulties. These children were very slow to progress and most had to be educated in special schools. Largely, on school-leaving, they were unable to obtain employment in the open market. The prevalence of this condition was low, around 4 to 5 per 10,000 in the UK child population (Lotter 1966). In looking for the causes of autism, Kanner noted that a high proportion of the parents seemed to have poor capacity for warm affection; he labelled them 'refrigerator' parents.

A year after Kanner's description of autism, in 1944, an Austrian paediatrician, Hans Asperger, described a similar but milder condition in children with normal intelligence. These children showed many of the same features as those with autism but were much less impaired. In 1977, a study led by Michael Rutter showed that the concordance rate for autism among identical (monozygotic) twins was much higher than that in non-identical (dizygotic) twins (Folstein and Rutter 1977). This put paid to the 'refrigerator parent' hypothesis which incidentally had been the cause of much distress among the parents of children with autism who had blamed themselves for their children's condition.

In 1981, a British psychiatrist, Lorna Wing, established Asperger's syndrome as a mild but distinct form of autism (Wing 1981). A movement grew up to merge these two conditions into one and, in 2013, in the American classification of mental disorders (DSM 13) and in the International Classification of Diseases (ICD 11) in 2018, Asperger's syndrome was formally integrated into the broader category of autism spectrum disorder (ASD). This meant that Asperger's syndrome, which had been a separate diagnosis in previous editions of these classification systems, was no longer recognized as a psychiatric disorder. Asperger's syndrome had been much commoner than autism, and, with a prevalence of autistic spectrum disorder of around 1.5 per cent (Baron-Cohen et al. 2009) the merging of the two conditions resulted in an enormous (about thirtyfold) increase in the number of children with a label of autism. The great majority of these would have previously been referred to as having Asperger's syndrome; now they were regarded as having a high-functioning form of autism.

There is a question as to whether there has been a real, albeit small increase in the prevalence of autism over the last fifty years. If there has, it is probably because of assortative mating. For example, people involved in engineering, computing and data analysis, who have an increased likelihood of showing autistic traits (Baron-Cohen et al. 1997), are more likely to meet people with similar traits socially or at work, develop partnerships with them and have children If there is an increase in the prevalence of autism, given the genetic influence, this is likely to be the explanation. In any event, paradoxically, the main effect of the coincidence in time of merging autism and autism spectrum disorder with the development of the concept of neurodiversity was to greatly increase the numbers of people, especially of children and young people, on waiting lists to see mental health professionals.

One result of the finding that genetic influences were important in the causation of autism was to stimulate a vast amount of research to identify the gene or genes responsible. All that has really emerged from this research is an awareness that no single gene or group of genes is identifiable. To the relief of many, this virtually removed the possibility of gene therapy to eliminate an 'autism' gene.

The twenty-first century saw considerable activity in the treatment of autistic spectrum disorders. Particular attention was given to early intervention to children at risk, aiming to improve the interactions between parents and their children with the aim of preventing autistic development. Applied behavioural analysis was used in more established cases. In general, the most promising results related to the milder forms of the condition that would previously have been diagnosed as Asperger's syndrome.

Overactive, inattentive children and young people

It has always been recognized that, from the first few months of life, some children are a great deal more active than others. Indeed, women who have experienced more than one pregnancy often report that foetuses vary greatly in their level of activity in the womb. As children move, round about the ages of three to five, from nursery to infant school, extremes of activity become obvious with nurseries sometimes excluding young children with levels of overactivity with which they cannot cope.

In the 1920s and 1930s, it was observed that some children who had suffered brain infections with confusion and delirium during the 1919 influenza pandemic showed abnormally high levels of activity and inattention even when their more obvious symptoms had cleared up. These were labelled as showing 'minimal brain dysfunction'. Already in the 1930s, it was noted that children with such behaviour problems quite often did not have a history of earlier brain disease. It seemed more likely that genetic influences were at work, and this was confirmed by systematic studies (Levy et al. 1997). Further, at this time, in the 1930s, it was noted that such children paradoxically often seemed to benefit if they were given stimulant medication in the form of dexamphetamine sulphate.

By the 1950s and 1960s, child psychiatrists and paediatricians were beginning to recognize that, although it was normal for activity levels to vary considerably, some young children were seriously disabled by their overactivity and inattention, and this clearly no longer had anything to do with the post-First World War influenza epidemic. The international classification systems introduced the labels 'hyperkinetic syndrome' and 'attention-deficit hyperactivity syndrome' (ADHD). Gradually, the term 'hyperkinetic syndrome' fell into disuse. By the 1970s, ADHD had become a reasonably well-recognized disorder though it was clear that the borderline between the condition and normal levels of overactivity was difficult or impossible to define. As well as overactivity in all situations (not just at school or just in the home), children with ADHD were generally restless and distractible, eating and sleeping poorly. They found it difficult to focus on tasks involving concentration. Their impulsivity meant that they were accident-prone and over-represented in children attending accident and emergency departments for major and minor injuries.

Survey evidence suggested that the administrative prevalence, based on the number of children identified as a result of contact with services, was in the region of 3–5 per cent. It increased fourfold between 1992 and 2008 (Sayal et al. 2018). However, survey evidence suggested that the community prevalence of ADHD changed very little over this time or subsequently, though awareness of the condition and of the effectiveness of medication meant that, with no increase in mental health professionals, waiting lists for assessment greatly increased. Boys were affected four or five times more commonly than girls (with some suggesting girls were under-diagnosed) as were children from poor families. There was a strong link with conduct disorders (see Chapter 6), with about a third of children with the one condition showing the other. The rate of administrative prevalence fell after the age of fifteen years though the condition began to be diagnosed in adults much more frequently in the twenty-first century.

Whereas previously it had been very infrequently prescribed, by the 1980s, methylphenidate, under its brand name, Ritalin, was being prescribed to a large number of American schoolchildren and a slowly increasing number of British children. During the first quarter of the twenty-first century, there was a marked rise in the number of UK children, especially six- to nine-year-old children, prescribed methylphenidate for ADHD. The other main intervention, behaviour therapy (see below), was less effective. Although changes to diet also became popular ways of intervening with ADHD, this approach only seemed effective for a small minority of children. When a child was found to show ADHD, there was often considerable pressure from both parents and teachers for at least a trial of Ritalin. The education of other children in the class was often compromised by the presence of just one or two hyperactive children. Pressure to treat with medication was increased when it became apparent that, although many of the symptoms of ADHD improved in adolescence, this was by no means always the case, and adult psychiatrists started to diagnose and treat medically ADHD in their patients with increasing frequency.

Seeing children and adults as 'neurodiverse' (see above) rather than as having medical conditions did not result in any reduction of research activity into the way the brains of those with ADHD are different from those without. Studies suggested that some areas of the brain are smaller in ADHD while others are larger; imaging studies suggested there is greater connectivity between frontal brain regions, which handle attention and control. Family and twin studies suggest strong genetic influences on whether an in individual develops ADHD. All the same, during the twenty-first century, it has become realized that the impairment experienced by children with ADHD can be considerably reduced if attention is paid to maintaining good general health and if those who interact with affected children at school or in the neighbourhood are understanding of the difficulties they face.

All the same, in it more extreme form, ADHD had a huge impact on the lives of affected children and their families (Sayal 2018). Children with this condition showed increased use of use of health, specialist education, social care and criminal justice services. There was also a wider cost to society because of its effects on parental employment and mental health, family-borne expenses, crime and offending.

Service responses to child mental health problems

After friends and family members, the first port of call for parents wishing to find help for children with emotional and behaviour problems was their family doctor. Indeed, Garralda and Bailey (1986) found that about a quarter of children seen by family doctors had significant psychological difficulties about which they were consulted. The filtering role that family doctors played in ruling out significant physical disease and pointing to possible relevant stresses probably meant that referrals to specialist paediatric and child psychiatry services were much reduced. Specialist services of some magnitude did however exist though there was controversy over their function and effectiveness.

The Underwood Report (see above) had revealed that, in the 1950s, over the country as a whole, there were 300 child guidance clinics (CGCs), most of which were part-time. About two-thirds were provided by local education authorities, a very few by voluntary bodies and the remainder by regional hospital boards and teaching hospitals, which also supplied the services of a psychiatrist for about half the clinics. Many parts of the country, particularly the Midlands, North-East, North-West and Wales, were very sparsely served. Scotland and some parts of England, such as Essex, were well served by educational professionals. London, particularly northwest London where the Tavistock and Anna Freud Clinics were situated, was particularly well-served with child psychotherapists. The Underwood Committee identified the lack of manpower resources to deal with the large number of children requiring help and set ambitious targets for increases in the number of mental health professionals, but these were largely not met (Stewart 2013).

As we have seen, in the 1950s and 1960s a substantial number of children, perhaps one in ten in the country as a whole, were showing mental health problems. Only a small proportion of these were in touch with health services for help. On the Isle of Wight, an area reasonably well provided with such services, in the mid-1960s only one in ten of the children with significant mental health problems was in touch with psychiatric services (Rutter, Tizard and Whitmore 1970, p.263). Only a tiny number were receiving treatment from their family doctor, though an additional number had consulted their doctor about the problem at some point.

There was a variety of reasons why disturbed children were not receiving psychiatric help when it was available. In nearly half the children with definite emotional and/or behavioural problems, the parents did not perceive there to be a problem more serious than most children showed. A similar proportion of parents of disturbed children, about a half, did not want help. Many parents did not grasp the fact that their children were impaired as a result of their psychological difficulties and many more did not realize that they might be helped by treatment. Fear that their children might be stigmatized if they were in contact with psychiatric services was another factor. Another reason for reluctance of parents to use the child guidance clinics that were available was that they were frequently not seen as helpful. Their name was misleading in that they largely did not provide guidance to parents about how to deal with their difficult children (Mills 1968). Instead, the child was seen for play therapy and the mother by a social worker who, rather than give advice, would probe for reasons in the mother's own upbringing that might be hindering her from providing good care for her child. Many mothers felt blamed for the fact that their child had a problem, inspiring an American child psychiatrist to refer to professional attitudes to mothers as 'mal de mère'. This led to a high drop-out rate among attenders at CGCs (ibid.).

Until the 1990s, the pattern of child and adolescent mental health (CAMH) services was relatively uncoordinated. However, in 1995 the Health Advisory Service published clear guidelines for a desirable pattern of services which received wide approval. These suggested that these services should be considered under four 'tiers'. Tier 4, the most specialist, should be reserved for the most complex cases, often requiring inpatient assessment and treatment. Tier 3 should be staffed by specialists who would only see complex cases. Tier 2 should be for the assessment and treatment of mild and moderate problems as well as for consultation with Tier 1 workers, such as general practitioners, community nurses, social workers and teachers. These were the first port of call for parents who were concerned that their children had emotional/behavioural problems. In addition, the guidelines suggested which problems should be referred to which tier of service and how communication between professionals working in different tiers should be established and maintained. These guidelines were widely adopted and went some way to improving shortfalls in services caused by inadequate levels of workforce supply. The guidelines were increasingly based on sound evidence, a development made possible by the establishment in 1999 of the NHS organization NICE (National Institute of Clinical Excellence, later renamed the National Institute for Health and Care Excellence). This recommended the most effective approaches to help children and young people with mental health problems.

A highly relevant new development in the lives of children emerging in the late 1990s and twenty-first century was the increasing use of the internet and, in particular, of social media platforms. This had many positive aspects. In particular, online therapeutic work was developed, as well as online training of mental health professionals. Opportunities for children and young people to engage in a whole variety of leisure pursuits increased, including social networking, communicating, expanding their interests, entertaining, gaming, connecting and learning (see Chapter 6). Ease of communication was particularly helpful for some children, such as those with autistic spectrum disorders who had difficulties interacting with others. Many children with autism had great difficulties with face-to-face interactions but could cope with and indeed enjoyed emails and participating on social media platforms. Further, children belonging to minority groups, such as the LGBTQ, were able to overcome stigma by communicating with others with the same or a similar orientation.

However, the arrival of the internet also meant there were new ways in which children and young people were put at risk (Bentovim 2021). Exposure to age-inappropriate material online, pornography, violence or hate speech became common. Some children were groomed into creating and circulating images of sexual activities. Sexual exploitation increased with perpetrators falsifying their identities and groomed young people, as a way of meeting and exploiting them sexually. Some websites depicted self-harm, suicide or unhealthy dieting behaviour. Children and young people not infrequently abused each other, sexting (sending sexual images), cyber-bullying, harassment, persuading them to disclose personal information which could then be used for blackmail. Threats of social exclusion sometimes triggered self-harm and suicidal responses.

During the twenty-first century, treatment approaches greatly diversified in a number of ways. In particular, in the second decade of the twenty-first century, vigorous attempts were made to provide relevant mental health services in schools. It became more common for members of the Child and Adolescent Mental Health Services (CAMHS) to be based in schools. The number of school counsellors, mostly dealing with mental health problems, increased, though a significant number of schools, probably about half of both primary and secondary schools, did not employ a counsellor. Schools began to establish their own withdrawal units staffed by specialist teachers. In 2019, a training programme for Education Mental Health Practitioners (EMHPs) was established to provide low-intensity mental health support to children and young people within schools and colleges. These primarily focused on mild to moderate anxiety, depression and behavioural difficulties. They offered interventions based on cognitive behavioural therapy (CBT) and guided self-help, often in group settings or one-to-one. EMHPs also supported school-wide initiatives to promote mental health and well-being. Unfortunately, this service was only patchily available and schools in general were able to provide appropriate psychological support for only a small proportion of the students they knew would benefit from it.

Treatment approaches during the twenty-first century were also adapted to provide trauma-focused responses. Indeed, the concept of trauma was broadened to include so-called adverse childhood experiences (ACEs), including not only physical, sexual and emotional abuse but other forms of harmful experiences, including challenging situations in the home and exposure to the harmful effects of social media (see above).

Throughout the period covered by this account, there have always been waiting lists for specialist services for disturbed children. However, during the COVID-19 epidemic (see Chapter 9) these grew exponentially, so that by 2024, there were over a quarter of a million children waiting for assessment and treatment. Given that, as we have seen, population surveys suggested that, except for a clear rise in rates of emotional and eating control problems in teenage girls, the prevalence of mental health problems remained relatively stable over this period, it seems likely that a much higher proportion of parents of disturbed children as well as teachers were seeking help in the 2020s than was the case even twenty years previously. If this were the case, it is possible that this occurred because of the decline in the availability of primary care services with loss of the filtering function they performed (see above). Further, there was a clear reduction in stigmatization of contact with mental health services over this period.

During the 2020s, the rise in the length of waiting lists for CAMH services and a sharp rise in the rate of school absenteeism following the COVID-19 epidemic (see Chapter 9) led to controversy over whether the children seeking help were 'really' disturbed or whether most of them were taking advantage of the system to avoid going to school. It is indeed quite likely that dislike of school is at the root of a significant amount of absenteeism (see Chapter 6 for students' attitudes to their school experiences). It was more difficult for parents to be firm about insisting their children go to school when many of their friends were 'off sick' with mental health problems and they themselves were far more often working from home.

In fact, throughout this period, it has been clear that the services for disturbed children are never likely to reach adequate levels. Mental health professionals are in demand, not only by the health services which employ them but by the courts and juvenile justice system, social services dealing with cases of child protection and education services concerned about disruptive children and others that teachers identify as distressed and in need of help.

Slow to learn children and young people

Both attitudes and understanding of children and young people who were 'slow to learn' changed considerably over the sixty-five years from 1959 to 2024. Changes in attitude were reflected by marked changes in the language used to describe the difficulties experienced by such children.

Terminology

Until 1977, when the ICD-10 (World Health Organisation 1977) was published, children who were severely slow to learn were referred to as 'idiots', those who were moderately slow to learn as 'imbeciles' and those with mild learning difficulties as 'feeble-minded'. These terms were then replaced by the considerably less offensive terms: mild, moderate and severe 'mental retardation'. By the time the ICD-11 was published in 2019, the term 'mental retardation' had itself come to be regarded as offensive and it was replaced by the term 'intellectual disability', which was now classified as one of a number of 'neurodevelopmental disorders'. This terminology brought ICD in line with the other internationally used classification of mental disorders, the American Diagnostic Statistical Manual (DSM). Intellectual disability in the ICD classification could be mild, moderate, severe or profound. Children who had intelligence within the 'normal' range but had a specific learning problem in, for example, reading or number work, were seen as showing 'developmental learning disorders'.

Intelligence testing

The testing of intelligence was first devised by a French doctor, Alfred Binet, in 1905, whose test was shortly afterwards modified by American psychologists into the Stanford-Binet test that remained in widespread use over much of the twentieth century. In 1949, a more widely used test for children and young people, the Wechsler Intelligence Test for Children

(WISC), was published. These tests were developed after use in large-scale population trials to ensure that the Intelligence Quotient (IQ) average score was 100, with two standard deviations from the average set at 70 and 130. For many years, it was thought that this standardization need not change with time, but Flynn (1984) showed that over the previous fifty years, probably because of increasing education, the average IQ had increased by about three points per decade.

IQ tests were used for a variety of purposes over this period. During the 1950s and 1960s, until the establishment of comprehensive schools, they were used in the UK to determine what type of school (grammar or secondary modern), children should enter at the age of eleven. They were also employed to decide on the placement of children in special schools of one sort or another (see Chapter 5). They were routinely used for clinical purposes when children were referred to specialist psychological or psychiatric services in order to assess whether they had learning problems that might be contributing to their difficulties. Finally, they were used for research purposes to assess whether children were adversely affected by, for example, a new form of medication or treatment that might have affected the brain.

After the 1980s, though they were still quite widely used, IQ tests fell out of fashion for a variety of reasons. First, it was realized that they only measured a part of what might reasonably regarded as intelligence. Indeed, some cynics suggested that the only skill they really measured was the ability to do intelligence tests! It was clear, however, that they did not measure what might be called social or emotional intelligence, both necessary ingredients for career and/or social success. Second, there was concern that the results of an IQ test might brand an individual with a label implying a permanent disability, whereas, in fact, many young people develop and change quite considerably over time. As a result of these and other concerns, intelligence testing was at least partly replaced by broader, though perhaps less reliable forms of assessment.

Education

Children and young people who are slow to learn may well require various forms of special education. These are discussed in the relevant section in Chapter 5.

Disability (see Chapter 8)

Children who are slow to learn form the largest group among those who are disabled, Indeed, among children with disability, children who were slow to learn, especially those who are severely slow to learn, imposed heavier burdens on their parents than any other forms of disability (Graham, Stevenson and Flynn 1997).

Conclusion

Over the sixty-five years covered by this book, there have been marked advances in research into child mental health, especially in epidemiological approaches. These have identified the fact that, in contrast to the situation with physical disorders, for which there were dramatic improvements, child mental health problems have, if anything, increased. This has been especially the case in the latter years, in teenage girls in whom there has been an increase in the prevalence of emotional disorders and eating control problems. An apparent massive rise in autistic spectrum disorders was probably largely due to changes in classification with many more children who would previously not have been diagnosed as autistic but as having Asperger's syndrome now being diagnosed as having autistic spectrum disorders. There has been a clear rise in the number of children being prescribed methylphenidate for ADHD, but this has probably not resulted from a rise in the prevalence of this condition, but because of the increasing awareness of its response to medication. Substantial rises in the size of waiting lists for CAMHS following the COVID-19 epidemic have arisen probably because of a combination of the decline in filtering primary care services, reduction in stigmatization and cuts in local authority spending, particularly after 2010.

The latter years have also been marked by increasing concern about the harmful effects of exposure to social media, these concerns sometimes masking the positive effects such exposure may have. Changes in approaches to assessment and treatment first involved a move away from a 'child guidance' approach to much greater use of family therapy and cognitive behavioural techniques. This was followed in the twenty-first century by increasing emphasis on trauma-focused approaches. Throughout, the vulnerability of children living in socially disadvantaged families has become more obvious, with treatment approaches increasingly taking into account the way children with emotional and behavioural problems have been exposed to adverse experiences.

5

Education

Introduction

This chapter reviews the very considerable changes in the British educational system over the sixty-five years covered by this book. After a description of the main changes following the Second World War, an account of the development of nursery schools following the publication of the influential Plowden Report (Central Advisory Council for Education 1967) is given. This is followed by an account of state primary and state secondary schools and a discussion of the National Curriculum. The significant private education sector, first preparatory and then secondary (public) schools, is then described and followed by a description of the link between poor academic achievement and low income. The development of the special education and disability (SEND) sector is then described. The voices of mainly secondary school students judging their own schooling are then heard.

The 1950s to the 1970s: Rapid change

The late 1950s saw the British education system in a state of transition. The 1944 Butler Act had made schooling compulsory for all five- to fifteen-year-olds. It had also envisaged a tripartite educational structure, with a separation of secondary education into grammar, secondary modern and technical schools. However, neither the Attlee government after its election in 1945 nor subsequent governments established technical schools, so post-war, virtually all secondary schools were either grammar or secondary modern. A gap in technical education was a major deficit in the British education system throughout the sixty-five years covered by this book.

The 1950s saw increasing dissatisfaction with the split between grammar and secondary modern schools. It became clear that the 11+ examination, taken in the final year of junior school to determine which type of secondary school a child should attend, was unreliable. A significant number of children well capable of an academic education failed to pass it and had to be transferred later from secondary modern into grammar schools. Second, taking the examination was experienced as seriously stressful by some students, especially those with parents who saw failure as condemning the child to a second-rate education. Third, the examination was seen to put working class at an unfair disadvantage compared to middle-class children who were disproportionately admitted to grammar schools, and finally, it was no longer seen as appropriate to segregate children into academic or non-academic or indeed to divide secondary schools in this way. The concept of the comprehensive secondary school for all children was born and translated into policy in England and Wales in 1965 with a circular from the Department of Education requiring local authorities to organize education along comprehensive lines.

The move to comprehensive schools was not the only change in the education system envisaged at this time. The education of the under-fives was also under scrutiny.

Nursery schools

The landmark Report of the Central Advisory Council for Education (1967), chaired by Lady Plowden, gave a contemporary account of the situation regarding educational provision before the age of five years. Despite the fact that during the Second World War a number of 'nurseries' for pre-school children had been developed to nurture underprivileged children, in the 1960s there were no state pre-schools or nurseries, so for most children just turning five years old, their first day at school was the first time they had been on their own, away from home. Most mothers did not work outside the home, so for many children this was also the first time they had been apart from their mothers. Consequently, the first day of school was often a very tearful event for both child and parent.

In the early 1960s, despite the almost complete absence of state-funded nursery schools, there was a wide measure of agreement among informed observers that state nursery provision on a substantial scale was desirable, not only on educational grounds but also for social, health and welfare considerations. Long before children were five, most were already familiar with books, toys and music. The issue was not whether they should be 'educated' before they reached school age because that was happening anyway. What had to be decided was how their education should take place in increasing association with other children and under the supervision of skilled people, as well as of parents, in the right conditions and with the right equipment.

The Plowden Committee thought that

> although there is no obvious break in children's development in the years below school age, we think that, since lines must be drawn somewhere, the day nursery is the proper place for those children who have to be away from their homes before the age of three. An institution with a more directly educational aim is right for children of three and over and for this reason it should be provided by the local education authority under the Education Acts instead of being administered by the health authorities. Some experts in early years education think, however, that, as in most of continental Europe, it would be preferable for formal education to be delayed until the ages of six or seven.

Whatever particular age was chosen for the break, the argument put forward all those years ago by the Plowden committee for universal nursery school provision seemed even more pertinent as time went on, given increasing evidence that by five or six years of age, children from low-income families were already significantly behind in their language development compared to those living in better-off families (Lawton 1968).

The reasons for the marked differences in language development between children from working-class and middle-class families were investigated by Tizard and Hughes (1984), who directly observed interactions between mothers and their children within three months of their fourth birthday. They found that there were no social class differences in the amount of mother-child talk or the length of conversations. However, middle-class mothers made more use of language for complex purposes and used a wider vocabulary. They more often gave children information of a wider range and more often took a role in imaginative play. They took their children's 'why' questions more seriously (ibid., p.158). There were clear implications here for approaches that could be used by nursery schoolteachers who wanted to tackle the social class gap.

After the 1960s, there was a gradual increase in free or subsidized provision for pre-school children. There were also many private providers for this age group. In 2010, fifteen hours free childcare was made available to three-year-olds, and this was extended in 2013 to include two-year-olds from disadvantaged families. By 2024, there were nursery school places in the UK for 136,000 three- and four-year-olds. This, however, only represented a little more than one in ten of the total population of this age group. At the time of its election in 2024, the Labour government was committed to funding a further 100,000 nursery school places. Although representing significant progress, this still left a considerable shortfall of places.

In the 1960s and 1970s, the philosophy of nursery school providers was greatly influenced by three pioneers in the understanding of child development. In a series of publications published in the late 1920s, Jean Piaget had proposed that a child's intelligence developed with age from the very early years up to around fourteen according to a series of stages: the sensori-motor from birth to two years, a 'concrete operational period' up to seven to eleven years and finally a phase of 'formal operations' when abstract thinking became possible. Teachers, according to Piaget, should tailor what they teach to the child's stage of intellectual development, expecting neither too much nor too little. For a summary of Piaget's ideas, see Donaldson (1978). Second, less well-known but probably equally influential were the ideas of the pioneer of child-centred education and early child psychoanalyst, Susan Isaacs (1930, 1946), whose books all those studying to be teachers of early years and infant children were required to read from the 1930s to the 1960s (Graham 2023). Gradually, over the years, the curriculum put more emphasis on the adult-led acquisition of language, literacy and number skills. Much later, the Department of Education (2008) laid down a framework, the Early Years Foundation Stage (EYFS), which all providers of education for under-fives were required to follow. This framework was heavily influenced by the third pioneer of early years education, Maria Montessori (1912), whose book published nearly a hundred years earlier had advocated allowing the child to play and explore in an environment prepared by the availability of specially designed Montessori equipment.

When, as was mostly the case during this historical period, nursery school places were not available, parents made alternative arrangements for their children when they went to work or wished to have time for themselves or felt it was important for their children to have the opportunity to mix with others. In particular, they sent them to play groups run on a voluntary basis, or to child minders who might be registered or unregistered with the local authority, or to family carers, such as grandparents. The quality of their experiences in these different settings varied considerably, but, at this age, there were no constraints against removing children from placements when they were unhappy, so aside from the need to find good, affordable care (often not easy), parents could and did look around for happier arrangements.

Primary (infant and junior) schools

Entry to infant school in the late 1950s took place at five years, with transfer to junior school at seven years. In the 1960s, there was a marked change in the methods used to impart knowledge to young children with a move away from rote learning to learning through play. Rote learning, or learning by heart, is an educational method that involves repeating a piece of information many times to embed it in a person's memory. The Plowden Report emphatically endorsed play rather than rote learning as the main route to the acquisition of knowledge in the young child. It claimed:

> Play is the central activity in all nursery schools and in many infant schools. This sometimes leads to accusations that children are wasting their time in school: they should be 'working'. But this distinction between work and play is false, possibly throughout life, certainly in the primary school. Its essence lies in past notions of what is done in school hours (work) and what is done out of school (play). We know now that play – in the sense of "messing about" either with material objects or with other children, and of creating fantasies – is vital to children's learning and therefore vital in school. Adults who criticise teachers for allowing children to play are unaware that play is the principal means of learning in early childhood. It is the way through which children reconcile their inner lives with external reality. In play, children gradually develop concepts of causal relationships, the power to discriminate, to make judgements, to analyse and synthesise, to imagine and to formulate. Children become absorbed in their play and the satisfaction of bringing it to a satisfactory conclusion fixes habits of concentration which can be transferred to other learning.
>
> (Central Council for Education, p.193)

To facilitate play, children were no longer seated in rows at desks but placed in small groups of four or five around a table so that they could engage more easily in joint activities, teachers moving between groups rather than standing at the front of the class. At pre-school and in the first year of infant school in reception classes, the emphasis was on indoor and outdoor play with 'home corners' where young children could 'mess about' or experiment with sand and water and move about on scooters. In the second year of infant and first year of junior school, six- and seven-year-olds were expected to transition to cooperative play and group learning.

There is no clear evidence as to whether so-called 'progressive' methods resulted in happier children or better or poorer academic attainment. However, British infant schools developed an international reputation in the 1970s for their 'progressive' methods. They probably suited some children but not others. In any event, subsequent years saw a backlash resulting from unjustified concern about lower academic standards and lack of classroom discipline.

A national curriculum

In 1969, much publicity was given to the so-called 'Black Papers', written by educationists and other largely right-wing figures, which, among other targets such as university student protests and the 11+ examination, attacked extreme forms of progressive education. In January 1974, a new headteacher was appointed to William Tyndale School, a primary school in a socially mixed area in the London Borough of Islington. He and his deputy introduced a radical child-centred approach in which for part of the day, pupils were free to choose what they did. They had great freedom and access to all parts of the school. Some middle-class parents withdrew their children from the school and some members of staff protested against the headteacher's methods and eventually went on strike. The Inner London Education Authority set up an inquiry as a result of which the headteacher and his deputy were dismissed. The furore led to increasing pressure for local authorities to take greater responsibility for ensuring that teachers were expected to ensure pupils reached recognized standards especially in literacy and numeracy and was one of the factors leading to a more interventionist approach by central government (Davis 2002). In 1976, the then Prime Minister, James Callaghan, in a speech at Ruskin College, Oxford, was supportive of this movement (Donoughue 2003). While making no criticism of the continuing move towards comprehensive secondary education, he pointed towards the possible need for a national curriculum.

Five years later, in 1979, Margaret Thatcher was elected prime minister. She had definite views about education. In particular, she was convinced that schoolteachers were engaged in an attempt to indoctrinate their students with left-wing ideology. At the 1987 Conservative Annual Conference, she made her views known in an uncompromising manner.

> Too often our children don't get the education they deserve. In the inner cities, where youngsters must have a decent education if they are to have a better future, that opportunity is too often snatched from them by hard left education authorities and extremist teachers. Children who need to be able to count and multiply are learning anti-racist mathematics – whatever that may be. Children who need to be able to express themselves in clear English are being taught political dogma.
>
> (McSmith 2011, pp.288–9)

The answer, she believed, was to ensure control of the curriculum was centralized. Her criticisms of an extremist left-wing conspiracy to indoctrinate children had little or no basis in reality, though her views were popular, at least partly because, in the previous two or three years, from 1984 to 1986, there had been a number of strikes by teachers over pay and conditions of work, which had made life difficult for many parents whose children had not been able to go to school. Just over a year after Thatcher's speech, her views and the pressure for higher standards led to the 1988 Education Reform Act steered by Kenneth Baker, the Secretary of State for Education, which made radical changes to the education system. For the first time, a national curriculum was indeed developed to make sure the same things were taught in schools throughout the country. From then on, all pupils were required to sit tests (SATS). Pupils sat these at seven, eleven and fourteen years. The results were used to draw up league tables which informed parents of each school's performance. Schools were encouraged to compete against each other so that parents would choose to send their children to the more successful schools, to which local education authorities would have to give increased resources. This marketization of schools led to competition rather than cooperation between schools.

The Act also laid down so-called Key Stages in a pupil's education. Key Stage 1 was from five to seven years and was assessed by a phonics and reading check at the end of the first year as well as a series of tests (SATS). Key Stage 2 was from seven to eleven years, at which point a further series of SATS is administered. This division of the curriculum into key stages led to criticism. For example, Donaldson (2015) concluded 'shifts in philosophy or approach at transition points can hinder progression and there was evidence that this could contribute to disengagement as young people progress through school. Successive stages can influence each other in unintended ways.'

In 2000 the Labour government introduced a new system whereby some schools came under direct control of the Department of Education. The development of these academy schools is described below in the section on secondary schools. During his tenure as Secretary of State for Education (2010–16), Michael Gove endeavoured to bring various aspects of the school curriculum, especially the teaching of phonics in infant schools and various secondary school subjects (particularly in English and History but also in other subjects) under more central control.

The promise or threat of an interventionist approach had already led to greater consideration of the purposes of education and of what might be considered a 'successful' school. Did this depend entirely or almost entirely on high achievement in academic subjects? Mary Warnock, a philosopher with experience as the head teacher of an independent girls' school, believed that the 'education of the imagination is by far the most important educational goal and should be central to any curriculum decisions' (Warnock 1994, p.173). Peter Mortimore (2013), a former director of the London Institute of Education, was highly critical of an exclusive emphasis on academic achievement and listed a number of other desirable outcomes. These included (ibid., pp.13–28) a 'moral compass' (the ability to tell the difference between right and wrong), good character, a sense of strategy, a trained mind, happiness, knowledge about a variety of subjects (including languages and the arts) and skills (including communication and IT abilities, as well as sporting skills).

The changes to the GCSE assessment, with overloading of the curriculum, allowed teachers less autonomy in the way they implemented the national curriculum. This meant that teachers were unable to tailor the content of the lessons they taught to the particular needs of their students. Too often, it was felt, were teachers merely delivering scripts prepared for them by people who had little idea of the circumstances in which their students lived. For some teachers, this plunged the teaching profession into a crisis, but this was by no means a universal perception among teachers, many of whom remained highly positive about their professional work (Towers et al. 2022).

State secondary schools

Though the technical colleges envisaged by the 1944 Butler Act had not been incorporated into the system, by 1959, most of the country's secondary schools were either grammar or secondary modern. While grammar schools generally enjoyed a good reputation, especially for their delivery of an academic curriculum, though there were many excellent secondary moderns, these were widely seen as 'dustbin' schools to which 11+ failures were consigned. The first comprehensive school opened in 1956, and numerous others followed, so that by the end of the century, only a handful of local authorities retained grammar schools.

Comprehensive schools were able to offer a wider curriculum than grammar and secondary modern schools with, for example, more foreign languages and greater opportunities to play musical instruments. They varied quite considerably, in the degree to which they 'set' children according to ability, with the most common practice being to 'set' by academic ability for some subjects but not others. Some, but by no means all, developed strong departments of design technology, carpentry or woodwork and domestic science. The degree to which there was social mixing in the schools was very variable, often with children from the same ethnic group sticking together whenever the school day allowed this.

The publication of *Fifteen Thousand Hours* (Rutter et al. 1979) was a major turning point in attitudes to the role of secondary schools in inner cities. This was the report of a research study focused on twelve comprehensive schools located in an inner London Borough. It showed that, after taking account achievement and social status at intake, schools could make a real difference to the academic levels and behaviour of their students. Those schools that focused on academic work as their main goal, that emphasized reward and praise rather than punishment and ensured that teachers acted as role models for good behaviour had student outcomes in achievement and behaviour that were significantly better than those that pursued other aims.

In 1988, the Education Reform Act, as already noted, brought for the first time a national curriculum which meant that children all over the country followed similar courses. The notion of Key Stages (see above) continued into secondary schools, with Key Stage 3 extending from eleven to fourteen years. At this point, compulsory national curriculum subjects were English; maths; science; history; geography; modern foreign languages; design and technology. Key Stage 4 took place between fourteen and sixteen years. All pupils of this age had to follow the national curriculum in the following subjects: English, mathematics, science, computing (England only), physical education, citizenship, careers education, religious education, work-related learning, Welsh (Wales only). The Key Stage ages were not extended even though the school-leaving age was raised to seventeen in 2013 and eighteen in 2015. The last two years did not need to involve full-time education. They could include academic learning but also apprenticeships, or work-based training. Students could also choose other options, such as going to college or getting a full-time or a part-time job. The Act also replaced the O-Level and CSE exams which had been set up in 1951, with the General Certificate of Secondary Examination (GCSEs) 'O' and 'A' levels.

The 1988 Act attracted much criticism. In particular, it was thought to over-burden the curriculum (and thus teachers) with far too much content for children to absorb comfortably. In 1995, a report by Ron Dearing reduced content by 20 per cent, a welcome respite and, in the 2000s, with Ed Balls as Secretary of State for Education in a Labour administration, content was further reduced with greater emphasis in the acquisition of learning skills.

An example of the centralization of the curriculum arose also in 1988, but this time as a section (28) of the Local Government Act. At the insistence of the Prime Minister, Margaret Thatcher, the section prohibited local authorities from 'promoting homosexuality' by teaching or publishing materials. It barred teaching the 'acceptability of homosexuality as a pretended family relationship' in maintained schools. Despite the fact that it was the object of much criticism and, indeed, embodied prejudice against homosexuality in a way which many thought sanctioned discrimination against gay people, the law remained in effect from 1988 until 2003.

The next significant change in the structure of education in the UK was the creation in 1992 of OFSTED, the Office for Standards in Education. This assumed responsibility for the inspection of all schools to ensure that they met required standards for safeguarding pupils and for academic achievement. OFSTED replaced the previous system of inspection, which had been the responsibility of Her Majesty's Inspectors. OFSTED inspection of schools was carried out virtually without warning and was the occasion of much anxiety among school staff as so much hung on the rating they gave to the school: 'Outstanding', 'Good' or 'Requires Improvement'. One focus of criticism of Ofsted was that it resembled a 'tick box' exercise, in which there was limited provision for the inspecting team to make suggestions for improvement. Thus, the tone of reports was widely thought to be overly judgemental with little content relevant to school change for the better. In 2024, following the suicide of a head teacher whose school had been rated as 'Requires Improvement', the Labour government announced it would bring in a more nuanced system of grading schools.

A further major change in the structure of British education was introduced shortly after the election of a Labour government in 1997. A number of schools, both primary and secondary, were converted to 'academies'. Whereas previously, all state schools had been responsible to local education authorities, governed by locally elected councillors, now, for some schools, this responsibility passed to the Department of Education which monitored the school's expenditure and quality of staff directly through the school's governing body. Initially academies were selected on the basis that they were 'failing' schools and needed 'sponsors', businesses which, in return for financial investment in a school, would have a seat on the governing body and a say in how the school was run. Gradually, sponsorship was discontinued, and the focus became a drive to convert all schools to academy status under central government control without involvement of sponsors. Indeed, schools were given financial inducements to apply to convert to academy status. By 2024, nearly half of all English schools had become academies and more than half of all students attended academies (Freedman 2022). There was no evidence that academies did better or worse than schools under local authority control (ibid.). Their existence was criticized by those who thought it was harmful and confusing to split the responsibility for control of schools in this way. In an important sense, in that power was removed from local authorities, the curriculum had been covertly nationalized.

In 1993, the Conservative administration introduced the concept of specialist schools, in which schools were given financial incentives to develop particular subjects, such as Science or Drama. This policy was continued under the 1997 Labour government and remained in place until 2011.

A further significant change introduced by the Labour administration was the injection of financial support for schools in inner cities that had suffered in the 1990s from poor academic achievement and high levels of behavioural disruption. In particular, support for London schools through a programme titled London Challenge had significant success in both these areas (McAleavy and Elwick 2016).

Michael Gove, Secretary of State for Education from 2010 to 2016, thought schools should be the engine of social mobility, reducing the achievement gap between students from poor and wealthy families. He rejected so-called 'progressive' approaches to education which gave priority to the individual needs of children and, instead, insisted on much greater standardization of the curriculum, especially in certain secondary school subjects: History, English and Modern Languages. These came under even greater central control. This approach ignored what many parents wanted from their children's education – more practical skills, for example, in budgeting and interviewing techniques. It also led to some schools becoming highly disciplinarian, with teachers demanding absolute compliance to their requirements for silence from students in the corridors and in the classroom. Gove also changed the means of assessment of student success, with emphasis on the results of written examinations, dropping modular assessments and results of course work. In 2011, he introduced the E-Bacc, a combination of GCSE subjects, English, Maths, Sciences and a language, that offer a range of knowledge and skills to young people. The E-Bacc was not, however, a qualification in its own right, but just a means of assessing students and schools. Another innovation of the Gove era was the establishment of 'free schools', the first of which started to take students in 2011. These were schools founded on the initiative of parents, businesses or other organizations, often religious, which came under the control of the Department of Education.

Gove was criticized for reducing the place of art and music in the curriculum, with many claiming there was just not sufficient time for them (Burley 2024). Between 2009–10 and 2022–3, there was a 42 per cent reduction in the number of students taking art at the GCSE level.

Gove's reforms, although leading to an improvement in achievement levels in the core subjects, came to be seen as a failure using his own criteria. At the end of his tenure and beyond, the attainment gap between the social classes remained very large. The coalition government inherited 300,000 disadvantaged students in 2019, and the same number existed in 2024 (Bailey 2025). According to the Department for Education's own data, the gap widened in 2020 and, after a brief improvement during COVID-19 (see Chapter 9), returned to the pre-COVID level. For this, much of the responsibility must be attached to the austerity measures taken by the 2010 coalition government from which schools as well as social benefits and other public services suffered (see Chapter 1). This gives credence to the view held by Sam Freedman (quoted in Bailey 2025) that what the poor need to catch up with the wealthy is not education, but money.

After its election in 2024, the Labour government set up an enquiry chaired by Becky Francis to point the way forward in education policy. An interim report published in 2025 indicated that the priorities for future policy would be equity in attainment, dealing with the imbalance between breadth and depth, digital literacy, dealing with the confusion in obtaining vocational qualifications as well as concerns about the excessive volume of examinations taken before the age of sixteen.

Independent schools

Over the whole of this period, somewhere between 9 and 13 per cent of children went to independent, private or public preparatory or secondary schools. (In the UK, paradoxically, private schools are referred to as 'public schools'.) The children who attended these fee-paying schools were a highly selected group. First, because the parents had to pay school fees, apart from a relatively small number on bursaries or scholarships, they came from well-to-do families, almost entirely from the business and professional classes. Second, there was a gender difference; boys were far more likely to attend them than were girls. Third, there were regional disparities. Children from the London area were more likely to attend these schools. Fourth, a high proportion of the children attending these schools went as boarders, either termly or, more commonly in the latter years, on a weekly basis. Fifth, there was a high number of children from overseas countries, some because their parents were living abroad, serving in the Foreign Office or in one or other of the armed forces, or posted overseas on business; others because parents from other countries wanted their children to benefit from what they saw as the superior education British schools provided.

Some of these schools were very old foundations, dating back many centuries. They were often linked to religious foundations, most commonly to the Anglican Church, but sometimes to the Roman Catholic, Muslim or Jewish religions. They were likely to have prayers in the morning at a whole-school assembly and grace was said before meals were served. Academic pressure was likely to be high, with some fee-paying schools recording very high levels of academic attainment. This was partly an effect of the above-average intake filtered by demanding entrance examinations and partly a result of smaller classes with more highly qualified teachers. Stress symptoms were common with high levels of anxiety and body-image problems (see the chapter on mental health disorders).

The very existence of these independent schools as bastions of privilege was controversial throughout the whole of this period (Green and Kynaston 2019). Attendance at a fee-paying prep school virtually guaranteed a place at a secondary age 'public school' at the age of eleven or thirteen when transfer commonly took place. In 2024, the newly elected Labour government proposed to charge VAT on school fees paid to private schools. At the time of writing, it is unclear what effect, if any, this will have on the number of children attending these schools. What is clear is that the existence of fee-paying schools was both a reflection of the inequalities in the British social system and contributed to it. The top positions in politics, the law, medicine, accountancy and business were held disproportionately by men (and, more recently, women), who had attended private schools and enjoyed the privileges of smaller classes, more highly qualified teachers and social contacts with other, more privileged children.

a) Preparatory (prep) schools.

These generally took children from seven to eleven or to thirteen years of age. Many of these schools, especially in the early days, had facilities for boarding pupils, some of whom would only go home during school holidays. Indeed, at the beginning of this period, most so-called 'prep schools' consisted largely of boarders. Gradually, as concern about the possible harmful effects of separating young children from their parents (see Chapter 2) became more acute, the proportion of fully boarding children declined significantly (Brendon, p.184). Those boarders that remained were now more likely to come from overseas. In the 1960s and 1970s, most prep schools were single sex, mainly for boys, but a few for girls. In the latter part of the twentieth century, needing to increase their numbers for financial reasons, a number became mixed sex.

The educational philosophy of the schools was very variable. Some, such as the Rudolf Steiner schools, and other progressive establishments were strongly child-centred while others exerted unusually firm discipline. Indeed, corporal punishment was freely administered in many private preparatory schools from the 1950s to the 1970s but was gradually used less and less. It was only finally abolished in independent schools in 1998, twelve years after it was abolished in state schools in 1986. Many of the unhappy memories of attendance at public schools at all ages centred around the recollection of fear of being beaten (Spencer 2024).

Indeed, the recollections of those who attended prep schools in the 1960s and 1970s do not make happy reading (Brendon 2009). An account of prep schools in the so-called 'swinging sixties' is taken up with stories of sometimes brutal physical punishment, bullying and sexually inappropriate behaviour of male staff towards pupils. Andrew Motion, later the poet laureate, claimed that the headmaster of the prep school he attended in the early 1960s, nicknamed the Beak, positively enjoyed beating students (Brendon 2009, p.162).

> He beat us if we did badly at work, if we were cheeky, if we walked with our hands in our pockets, if we left the middle button of our jackets undone, if we walked on the grass by the statue standing on one leg, if we slammed doors, if we barged ahead of masters, if we swore, if we made a mess in our lockers, if we didn't have our towels, if we had fights, if we damaged the flowers, if we hid our food.

Nor, according to Vyvyen Brendon's informants, did the situation improve much in the 1980s. Some, at least, continued to endure 'terrible homesickness', of suffering under 'bullies and beastly matrons', of getting the cane or the size 14 slipper for talking after lights out'. In truth, she writes, 'the 1980s did not witness radical transformation of prep schools, although some headmasters ran them more benevolently than others – as had always been the case' (ibid., p.181). Despite this unhappy picture of prep schools painted by many of their alumnae, it is also clear that a significant number of children who attended them had excellent teaching as well as opportunities to participate in art, music, drama and sport often denied to those in state schools, though the quality of their educational experience was seriously limited by the social exclusiveness of the schools they attended.

Independent secondary (public) schools

Over the period in question, a steady 8–12 per cent of children of secondary age attended these fee-paying schools that took children from eleven or thirteen to eighteen years. Most, as described above, were entirely fee-paying and so restricted to students with wealthy parents but a minority were so-called 'direct grant' schools, which, following the 1944 Education Act, took a substantial number of children on scholarships from state primary schools. The direct grant arrangement was abolished by the Labour government in

1976, when a minority of direct grant schools went into the state system, though most became fully independent.

During the late nineteenth and twentieth centuries a large number of single-sex boarding schools for girls were founded; previously such schools had been restricted to boys. Girls' public schools were more commonly for day pupils as well as boarders. During the twentieth century a number of boys' public schools began to take girls at sixth form level, and a minority became fully co-educational.

Children who attended secondary public schools, like those attending prep schools, were disproportionately successful in the law, medicine and the other professions as well as in business and commercial affairs. They were particularly high achievers in politics with virtually all prime ministers until the 1990s having been educated at Eton or Harrow, two of the leading public schools. It was only in the 2024 Labour cabinet that the numbers educated at fee-paying schools were roughly proportionate to those in the general population.

Educational achievement and social disadvantage

Throughout the sixty-five years covered by this book, socially disadvantaged children made much poorer academic progress than did those from more affluent families. From the early years of children's lives, the limited access to books and an upbringing in which language usage was more limited, meant by the time children entered school at the age of five years, there were already marked differences in language development (Lawton 1968) arising from a language-deprived environment. The results of the 11+ examination during the 1960s and 1970s strongly disfavoured the poor. Children from the north-east and north-west of England, where economic deprivation was greatest, consistently did less well in 'O' level and 'A' level public examinations. Until the 2010s, it was unusual for a child from a poor family to gain a university place. In fact, income inequalities did not increase during the 1960s and 1970s, but examination of time trends in the Gini coefficient (a measure of income inequality) reveals that this gap increased after the election of the Conservative government in 1979 (Francis-Devine 2024). So, it is not surprising that the social class differences in educational achievement widened as children advanced through the education system. Further, children from socially disadvantaged families were highly over-represented in the special educational needs (SEN) system. Again, this is not surprising as many SEN children were in the system because they were slow learners, on a continuum with slow learners in mainstream schools.

At various points, government and local initiatives have been put in place to compensate for this disadvantage. In the late 1960s, educational priority areas were established in socially disadvantaged parts of the country to which additional funding was made available. However, the emphasis on competition between students and between schools after 1979 created problems for both students and teachers with schools feeling incentivized to exclude poorly performing students to improve their performance in league tables. Teachers' strikes from 1984 to 1986, though ostensibly about pay and contractual arrangements, in fact reflected poor morale among teaching staff. Poor children were disproportionately affected by this industrial unrest. The chaotic atmosphere in many inner-city secondary schools in the late 1980s and 1990s with disruptive students more frequently out of control was probably a further product of teacher disaffection and under-funding. As described above, in 2003, the London Challenge programme was put in place, increasing resources to schools in under-privileged areas in the metropolis. Combined with efforts to appoint inspiring headteachers and reduce tolerance to even mildly disruptive behaviour, these initiatives had significant success. At the turn of the century, a number of head teachers developed reputations for being able to 'turn around' schools that had high rates of students showing disruptive behaviour.

In 2011, the Coalition government introduced a so-called 'pupil premium' aimed at giving a significant financial supplement to schools depending on the number of their students receiving free school meals. This made a significant difference to schools in socially disadvantaged areas, but the impact of social disadvantage on academic achievement was as great in the 2020s as it had been in the 1960s (Tahir 2022). The effects of the cuts to social benefits during the austerity years following 2010 clearly did not outweigh the positive effects of the pupil premium.

Special education

It had been recognized since the eighteenth century that some children with disabilities need education but cannot receive their education in mainstream schools. They need special teaching or special facilities or both. The 1945 Handicapped Pupils and School Health Service Regulations defined eleven categories of pupils: blind, partially sighted, deaf, partially deaf, delicate, diabetic, educationally subnormal, epileptic, maladjusted, physically handicapped and those with speech defects who needed special education. Of these, by far the most numerous group (over two-thirds) were those known by the stigmatizing name of 'educationally subnormal', or slow-learning children. During the 1950s and 1960s, the education of all children, except those who were markedly slow to learn who were regarded as ineducable and the responsibility of health authorities, was the responsibility of local education authorities. This arrangement remained relatively unchanged until 1971, when the Education (Handicapped Children) Act 1970 transferred the responsibility of very slow-learning children from health to local education authorities. From this point onwards, all children were regarded as educable.

These arrangements were greatly altered by the 1981 Education Act which legislated along the lines recommended by the Report of the Committee of Enquiry into Special Educational Needs (Department of Education 1978), chaired by Mrs (later Baroness) Mary Warnock, of which I was a member. Amongst other provisions, the Act proposed that children hitherto referred to as being 'educationally subnormal' should henceforth be described as showing 'learning difficulties'. The medical categories should be abolished and replaced by a 'statement' of special educational needs prepared by a multidisciplinary team. It was the responsibility of the local authority to meet these needs. There should be maximum collaboration between education, health and social services to meet the needs of the child.

Special education should begin as soon as it became apparent that a child was in need of it, and this might be as early as immediately after birth, certainly before the age of five. Where possible, a child's special needs should be provided for in an ordinary school, perhaps in special classes or units. Special schools should be sited in the same vicinity as ordinary schools so that there could be maximum contact between pupils attending both types of school. Too often, parents had been seen as obstacles to the provision of special education. From now on, parents should be seen as partners in the education of their children. There should be a Named Person for each child with special educational needs who would help parents understand the educational system and contribute to the education of their child. Special schools should prepare their students well before leaving age for life after leaving school. There should be a smooth transition from school to special forms of higher education if these were indicated.

The arrangements put in place by the 1981 Education Act remained in place for the remainder of the period covered by this book, though there was gradually a greater focus on every child reaching a specific outcome. In 2014, the Children and Families Act replaced statements with 'education, health and care plans' (EHCPs) with an extension of the responsibility of local authorities for students in need up to the age of twenty-five. An attempt was made in this Act to streamline the assessment procedures though the changes made were largely cosmetic. Mainly because of under-funding, by the 1990s, the Special Educational Needs (SEN) system was far from satisfactory. The number of children requiring EHCPs became far greater than that envisaged by Warnock. A lack of an adequate professional workforce meant that many children and parents had to wait far too long for statements (or later EHCPs) to be formulated. Local authorities, strapped for cash, were often reluctant to accept recommendations made by multi-disciplinary teams. This led to many formal appeals by parents against the local authority decisions, most of which were successful but again the bureaucratic process often led to long waiting lists and consequent delays. By 2024, the special education system was in serious disarray.

Nevertheless, the overall effect of the legislation which followed the publication of the Warnock Report was distinctly positive. It led to the closure of a number of schools for children with mild and moderate learning difficulties, previously termed 'educationally subnormal'. The students in these schools were integrated into mainstream schools, sometimes in special units in such schools with generally positive results. The 1981 Act enabled children with severe disabilities who would previously have had extremely limited lives to enjoy a much fuller existence. For example (Graham 2021, p.192), a child born in 1980 with Down syndrome and a mild hearing impairment was placed in a special school but was able to attend several school clubs at a nearby primary school. When the family moved from the south to the north of England, the fact that he had a Statement of Special Educational Need meant that his new local education authority had a duty to find him a suitable school placement. When he left his secondary school, to improve his literacy level, he attended classes at the local further education college and also at a local community art project. In his early twenties, he moved into a supported living arrangement (a shared flat) with regular support and practical help with daily living. During one of his annual reviews, he claimed 'life is great'. His mother, looking back at this point, commented:

> We were upset that X couldn't go to the same school as his brother. But now we are pleased that he went to schools which could give him the skills for everyday life. He's been able to make choices, to get a home of his own and, when he walks down the street, he seems to know more people than we do! He is really part of his local community, and he has got a life.
>
> (ibid., p.194)

The Report led to more sharing of facilities between special and mainstream schools. For example, the rebuilding of a special school, Riverside, in Tottenham, a deprived part of London, provided the opportunity to site the school on the same campus as a mainstream comprehensive school, Woodside High. Riverside mainly took children with autism and moderate-to-severe learning difficulties. There was active engagement between the two schools. The headteacher of Riverside School attended Woodside governing body meetings and vice versa. Although this was unusual, where Riverside students had the potential to take public examinations, they joined classes at Woodside. Riverside students were taken on tours of Woodside and vice versa. Students from Riverside who set up a breakfast club joined students in the Woodside canteen. Riverside/Woodside ran a joint Red Nose Day with shared activities. Riverside's after-school club visited Woodside's open-air Windrush anniversary celebration. Riverside partnered with Woodside in completing the Duke of Edinburgh's Silver Award. Students from the two schools worked together to support one another, hike and navigate through the planned route. They socialized and played rounders together in the evenings (Graham 2021).

There were a number of local and national charitable organizations which promoted the social integration of children with disabilities. Probably the best known was PHAB (Physically Handicapped/Able Bodied) which organized local and residential activities mixing disabled with non-disabled children and young people. In 2024, it had 180 clubs. PHAB was founded in 1957 and so was active throughout the whole period covered by this account.

However, a much less rosy picture emerges from a survey of the views of children and young people with disabilities carried out by the Children's Commissioner for England (2023b). The Report lists a number of barriers to a good life voiced by children with disabilities.

These included delayed identification of needs:

> I was not given a language system until I was 9 and so I had no way of communicating even my most basic needs. [...] It also meant I could not make friends and didn't have a single friend. I was hurt by other children
>
> – Boy, 13, attending a school for deaf children

Sometimes a condition was not identified until early adulthood with devastating consequences. One 22-year-old woman with a disability in the care of a local authority, looking back, recalled:

> Nothing was diagnosed until adulthood ... To some extent I think I probably wouldn't have ended up in care if I'd been diagnosed earlier because I think looking back and reflecting on the circumstances that led to me being in care I think a lot of those were difficulties which were exacerbated by [my condition] and that we didn't know was [my condition] at the time ... the support I was getting wasn't what I needed ... I think it would have made everything 10 times easier.

A host of other complaints were made:

> I think accessibility is a huge thing that needs sorting out. Because, for example, in my school we've got one lift that's completely broken and it needs fixing, but they've just not got the money to fix it. And there's plenty more upstairs classrooms that are inaccessible for some people
>
> – Girl, young carer, 15.

> Our current education system is not suited to ... those with ADD, ADHD and autism. Teachers aren't educated in the teaching styles that are appropriate
>
> – Girl, 16

> There aren't enough school places for young people with SEN (special educational needs). Mainstream school is really hard to cope with. I have been out of school for a very long time, and I don't see friends, it

> can be really lonely. I don't think people always understand autism and it's hard to fit in. I need an education so I can get a good job, but I am stuck because there is no school where I fit in
>
> – Girl, 16, not in education.

As was the case with children without disabilities, a major reason for unhappiness was bullying and a sense of being discriminated against.

> If somebody has a mental disability or is bullied they will feel bad about themselves and possibly become depressed, which makes them sad, so they won't want to come to school because they'll think that they'll just get bullied more if they go in
>
> – Girl, 10

> A friend of mine with autism found she had little learning support and no protection from the bullying she was put through as a result of her autism
>
> – Girl, 17

It needs to be taken into account that this survey was conducted in the summer of 2023, three years into the COVID-19 epidemic. The social isolation imposed by the regulations during the time of the epidemic may well have worsened the experiences of children with disabilities, but it should be noted that many of the comments relate to a period before the epidemic began in 2020.

In fact, it became clear shortly after the Warnock Report was published and the 1981 Education Act had passed through its various stages that special education, in an era of declining resources, was going to suffer disproportionately. Indeed, Mary Warnock expressed her misgivings early on (Warnock 2005) and the situation of children with special needs gradually deteriorated through the late twentieth and early twenty-first centuries. By the end of this period (Harris 2024), there were widespread delays for assessment, with, in particular, long waiting lists for the diagnoses of autism and attention-deficit hyperactivity disorder (ADHD), followed by long delays in local authorities finding suitable and affordable placements. The fact was that, as a result of austerity cuts, local authorities just could not afford to send children to special schools and so tried to 'make do' with placing children in mainstream schools supplemented by increased numbers of teaching assistants. However, financial constraints meant that even the number of teaching assistants had to be reduced.

Finally, in this section on special education, and this is a theme taken up both elsewhere in this chapter and in other chapters, it should be noted that a major factor determining the quality of life of children with disabilities was family income. The Children's Commissioner's Report (2023) points to a strong '(the) link between SEND and poverty is particularly strong, with 41.1% of pupils with an EHCP and 37.5% of pupils with SEN support eligible for free school meals in 2023, compared to 23.8% of all pupils in schools' (ibid., p.17). The negative effects of poverty are perhaps most marked in such children, especially those with conduct disorder, attention-deficit hyperactivity disorders (ADHD) and learning difficulties (ibid.).

Education in the devolved administrations

While there are broad similarities between the history of education in England and the devolved administrations, there are also some significant differences. This is not surprising as education was one of those areas for which responsibility was devolved at the time these administrations were established in 1999. (Northern Ireland had also had a devolved administration for education before 1972.)

Northern Ireland

The English National Curriculum is largely followed. The phasing out of grammar schools has also largely followed England though progress has been much slower and was still far from complete in 2024.

The role of religious organizations in the running of schools was far greater than it was in England. In the 1950s, the majority of primary and secondary schools were so-called controlled schools. These were administered by the State to which the Protestant churches had previously transferred authority. A majority of pupils (59 per cent) in these schools were Protestant but there were a significant number of Catholic pupils as well as others. There was a slightly smaller number of Catholic-maintained schools run by the Catholic Church as well as a smaller number of voluntary grammar schools. As a result of parental initiatives, since 1981 there were a small number of grant-maintained and controlled integrated schools with roughly equal numbers of pupils from the two main religious faiths.

Wales

Selection by academic achievement was ended by 1980. Mostly the curriculum and governance arrangements followed those in England, although about 16 per cent were Welsh medium schools. However, all state exams were taken in English. Welsh was a compulsory subject up to the age of sixteen.

Scotland

The Scottish system of education was distinctive in that, traditionally, at secondary school level it emphasized breadth across a range of subjects, while the English, Welsh and Northern Irish systems had emphasized greater depth of education over a smaller range.

The Scottish education system differed from England's in several other ways, including:

- Curriculum
  Scotland's Curriculum for Excellence (CfE), established in 2010 after a national debate, focused on developing skills for learning, life and work, and was more flexible than England's national curriculum. The CfE had three core subjects: health and well-being, literacy and numeracy, and schools had more autonomy to shape the curriculum. The CfE was divided into levels, rather than key stages, and included Early Level (pre-school and P1), First Level to Fourth Level (ages five to fifteen) and Senior Phase (ages fifteen to eighteen). Unfortunately, this curriculum had to be considered a failure as Scotland's Pisa (Programme for International Student Assessment) points fell well below that of the other devolved administrations by the 2020s (Bailey 2025), suggesting a relative decline in performance.

- School year
  The Scottish academic year ran from August to June, while England's ran from September to July.

- School structure
  Scotland's schools included early years education and childcare, seven years of primary school (P1–P7), and secondary school (S1–S6), also known as high school or academies. The first four years of secondary school were compulsory, while S5 and S6 were optional.

- Qualifications
  Scottish students took examinations called Standards and/or Highers instead of GCSEs and A Levels, and secondary school qualifications were awarded by the Scottish Qualification Authority.

What have children thought about their schools?

In general, the recollections of primary school children both contemporary and retrospective have been largely positive. The contrast between recollections of primary and secondary schools is encapsulated by this quotation of the comparison made by a thirteen-year-old boy (Blishen 1969, p.7).

> At present, the main difference between secondary and primary schools is that primary education is enjoyable and secondary education is absolutely dreary and boring. Primary education ... that golden land where the revolution has at least partially taken place. May it soon take place in our secondary schools.

A couple of nearly seven-year-olds said of their primary school (Tara Midgen, personal communication):

> I like doing homework. I love school. I love that really much – it lets me learn more stuff! I like literacy, Maths, and DT.

> I like school. I don't like going home. I like to have play dates after school.

Apart from the Children's Commissioner's survey of the views of children with special needs (see above), there are two more comprehensive sources of information about the way British children themselves have thought about the schools they have attended. In December 1967, *The Observer* invited all secondary schoolchildren to enter for a competition by writing an essay with the title *The School I'd Like*. A selection of these essays was published in 1969 in a book edited by Edward Blishen (1969). In 2001, thirty-four years later, *The Guardian* invited all UK schoolchildren (not just those in secondary school) to enter into an identical competition, writing an essay with the same title. The results were summarized in an article in *The Education Guardian* in 2003 and then presented in expanded book form in the same year and in a revised second edition, twelve years later (Burke and Grosvenor 2015). This revised edition makes many comparisons with the 1967 book so that it is possible to see what changes, if any, occurred in children's views of their schools over this period.

The title of the essays schoolchildren were asked to write with its focus on how schools could be better than they were inevitably meant that the content of what children wrote emphasized the shortcomings of their schools. Further, those who responded were clearly a selective group, probably meaning that those with complaints about their schooling were over-represented. All the same, it is striking how the essays overwhelmingly conveyed two extremely depressing messages. The first was the degree to which the schools these children attended left a great deal to be desired and the second was how little had changed in the thirty-four years between 1967 and 2001.

The following quotation (p.99) encapsulates many of the criticisms voiced by other students:

> I left school last year at the age of thirteen and enrolled at a local college ... I left because I felt that the regime was oppressive and, like most oppressive regimes, coercive and difficult to change. I resented

> being told what to do, what to think, what to believe, what to say and when to say it, in the average school, the children are the underclass, so low in status they are not worth listening to.
> In the present state system, there is a set curriculum that is concerned with efficiency rather than fulfilment. It prioritises the preparation of a useful workforce and makes little allowance for individual preference and talent.
> The school I'd like would stand for freedom, tolerance and flexibility
>
> (Lorna, 14, Ipswich)

The same student expressed widely shared criticisms of teachers.

> Rightly or wrongly, the power relationships between pupils and teachers are unequal in most schools, but I think that teachers frequently abuse their authority. It is often seen to be acceptable for the young to be treated with disrespect or to be humiliated. A 'ticking off' tends to have more to do with power and punishment than with logic or negotiation.
>
> (Lorna, 14, Ipswich)

There was a widespread plea for more time to be spent out of the classroom.

> In my view, the sooner we all get out of the stuffy classroom, the better it will be for everybody. Life is much more interesting if you can go out and see something instead of just sitting at a desk and being loaded with information about it.
>
> (Lynne, 15)

> What a bore school is nowadays, the same as it has been for hundreds of years. What we get is the same old thing- teacher, outdated textbooks and a class fed up to the teeth with the teacher and the school. What we need is one vast change in the educational system of this country. Children do not want to be taught at, but want to find things out for themselves.
>
> (Robin, 16)

Edward Blishen summarizes such complaints by reporting that in many of the 1967 essays, children were (p.67)

> begging to be allowed to get out of the dead air of the classroom – to be freed from that sterile and cramped learning situation in which the teacher, the textbook and the examination-dominated syllabus have decided what should be learnt and how it should be learnt, and that virtually everything should be presented as a hurried intellectual abstraction.

It is depressing to read how little changed between 1967 and 2001 when it came to the basic necessities of life, especially clean toilets and edible food. Typical of descriptions of the state of toilets is an account of Leeds schools in which the toilets are described as: *dirty, smelly and unpleasant places which suffered from vandalism, particularly in the girls' toilets. There were broken toilet seats, no lids, insufficient supplies of toilet paper, poor handwashing facilities and string in place of chains to flush the toilets.*

School meals are also a cause of plaintive comments in both surveys.

> School meals are ghastly affairs, which always cause disturbance among pupils and adults.
>
> (Angela, 15)

It should be noted that these negative comments were made well before the reforms introduced by Michael Gove in the 2010s. No similar survey of students' views was conducted after then, but it is difficult to imagine that the results would have been more positive if they had been.

Conclusion

It has been said that childhood is not just a preparation for life; it is a part of life. It follows that education should be judged not only on the degree to which it prepares children for adult life but on how enjoyable it is. It has to be said that, as a result of the educational structure imposed by successive governments, the sixty-five years of British education from 1959 to 2024, despite the efforts of countless brilliant teachers, was only partially successful as preparation for later life, especially in relation to technical skills, and was largely a failure with respect to enjoyment. The quotations from children in the previous section provide chapter and verse for the dismal nature of the experience of secondary schooling for many students over this period.

Despite the strong evidence that success in virtually all areas of life depends on the ability to cooperate with others rather than to compete against them, the ethos of schools over the whole of this period but particularly after 1979 was on competition rather than cooperation. Examinations and tests set individual students against each other; league tables set schools against other schools.

Knowledge advances through the light that one subject sheds on another. History sheds light on geography, mathematics on evolutionary biology, English literature on religious studies and vice versa. In contrast, as the children's essays reveal, the school curriculum was strictly compartmentalized with sharp demarcation between subjects in the twentieth century and probably became more so in the twenty-first.

While at the beginning of our historical period, creative subjects such as music, art and sport were well represented, the time devoted to these subjects, vital for spiritual and physical development, was gradually eroded in favour of academic bookwork. This impoverishment of the curriculum meant that, as time went on, the school experience of children was far less enriching than it might have been.

It is a matter of common observation that, while the rate of unemployment of young people is high, there is a lack of people available to work in technical or 'trade' subjects. Britain has to import electricians, plumbers, decorators and electronic engineers from overseas because there are too few 'home-grown' workers in these fields. The failure to develop technical education as envisaged by the 1945 Labour government and by subsequent administrations has cost the country dear.

This is not to say that British education has failed to deliver in all respects. The UK remains high in the list of countries producing top scientists and doctors. Schools must take a good deal of the credit. Further, schools have facilitated the making and maintenance of friendships that have often given lifelong satisfaction. In the light of highly relevant research findings (Olweus 1993), bullying in schools has reduced in frequency and is much less tolerated. Finally, many adults do look back on at least some aspects of their school experiences with great satisfaction. It is just such a pity that more positives cannot be expressed.

Every year, the Children's Society publishes in its Annual Report an account of how children themselves feel about the quality of different aspects of their lives. In 2024, more children and young people (14.3 per cent or one in seven) were unhappy with school than with the nine other areas of life they were asked about (Children's Society 2024). Let us hope that future governments take the views of children and young people into account when they embark on their next round of school reforms (see Chapter 10).

6

Free Time

Introduction

Over this period, children and young people spent a substantial amount of their time in school. After the age of five years, attendance at school was compulsory up to fifteen years when, in 1972, the school-leaving age was raised to sixteen years. After 1972, although the school-leaving age remained unchanged, many young people remained at school for some years, and in 2013 it was made compulsory for them to participate in some form of education, employment or training until the age of seventeen (raised to eighteen in 2015). All aspects of schooling are considered in Chapter 5. In this chapter, the way children and young people spent their time when not in school is discussed.

Killian Mullan (2022) drew together the findings of three studies carried out in 1975, 2000 and 2015 in which children and young people kept diaries of the way they spent their time. These revealed that while the total amount of non-school time remained remarkably constant over these three periods (2022, Table 1, p.19), the way this time was spent changed considerably. Obviously, how children spent their time varied considerably depending on their age. Mullan (2022) presented his findings separately for children aged eight to eleven years and those aged twelve to sixteen years. He also presented separately how children spent their time when not at school on days they attended school, and on non-school days. Children were not asked to keep diaries for the school holidays (about thirteen weeks a year) but one can assume they mostly spent their holidays in the same way they spent the time during the weekends of term-times. So, over the year as a whole, about half their time was taken up with school days and the other half with weekends and school holidays. I have drawn heavily on Mullan's data for children aged eight to sixteen years; for younger children, I have drawn on other sources.

Over the whole age range eight to sixteen years, during school days about nine and a half hours and about ten and a half hours on non-school days were spent in bed (2022, p.19). There was a slight increase in time spent in bed from 1975 to 2015. This is perhaps a little surprising as it is often assumed that with more time spent on the phone and on screens, this would mean less time in bed, but this was not the case. A little less than two hours was spent on eating and personal care on school days and a little over two hours on non-school days, again with little change over time. There was a slight increase in the amount of time both younger and older children spent on homework from 1975 to 2015, reaching an average of forty minutes on school days and thirty-three minutes on non-school days (Mullan, Table 2.1, p.35). Altogether, children spent about three-quarters of an hour doing housework on non-school days but much less on school days, with girls doing more than boys. This left about four and a half hours on school days and nearly ten hours on non-school days as 'free time', with little change over the years in the amount. Most of the rest of this chapter considers the use of this free time.

Five to eleven years

Throughout the 1960s and 1970s, the great majority of the children at the younger end of this age group spent most of their time when not in school with their mothers. During the later part of the 1970s and for the rest of our period, an increasing number had mothers who went out to work part or full-time (see Chapters 1 and 2) and so were looked after at home or elsewhere by others until their mothers or sometimes fathers returned from work. After school, at weekends and during the school holidays, children aged up to eight or nine years usually also spent most of their time at home with their mothers and whoever else was living at home, especially younger children. After school, when they weren't having their tea or supper, during the 1960s to the 1980s, they were usually watching TV or playing games indoors or outdoors depending on the weather, until it was time to go to bed. From the 1990s onwards, they were increasingly spending this time before going to bed on their phones to their friends, or on their iPads or other screens, playing video games. A small number were practising the musical instruments they were learning.

In 1975, eight- to sixteen-year-old children spent, on average, two and a quarter hours watching television on school days and just over three hours on non-school days. With the advent of other devices, this went down to an hour and three-quarters in 2000 and an hour and a quarter in 2015. The reduction in time on television was mostly made up on school days in 2000 and 2015 with time spent on computers and playing video games. On non-school days, time spent on computers and video games was around three-quarters of an hour in 2000 and an hour and a half in 2015. Thus, the reduction in time spent watching television was more than made up for in the later years by computers and video games (Mullan, Table 5.1, p.121). At all time periods, girls spent less time watching television, using computers and playing video games than did boys (ibid., Table 5.2, p.122). By 2015, eight- to eleven-year-old children were spending an hour and a quarter on their devices on school days and, on average, just over two hours on non-school days (ibid., Table 5.3, p.124).

Occasionally, mothers would invite other similar-aged children from the neighbourhood or from the same class at school into the home or accept invitations from parents of other children for a couple of hours to play games. Birthdays were usually marked by inviting such children home where there would be games and, in wealthier households, some fun from a children's entertainer. Alternatively, under adult supervision, a group of younger children might be taken as a treat to a local cinema or similar venue.

For most children of this age, the way they most wanted to use their free time was to see or, later in the period, to talk to their friends. Interaction with friends was seen as an essential part of social development. In the late 1950s and 1960s where children saw their friends depended very much on where they lived. Over those years, in many parts of London and other big cities, bomb sites and the back streets were still available for children to play on. These were largely unsupervised and, although often dangerous places to play (see Chapter 2), there was so little for children to do at home (often in poorer homes with no television), mothers felt they had no option but to let children play on them. Boys would usually play football or other ball games or split up into groups with one lot, for example, playing Germans and defending a broken-down ruined building against the other lot, playing the Allies. Versions of tag and 'last in' were also popular. Mildly antisocial behaviour such as knocking on doors or ringing on doorbells and then running away before the door was opened was a popular pastime, though one had to keep an eye open for the local policeman.

By the middle of the 1960s, the bomb sites and small back streets in large cities had largely been cleared and replaced by tower block housing. By then, nearly all households had a television. In many ways, with their greater space, indoor toilets and modern furniture, the flats in the blocks were a great improvement on the back-to-back slum housing they replaced. But, when it came to fun and play, football and cricket and chatting to your friends, the narrow terraces and large featureless, concreted spaces at ground level were no substitute for the bomb sites and the back streets. The bomb sites were, to some degree, replaced by adventure playgrounds, but these were much less popular as their health and safety features made them less exciting places to visit. By the late 1960s, children were spending more and more time indoors watching television, especially but not only the children's programmes (see below). In places where the back streets had been demolished to make room for the development of tower blocks, there were still parks and back gardens to play in for those lucky enough to have access to them. Further, streets and fields were still used for games like Boatman, Boatman and British Bulldog in which children had to run across the road without being caught. In the early years, in parts of inner cities, the volume of traffic was so low that children could play football for hours without needing to stop for a passing car.

Toys, outdoor games and indoor activities

In the 1960s, new toys for boys such as sparking space guns and action figure heroes like Captain Scarlett and Action Man dolls appeared on the market. Indoors, stamp-collecting and filling in scrapbooks were frequent diversions. Children, more boys than girls, would also play doorstep games such as five stones, jacks and marbles. In the autumn, conkers were a popular form of game with the hardest specimens much prized. The 1960s and 1970s also saw many more diversions for boys with clockwork cars, construction toys like Meccano, Lego and model aircraft construction kits, with play doh and plasticine for the younger ones.

Both boys and girls played at skipping, ball games, hopscotch and various forms of run-out. There were also cheaper forms of wheeled vehicles, such as roller skating, scooters, tricycles and children's bicycles available. Girls were often building dens and playing at housekeeping (Webb 2012, p.21). *Cat's Cradle* was a game for two played by girls who made a series of patterns with a ball of string. There were also new toys for girls with dressing-up clothes. Girls and much less commonly boys were often taught to sew and knit, bakery and cooking by their mothers. But in the school holidays and at weekends, it was not unusual for children as young as nine or ten to disappear out of the door after breakfast and not be seen again until suppertime (Feeney 2010, p.61). The pattern of play was, of course, seasonal, with much more outdoor play in the spring and summer than in the winter months.

Whether a child could have friends come home to watch TV or listen to music or just to chat depended on a range of matters such as how welcoming and 'houseproud' mothers were, whether a child had a room of his or her own and how many children there were in the family. Meals were not often shared with children from other families, so the arrival of teatime or supper often meant that guests had to depart back to their own homes. Friends staying for a meal and 'sleeping over' gradually became more common in the 1970s and 1980s. Whether this happened often depended on how happy a child was to be away from its parents for a whole night, and this did not usually occur until children reached secondary school age (11+).

Television

Children's television, especially aimed at the younger age group, was a prominent feature of television programming from the start, gradually superseding children's radio. Thus from 1952, *Watch with Mother* was first run parallel with *Listen with Mother* and gradually replaced it. *Blue Peter*, the longest running children's TV show in the world, began in 1958 and continued with varying frequency until after 2024 when it was still popular. Its content always followed a magazine/entertainment format, with viewer and presenter challenges, competitions, celebrity interviews, popular culture, and sections on making arts and crafts creations from household items. It was meant to be suitable for eight- to twelve-year-olds but was watched by older and younger viewers. In 2002, two new children's programmes were launched by the BBC: CBeebies for those aged under six, and CBBC for those aged six to twelve. Over the years, there were numerous highly successful programmes for younger children, including the Muppet shows (1976–81) and Bagpuss (1974). Grange Hill (1978–2008) was particularly popular with younger teenagers.

Reading

Before the 1960s and indeed well into the 1970s, many children started to learn to read from the Janet and John books, the first of which, *Here We Go*, was published in 1949. These became notorious for their class and gender bias. The children in them lived in large houses with extensive gardens. No boy ever became a nurse, and no girl aspired to be a doctor. Many middle-class children went on to read the comic magazine, Sunny Stories, founded and initially edited by Enid Blyton (though she no longer edited it after 1953) which led on to her many children's books. Many children would graduate onto action comics such as *Hotspur* and *Roy of the Rovers*.

Following learning to read, much reading by children was related to schoolwork. Most subjects, other than Maths and Science, required a good deal of reading. Such reading is dealt with in Chapter 5. In this chapter I shall only discuss reading for pleasure, undertaken as a free choice in preference to other activities. In fact, such reading, on average, took up relatively little of the free time available to young children, only about ten minutes on a school day and twelve minutes on a non-school day (Mullan 2022, p.38), but, of course, there was wide variation with some children reading not at all and others reading a great deal more than the average.

Up to the 1990s, nearly all children's reading for pleasure was from books, magazines and comics. Since the late 1990s, text messages, websites and emails as well as magazines have been the most common reading choices for children and young people. There are no reliable data for the number of children who enjoyed reading for pleasure from the 1960s up to the mid-2000s. A survey carried out by the National Literacy Trust (Clark et al. 2024) established that 51 per cent of young people enjoyed reading either very much or quite a lot. Over a third only enjoyed reading a bit, while 10 per cent did not enjoy reading at all. Significantly more girls than boys said that they enjoyed reading, with 43 per cent of boys and 58 per cent of girls enjoying reading either very much or quite a lot.

Enjoyment of reading declined with increasing age, with younger children enjoying reading more than older ones. Most children read outside of class every day or two or three times a week (61 per cent). Only 7 per cent did not read outside of class. Fiction was read outside of class by two-fifths of the children and young people. Girls were more likely to read technology-based materials as well as fiction, poems and plays, whereas boys were more likely to read comics, newspapers and manuals.

This population of children and young people became well connected to the outside world for the first time in the twenty-first century. By 2010, eight out of ten had their own computer or access to one as well as a mobile phone. Half had their own profile on a social networking site. Slightly more girls than boys owned their own books. Slightly more younger children owned their own books and had a desk. Children on free school meals were less likely to have all of these – Asian children more likely to possess them than all other ethnic groups, including white British. The numbers connected in this way had increased between 2006 and 2009 (Clark 2011), and the numbers further increased between 2009 and 2024 when a further survey by the National Literacy Trust was carried out (Clark et al. 2024). Just one in three (34.6 per cent) children and young people aged eight to eighteen said that they enjoyed reading in their free time in 2024. Reading enjoyment levels had decreased by 8.8 percentage points over the previous year alone. Of course, reading for pleasure is not always the key reason for children reading. Other reasons given by children included the wish to obtain new skills or for learning and understanding. Another popular reason given is emotional – relating to the way reading made children feel.

A significant number of children visited public libraries with a children's section. Excluding school libraries, the Taking Part Survey (Department of Culture, Media and Sport 2011) revealed that 61 per cent of children aged five to fifteen had visited a library in the previous twelve months. A significant portion of these visits, approximately 64 per cent, were by children aged five to ten. Library closures during the austerity years after 2010 were at least partly responsible for a decline compared to earlier years, particularly among eleven- to fifteen-year-olds. For instance, in 2019/20, only 58 per cent of this age group visited a library, a decrease from 72 per cent in 2006/7. Library closures were four times more likely to occur in socially deprived areas than in affluent ones. About 15 per cent of public libraries closed in the UK, most of which had children's sections. Some libraries would otherwise have closed but were kept open by volunteers.

The type of content of the books children read as well as the favourite authors changed over the years. Before the 1960s, the fiction read by young children was dominated by authors such as Kenneth Grahame, Beatrice Potter and AA Milne, whose content was largely fantasy. Kenneth Grahame's Wind in the Willows, Beatrice Potter's little rabbits, Flopsy, Mopsy and Cotton Tail, as well as AA Milne's Winnie the Pooh, retained their popularity well into the 1960s. But then more realistic children's fiction began to appear. In the 1960s, Roald Dahl's first books were published – *James and the Giant Peach* (1961) and *Charlie and the Chocolate Factory* (1964). Dahl's books had memorable characters and were characterized by their unsentimental approach. In the 1970s, for younger children, the American children's writer, Dr Seuss, was widely read even in the UK, for his wit and ingenious rhymes in, for example, *Green Eggs and Ham*, while the 1980s saw the first appearance of Michael Morpurgo's books, especially *War Horse*.

Music

In the early years, and until they reached seven or so, the music children listened to was greatly influenced by their parents. Until ten or eleven, they would listen with their parents, especially their mothers, first, in the late 1950s and early 1960s, to radio programmes and then to whatever was on the television. Once they reached ten or eleven, they began to develop their own musical tastes, often influenced by children their own age. To begin with, they were likely to listen to offshore musical stations such as Radio Luxembourg and Radio Caroline. Radio Luxembourg, which broadcast popular music from 1933 to 1992, was, for a long time, the only international radio station on which one could listen to such music in the UK. Radio Caroline, an initially illegal station, broadcast music twenty-four hours a day from 1964 to 1990 after which it broadcast via satellite. After their bedtime, children and teenagers would pull their blankets over their heads to listen to them (Feeney 2010). In addition, from 1954 onwards, a musical request programme for children, Children's Favourites, was broadcast on the BBC Light Programme on Saturday mornings until 1982. It was initially presented by Derek McCullough or Uncle Mac, whose introduction 'Hello children, everywhere' was familiar to many children of that era.

Music in junior schools was usually rather limited, especially as far as popular music was concerned. A minority of schools played popular music at the School Assembly. Junior school discos, generally for ten- and eleven-year-olds, organized by enthusiastic teachers or parent teacher associations (PTAs) were generally very popular and well attended throughout this period, with the opportunities they provided for supervised mixed gender interaction.

Children and young people aged twelve years and over

Television

Gradually, as described above, during the late 1950s and 1960s, nearly all homes possessed a television, either by buying or, initially, by renting one.

This meant that, for the first few years, though this situation did not last long, children from poor families were excluded from watching television unless they went to friends. Initially, there were only two national channels, the BBC and the commercial channel, ITV, but in 1964, BBC 2 was launched. There were, however, numerous analogue terrestrial programmes available before this, and, in 1957, BBC broadcasting for schools had begun.

The fact that, in the 1960s and 1970s, there was usually only one television set in the home meant that all members of the family had to watch the same programmes and this often led to tension. There were often arguments as to whose finger was on the remote-control button. Although the first portable television sets were available in the 1950s, it was not until the late 1970s that children and young people began to have television sets in their own bedrooms. Many parents tried, often unsuccessfully, to retain control of the amount of television their children watched, again a focus of disagreement and arguments.

As was the case for listening to music (see below), older teenagers generally preferred to watch programmes primarily intended for older audiences. Thus, the most popular programmes for adults (for example, events like the wedding of Princess Margaret and Lord Snowdon in 1960, the landing on the moon in 1969, the release of Nelson Mandela in 1989 and the funeral of Diana, Princess of Wales in 1997) were watched by a large number of teenagers, as were series mainly aimed at adults such as Fawlty Towers (1975–9) and Monty Python (1969–74). Other television much watched by children and young people but intended for adults were sports programmes, especially ITV's Sports World broadcast on Saturday afternoons from 1965 to 1985. Increasingly, from 1991 onwards, sports programmes were only available on subscription, especially to Sky Sports or the BBC subscription programmes such as BBC Sport, so, once again, children from poor families were excluded from watching them.

A massive expansion of the availability of television began in the early 2000s with digital streaming. The first popular video-streaming site, YouTube, was launched in 2005, with Netflix opening its video-on-demand service in 2007. However, in order to stream television, it was necessary to have a high-speed internet connection, a streaming device like a smart TV or a computer/tablet, and a subscription to a streaming service like Netflix or Amazon Prime Video.

Communication with friends

Friendships, particularly friendships with other young people of roughly the same age, have always been a highly important part of the life of the young. Indeed, friendships are not just part of the way children spend their free time, they are also part of school time. If one asks children what they look forward to when they return to school after a holiday or a weekend, the most common answer is to see their friends. Who were friends? Friendship was defined as a dyadic, reciprocal and affectionate relation between peers (Bukowski et al. 2009). A relationship with a close friend, in particular, was characterized by spending time together and having fun, providing each other with social and emotional support, and sharing common interests as well as intimate information.

From the 1950s to the 1980s, face-to-face contact within or outside the home was by far the most common type of interaction with friends. This was supplemented by conversations over the phone. This was made possible by the fact that nearly all homes owned a phone and, for those who did not, a public telephone box was available nearby. Most parents allowed their children to use the home phone although, because long calls were expensive and others might want to use the phone as well, they sometimes placed a time limit on the amount of time their teenage children were allowed to spend on the phone. The disadvantage of home phones or landlines was that access was limited and, because the phone was often situated in a common area, conversations could usually be heard by others in the family. The advent of the cordless phone in the early 1980s meant that children could take the phone up to their own room for a private call. However, this could be unpopular if others also wanted to use it.

The arrival of the internet in 1983, making it possible for different computer networks to communicate with each other, made a massive difference to the way children and young people communicated with friends. In the rest of the 1980s and 1990s, it made it possible for much more rapid and private communication between friends, and those young people with access to a computer (an increasing minority gradually becoming an overwhelming majority) quickly took advantage. Then, in the late 1990s, when mobile phones became cheaper and much more widely available with, shortly afterwards, the connection of the internet to them to create the smartphone, this opened up a new world of possibilities.

Children and young people could now communicate with their friends wherever they happened to be. Further, if they wanted to talk to someone or make a new friend, all they needed was access to the mobile number. Once texting became possible in the late 1990s with communication between different mobile networks, one could even contact someone without disturbing them and they could reply or not as they pleased. This laid open the possibility of unwanted or even harmful communications, one of the many negative features of the internet discussed in Chapter 7. Those young people who had previously had difficulties in communication with others, perhaps because of mental health problems such as autistic features or because of anxiety about ostracism, such as those from LGBTQ groups (see Chapter 8), could now communicate with much greater ease.

Using the internet, it soon became possible to make contact with vast numbers of other young people with whom one would never otherwise have had any interaction. In 2004, the first social networking site, Facebook, was launched by Mark Zuckerberg. By the 2010s, other social media sites, each with its own claim to uniqueness, soon followed. In 2005, YouTube, an American social media and online video-sharing platform owned by Google, was launched. In 2006, Twitter (later X), a platform enabling users, including children and young people to 'tweet' or post opinions to elicit positive and negative reactions, came into the public domain. Soon, popular users of Twitter accumulated thousands and then hundreds of thousands of followers who found their tweets interesting or enjoyable. In 2009, WhatsApp, a messaging service, was launched and rapidly became widely used as an inexpensive form of communication.

A particular feature of Instagram, launched in 2010, was the facility to post photographs taken with mobile phones. This was rapidly followed by Snapchat, launched in 2011 which had the same facility for sharing of photographs and became equally popular. In 2016, TikTok, a popular social media app that allowed users to watch and share short videos shot on mobile devices or webcams, became available.

Users of mobile phones had always been able to view television programmes on their devices and indeed this soon became the preferred mode of watching television. However, the social media platforms served as streaming services, allowing users to download anything from short clips to full-length films specifically made for the purpose of streaming. By 2016, streamed content had overtaken television in popularity.

'Hanging out'

'Hanging out' with friends, playing games, chatting in groups on the street, in coffee shops or parks was common from the 1960s to the 1980s but became less popular later, especially during the 1990s with the arrival of different modes of communication. During the earlier period, boys met to play football in the street or in parks. Girls met similarly to chat and share gossip. Attendance at youth clubs (see below) became less common as these declined in number in the 1980s. Attendance at church services and clubs was unusual unless parents were observant, most commonly in immigrant groups (see Chapter 8).

Other uses of the internet

As well as enhancing communication, the internet provided unparalleled access to information. In 1998, Google, a search engine enabling users to find out pretty well anything they wanted, was launched and remained the most popular source of information throughout the first quarter of the twenty-first century. Soon, preferring to use Google, previously proud owners of the *Encyclopedia Britannica*, which had reached thirty-two volumes in 2000, decided to take them to recycling or, if it would accept them, to the nearest public library. Indeed, in 2012, the *Encyclopedia* went online, thus dispensing with the need for a print version. The availability of such extraordinary amounts of information had obvious implications for schools, and these are discussed further in Chapter 5.

Other practical uses of the internet, fully exploited by children and young people, included online purchasing. By the 2010s, going into a shop to look for something to buy had largely been overtaken by browsing the internet, which had rapidly become an alternative to window-shopping. Similarly, buying tickets for an event such as a pop concert was now far more frequently done online than by telephoning or going into a box office. Playing games or 'gaming' either by oneself or with other children and young people on the internet was also a popular activity. In the early 2020s, the most frequently played online games were *Roblox, Minecraft, Fortnite, FIFA* and *Call of Duty*.

The mobile phone was the most popular device used by children and young people to access the internet, but the introduction by Apple in 2012 of the iPad gave them an alternative that many took up. The iPad was a portable device that offered a more substantial computer experience than a smartphone but wasn't as feature-rich as a laptop.

The amount of time that children and young people spent accessing the internet was a cause for concern from the 1990s onwards. By the early 2020s, the average amount of time spent by teenagers was just over three and a half hours daily but quite a large number spent significantly more than this, with a quarter spending more than five hours, thirty minutes (Mullan 2022). One study suggested that teenagers, on average, spent nine of their fifteen hours waking time on one or other of their screen devices, including smartphones. The vast majority of teens were using social media with 94 per cent checking their phones after going to bed and nearly half keeping their phones next to their beds at night. On any given day, only 6 per cent did not use social media at all. Many of these social media platforms had an addictive quality that made them difficult for young people to resist, and this is discussed further in Chapter 7.

From the 1980s, even from about the age of ten, children spent much time on the family phones talking to their friends. Phone contact with others of the same age increased vastly in the early 2000s when to begin with some and then, by 2004, nearly all teenagers had a mobile phone of their own. Social media began to gain currency in the mid-2000s and from that time became an almost universal mode of communication by teenagers. In 2006, Facebook opened its site to all over thirteen years of age and, since then, teenagers have used all the most popular social media, including Twitter (later X), TikTok, YouTube, Instagram and WhatsApp. By 2024 the average teenager was spending four to five hours a day on social media.

Music

From their early teens listening to music in their own home or in the home of friends became a highly popular activity. Throughout this period, rock and roll, hip-hop, rhythm and blues and pop were the most popular genres with a small minority listening to classical music. Each decade saw particular popular singers and groups dominate the charts and then decline in popularity, though some such as the Beatles and the Rolling Stones remained remarkably durable.

Once they reached their early teens, the young wanted to listen to popular music aimed at young adults. They aspired to experience the emotions of those older than themselves. This is well expressed in the lines of the lyric sung by Nat King Cole to a song that reached Number One in the United States in 1951 and was highly successful in 1972 in the UK when sung by Donny Osmond.

> They try to tell us we're too young/Too young to really be in love.
> They say that love's a word/ A word we've only heard
> And can't begin to know the meaning of.
> And yet, we're not too young to know/This love will last tho' years may go
> And then some day they may recall/We were not too young at all.

By the mid-1960s, nearly all homes possessed a television, and popular music was a staple content of many TV programmes. Some, such as *Top of the Pops (TOTP)*, were long-lasting. It was shown from 1964 to 2006 and, at its popular height, its audience reached 17 million, many of whom were in their mid- to late teens. The format involved the performance of the highest-selling records of the previous weeks interspersed with shots of young people dancing to the music in the BBC studios. The first presenter, always a celebrity, was Jimmy Savile (see Chapter 7). Initially, the programme was broadcast twinned with Radio One and the performances were mimed, but this was soon discontinued and from then on, the music was broadcast live. In 2024, repeats of TOTP were still being shown regularly on BBC Four.

Two revolutions in popular music took place in the 1950s at the beginning of our period: rock and roll, enhanced by the introduction of electronic music which was given impetus when Bob Dylan plugged in at the Newport Folk Festival in 1965, and folk music more generally. The blues formed another genre popular at the beginning of our period. Initially expressing feelings aroused by slavery, oppression, discrimination and injustice experienced by the American Black population, the British invasion of popular music in the United States in the 1960s and 1970s ensured the integration of the blues with popular culture. Rock and Roll was 'teen' music that gave young people the opportunity to express themselves exuberantly in a way that separated them from their parents. This was the first time most young people had enough money to buy their own music and, from 1954 with the appearance of Bill Haley's Rock around the Clock shortly followed by the rock music of Elvis Presley, they bought in their millions. The lyrics were youth orientated. Soul music also drew on the sadness experienced in the American deep south, narrating the predicament of blackness and the hope of better times to come.

Still influential in the 1960s was the music brought over from the Caribbean by the Windrush generation in the 1950s. Commercially exploited by Chris Blackwell, this was music which broke down class barriers with its appeal to the highly educated as well as to working-class Black people. Blackwell was responsible for bringing Bob Marley and the Wailers to England in 1976.

It is not just the music children and young people have listened to over the years that changed, but how they accessed it. From radio, the gramophone and record players with vinyl discs in the 1950s, they moved on to television in the 1960s. The development of cassettes in the 1960s made it possible for young people to record their own music much more easily. In 1979, the Sony Walkman then meant that they could carry around their music and play it with friends wherever. A standardized compact disc (CD) was then developed in the early 1980s by Philips and Sony which meant many more tracks could be contained in a small space. In 2001, Apple then developed and sold 450 million iPod devices which could be stored in a small space including vast numbers of tracks which two young people could listen to simultaneously through their earphones. A big advance came at the turn of the century with streaming. Streaming media involved direct transmission with multimedia through a network for playback. Throughout the twenty-first century, as well as dedicated music sites such as Spotify and social networking sites like Facebook and MySpace created the possibility of shared lists of popular music.

The development of music festivals, following a pattern set in the United States, began on the Isle of Wight in the 1960s, followed soon after by Glastonbury in 1970. These were attended by many young people given their first taste of live music performed by celebrities. Often televised live, these festivals made popular music much more widely available right through to the mid-2020s.

From the early 1980s, there was a growing interest in the lives of popular performers. This led to the production of music magazines such as NME and Rolling Stone, read widely by young people. They used interviews and profiles to bring the music customer nearer to the performing artist, giving the illusion of personal familiarity.

There was a marked contrast in this period between the development of popular and classical music. Musical education in schools is dealt with in Chapter 5. As well as singing in school choirs, most children had the opportunity of learning a musical instrument during their time in school. A minority went on to play classical music for pleasure in their own free time.

The highly talented went from schools to music schools such as the Purcell and Chetham's in Manchester.

Cinema

For many children, in the 1960s and 1970s, cinema provided the great cultural experience of the week. The Saturday morning performances put on by all the large cinema chains which continued until the late 1970s were attended in 1971 by 800,000 children a week. As entrance was cheap, sixpence or two and a half pence, even children from poor families were able to attend. Performances were often noisy with much booing of the villains and cheering of the heroes. Sometimes performances had to be stopped because of fighting among audience members. But these Saturday morning shows which featured a whole variety of genres, including comedy classics, cowboy and adventure films, and cartoons, gave enormous pleasure to large numbers of children. Paul Feeney (2010) describes the 'great joy of going along every Saturday morning to watch your screen heroes'. The rowdiness of the atmosphere meant that some middle-class parents would not allow their children to attend. Alan Johnson, in his autobiography which describes his poverty-stricken upbringing, recalled that one of the three places in his neighbourhood that he took care to avoid was the Electric Cinema in the Portobello Road, London, known locally as the Fleapit or the Bughole, because of its derelict state. 'It never showed anything we wanted to see and its clientele, we heard, consisted of nutcases who would carry us off to be mutilated and murdered' (Johnson 2013, p.73).

Of course, children whose parents could afford it went to the cinema at other times of the week. But they were not allowed to attend excessively violent or sexually explicit films. The British Board of Film Classification (BBFC) rated films as X if they were thought unsuitable for children. Films rated X were forbidden to children before they reached their sixteenth birthday, and this was raised to eighteen in 1982. Many younger children found ways to circumvent these restrictions. Under the aegis of its long-serving Director, James Ferman (1975–99), the BBFC became less restrictive of sexually explicit films and videos and more restrictive in relation to violence. This trend was reversed after his departure.

Reading for pleasure

Fantasy novels dominated the market for teenagers during the second half of the twentieth century. Among the most popular authors in the earlier years were Arthur Ransome, whose books such as *Swallows and Amazons* remained widely read since they were published in the 1930s, *The Little Prince* by Antoine St. Exupery, CS Lewis's *Chronicles of Narnia* and *The*

Lion, The Witch and the Wardrobe, Where The Wild Things Are by Maurice Sendak, *Charlotte's Web* by EB White and the *Hobbit* series by JR Tolkien.

In 1997 came the blockbuster Harry Potter series, which, with its compelling mixture of fantasy and reality, dominated the children's reading market well into the 2000s. The first book, *Harry Potter and the Philosopher's Stone*, was followed by several others, finishing with *Harry Potter and the Deathly Hallows* (2007) but the author, J.K. Rowling remained popular during the first two and a half decades of the twenty-first century. Although infiltrated with much fantastic elaboration, there is much grim reality in the Harry Potter books which were seen to have transformed children's literature. In fact, Jacqueline Wilson, by the mid-1990s, had already broken the ground with books featuring children living in families stressed by divorce, separation and mental illness.

The average amount of time spent reading went up from five to ten minutes a day for eight- to eleven-year-olds and remained the same for twelve- to sixteen-year-olds on school days between 1975 and 2015 and on non-school days it remained the same for eight to eleven and went down from nineteen to ten minutes for twelve- to sixteen-year-olds (Mullan 2022, p.38, Table 2.2). These averages mask wide variation in time spent reading.

Youth clubs

In the 1960s and 1970s, various types of youth clubs and other organizations for young people, including sports clubs, Girl Guides and Boy Scouts, flourished and were a significant part of the youth landscape. There were a large number of youth workers and volunteers involved in running the activities that took place in them. During the 2000s, as concern grew about the social and emotional problems commonly experienced by young people, these gradually extended their activities to include guidance and advice. Umbrella organizations such as Youth Clubs UK grew to play a key role in supporting clubs and providing advice to youth in problematic situations. However, following the 2008 financial crisis, youth clubs and associated organizations were seen as the most dispensable bodies supported by the State and Local Authorities. More than 760 youth centres closed in the UK after 2012, and there was a strong decline in youth services generally. This reduction was blamed for larger numbers of young people being out on the streets with nothing to do and turning to crime in the absence of more positive activity (see below).

Games from the mid-1970s onwards

The world of children's and young people's games was transformed in the 1970s and 1980s with the introduction of video games. The term 'video games' was first introduced in around 1973 to describe electronic games played on a video display. To distinguish them from board games played on a screen, they were required to have some degree of interactivity. The first such game was Computer Space which was only available in arcades in coin-operated form. In 1972, Pong, a form of electronic table-tennis, was introduced and gained popularity. Since that time, video games became much more sophisticated but the basic principle, namely that the point of the game is to accumulate points to reach a target or beat a competitor, has remained the same.

Originally, games were played on personal computer or home console, but, during the 1990s and 2000s, these were gradually superseded by the introduction of smart phones and mobile device gaming became the dominant mode of playing. However, playing on machines in arcades remained popular with teenagers. During the 2000s a number of refinements were introduced, particularly the involvement of virtual reality which required the user(s) to wear a special head-mounted unit. Most video games were played for solely entertainment purposes, but increasingly, video games were used in schools and at home for educational purposes.

Soon after video games became popular in the 1980s and 1990s, concern was expressed about the violent nature of the content. Various content rating systems were devised, including the Pan European Game Information (PEGI) covering the UK and most of the European Union and other European countries. The PEGI system used content rated based on minimum recommended ages, which include 3+, 8+, 12+, 16+ and 18+. Further concern was expressed after the murder of Jamie Bulger, a two-year-old, in 1993, with some suggestion, probably unfounded that one of the ten-year-old perpetrators had been influenced by video game content. Games such as Mortal Kombat and Grand Theft Auto lll continued to cause anxiety in the 2000s. There was further concern about the degree to which children and young people could develop an addiction to playing games. In 2022, the World Health Organization included 'gaming disorder' in the Eleventh Revision of the International Classification of Diseases. Certainly, towards the end of our historical period, the amount of time spent by the young in gaming was considerable. Screen time for children aged five to sixteen rose dramatically from approximately 3 hours in 1995 to 6.5 hours a day in the 2010s. Astronomical amounts were made by the companies such as Nintendo, Sega, Sony and Xbox, with the value of the video games industry estimated at $159 billion.

Holidays

The 1950s and 1960s were the golden age of the British family holiday by the seaside. Most people in employment had at least two weeks, holiday a year, as well as bank holidays. Into the 1960s, partly as a result of the cuts in railway lines, more families owned a car. Families with children up to the age of fifteen went to seaside resorts, especially on the south coast, Brighton and Bournemouth being the most popular. Resorts on the east coast such as Clacton and Southend offered many small hotels and boarding houses. Those living in the north of England went to Blackpool, Morecambe and those in the west to resorts in Somerset, Devon and Cornwall. This was also a time when holiday camps, run mainly by Butlins and Pontins catering for families with children up to the age of sixteen, expanded. They offered modest accommodation with much entertainment aimed at both parents and families in the evenings. Many had crèches for young children available during the day.

In the 1970s, wealthy parents began to buy second homes in the countryside or on or near the British coast, which were often used not just for family holidays, but at weekends. By the 1980s, such families began to buy homes abroad, especially in Spain, but, to a smaller extent, in France and Portugal. In the 1990s with cheap, budget air travel to overseas destinations, pioneered by Easyjet, made travel abroad much more affordable. By the 2000s, with a minority of families now with much larger disposable incomes, holiday travel to the Caribbean, the United States and Southeast Asia, especially Thailand and Sri Lanka, became popular.

Among low-income families, during the whole of this period, holidays were an unaffordable luxury, and many families did not go on holiday for years at a time. In general, families dependent on state benefits did not go on holiday. Of families of all income levels, holidays in the UK remained popular, with about 40 per cent of families not going abroad for holidays. By the twenty-first century, however, a significant number of families with children went abroad more than once during the year, perhaps once in the winter to ski, and once or more during the summer months.

Mixed-gender relationships

At the ages of fifteen or sixteen the single-sex groups which had thus far predominated often became mixed gender with gradual pairing off into couples, usually in short-term but sometimes in long-lasting relationships. The age of first sexual intercourse reduced markedly over this period. In the 1960s, it was around twenty years for young men and nineteen years for young women. By the 1990s, this had reduced by three years for both genders (Mercer et al. 2013). Unplanned pregnancies were relatively common until the 2000s when contraception became more widely used. Attitudes to same-gender sexual relationships also changed greatly, such relationships always being covert in the early decades, indeed illegal until 1967, and more often overt by the early 2000s (see Chapter 8).

Watching pornographic material

Pornography has been defined as 'any material that is sexually explicit and intended primarily for the purpose of arousing sexual desire' (Graham 2017). Until the arrival of the website Pornhub in 2007, pornographic material in any meaningful sense was not widely available. Subsequently, the porn industry became huge, with an estimated value of 15–97 billion dollars a year derived almost entirely from advertising revenue.

Up to the first few years of the twenty-first century, children and young people could and indeed did see pictures of nudes they obtained either by sneaking looks at magazines such as *Playboy*, that their parents had bought or by buying them themselves from the top shelves of newsagents. From then on, porn was not only available on Pornhub but on all the most widely accessed websites, including Twitter, Snapchat and Instagram. Further, although the Online Safety Act (2024) made it illegal to show or distribute such material to children under the age of sixteen years, before then, there were no serious age checks on those viewing this material.

According to a report by the Children's Commissioner (2023), the average age at which children first saw porn in the early 2020 was thirteen and by the age of nine, 10 per cent of them had seen such material. Nearly four in five young people had viewed violent porn before the age of eighteen years, with depiction of sexual degradation, violence, aggression and exploitation as commonplace. Half the girls in the population and a third of the boys were sent explicit images of a person known to them between the ages of sixteen to twenty-one years. Young children, before the age of puberty, were not infrequently exposed to porn that they tended to find funny as well as puzzling, but they did not spend much time watching it. In contrast, the onset of puberty, with the accompanying increase in intense sexual desire, often meant much more time was spent watching porn though the average amount of time spent in this activity is unknown. However, it is known that a fifth of teenage males watch porn at least once a day compared to 7 per cent of girls. What is clear is that at least a small number of teenagers became addicted to watching porn, sometimes of a violent nature and were unable to stop viewing despite their wish to do so.

It was widely thought that viewing porn had various negative effects on sexual expectations, with unrealistic thoughts about the experience of sexual pleasure, and, for example, girls thinking that aggression was a normal part of sexual activity. Some longitudinal research found exposure to violent porn to be a strong predictor of sexual violence (ibid.). The exploitation of children in the manufacture of pornographic material is discussed in Chapter 7.

Antisocial use of free time

Since recorded time, a number of children and young people have spent their free time engaged in antisocial behaviour. Until 1792, those who were caught and convicted were treated like adults. At that point the Royal Philanthropic Society opened a Centre to look after convicted children who might otherwise have been transported. From then, a variety of measures have been taken and institutions established to deal separately with children with delinquent behaviour (Bateman and Hazel 2014). In 1963, the Children and Young Persons Act raised the age of criminal responsibility from eight to ten years at which age it remained, except in Scotland where it was eventually raised to twelve years. In 1989, the Children Act gave responsibility for child welfare matters to Family Proceedings Courts, while Youth Courts continued to deal with children charged with offences. Children received different sentences from adults and, throughout, were sent to different custodial institutions from adults. Over the years, government and public attitudes to youth crime, or juvenile delinquency, veered from putting emphasis on punishment to prioritizing prevention and rehabilitation.

Measuring the number of children and young people engaged in antisocial behaviour is problematic. Sometimes, in published data, as well as convictions, children are included who have only been cautioned by the police. Further, most antisocial behaviour goes unrecorded as it is undetected. Surveys of self-reported offending behaviour provide a very different picture from that of convictions (see below). The number of children convicted of offences gradually rose after the Second World War. This was attributed to family disruption consequent upon the war and rising affluence leading to an increase in relative deprivation. It then fell sharply during the 1980s. There was an apparent rise in the early 1990s, but this was because seventeen-year-olds were included for the first time (Pitts 2002). In fact, the fall continued until the early years of the twenty-first century when it rose for five to six years after which it continued to fall until a small rise occurred again in 2022. The reasons both for the increase and for the subsequent decline are unclear. However, the prevalence of convictions of children and young people is closely linked to family income. The policies of the 1997–2010 Labour government did result in a substantial reduction in the levels of child poverty (see Chapter 1) and this may have had an effect. There is another, much less frequently considered possibility. The mid-1990s saw the introduction of the internet and, shortly afterwards, the widespread engagement of children and young people in playing video games (see above). On the principle that 'the devil finds work for idle hands to do', it is not impossible that children in poor families found other, more pleasurable uses of their free time than engaging in antisocial behaviour.

At various points, the number of children and young people charged has increased or declined depending on government policies. For example, in the 1980s, probably as a result of Thatcherite concerns for restricting public expenditure, the number of children in custodial care greatly declined. Under the New Labour administration, the introduction of antisocial behaviour orders in the late 1990s resulted in the criminalization of large numbers of children who would not previously have come in contact with the judicial system. The attitudes of the Coalition government elected in 2010 greatly reduced the number of convicted children because of a new emphasis on using diversionary measures to reduce the number of first-time entrants to the justice system, as well as reoffending and the numbers of those in custody (Bateman 2014). At the beginning of the twenty-first century, nearly half the offences for which children and young people were convicted involved theft, with about 16 per cent involving burglary and roughly the same proportion, violence against the person. Drug offences accounted for only about 6 per cent (Pitts 2002 p.15, Table 2.1).

In fact, official figures for convictions of children and young people provided a very inadequate and misleading picture of the numbers engaged in antisocial behaviour (Auty, Farrington and Coid 2015). When children and young people were asked to disclose whether they had engaged in illegal behaviour, a much larger number admitted to such behaviour than were convicted. Indeed, about a quarter of the child population said that they had committed offences and this was on the low side compared to other studies of self-reported offending. Most of the offences admitted to were not serious, involving theft and minor aggression. The peak ages of offending were between fifteen and seventeen years, after which it declined. In fact, on all measures of offending behaviour, it rose during the teens, after which it declined during the late teens and early twenties. Throughout, the great majority of offenders were male.

Throughout the 1960s and 1970s, there was controversy whether children whose antisocial behaviour is shown by severe disobedience, aggression and criminal behaviour such as shoplifting and interpersonal violence should be seen as having mental health problems requiring diagnosis and understanding rather than being seen as 'just naughty' and requiring firm discipline and/or punishment. In the early part of this period, the antisocial behaviour shown by children and young people was classified as 'socialized' (if the behaviour generally conformed to the norms in their neighbourhood) or 'unsocialized' (if the individual's behaviour did not conform to social norms). In the 1970s, a further distinction was drawn between 'oppositional defiant disorder (ODD)' and 'conduct disorder (CD)'. Both were destructive behaviour patterns that involved repetitive, persistent patterns of behaviour. ODD was characterized by defiant, disobedient or hostile behaviour, CD by serious violations of social norms, rules and the basic rights of others. CD was associated with a higher risk of persistent antisocial behaviour, substance abuse and legal issues later in life and a generally worse outcome. In the Isle of Wight and Inner London Borough studies (see Chapter 4), about half the children regarded as having a significant mental health problem were showing conduct problems. It is also relevant that a high proportion of children with attention deficit hyperactivity disorder (ADHD) showed antisocial behaviour (see Chapter 4).

The evidence suggests (Maughan et al. 2008) that there was a sharp rise in delinquency rates or recorded crime by children and young people from 1960 to 1985. In fact, the rise probably continued until the mid-1990s (see above). Plausible reasons for this increase (Farrington 2011) include increasingly poor parental child-rearing techniques, increasing numbers of criminal and alcoholic parents, increasing numbers of children in families dependent on welfare benefits (experiencing relative economic deprivation), increasing substance abuse, increasing truancy, increasing opportunities for crime and decreasing deterrence. However, as the rise was based on recorded crime, it is also possible that differences in the way crimes were recorded rather than an actual change in prevalence were responsible.

Collishaw et al. (2004) compared the prevalence of parent-reported conduct problems in three national UK cohorts of fifteen or sixteen-year-olds assessed in 1974, 1986 and 1999. They found there had been a substantial increase in adolescent conduct problems, particularly nonaggressive behaviours (lying, stealing, disobedience), over this twenty-five-year period, with similar increases for boys and girls, and for young people from socially advantaged and disadvantaged homes. Rates of conduct disorder remained relatively stable in the first quarter of the twenty-first century. In 2017, the NHS Digital survey found 4.6 per cent of five- to nineteen-year-olds in England had a behavioural or conduct disorder (NHS Digital 2018). Rates were higher in boys (5.8 per cent) than in girls (3.4 per cent). Oppositional defiant disorder was the most common type, present in 2.9 per cent of children. Rates of conduct disorder were highest in white British children (5.7 per cent) and lowest in those who were Black/Black British (0.7 per cent) or Asian/Asian British (0.8 per cent). Children living in the lowest income households were three times more likely than the most affluent children to have a behavioural disorder.

Conclusion

Children and young people spent their free time, the time they were not at school, in many different ways, depending on their age and preferences. Over the years, seeing and communicating with their friends gave most pleasure. The arrival of the internet made possible a dramatic shift in the ways they communicated with much greater reliance on their various devices as time went on. Some pastimes, such as cinema-going and, to some degree, watching the television, declined, while others, such as playing video games, took up much more of their time. Listening to music was a constant pleasure throughout, though the means of accessing music changed considerably. Throughout, those from low-income families were either excluded from participation or were slower in being able to take advantage of the considerable advances in technology that took place.

7

Child Protection

In this chapter I shall first describe the main changes in the law as well as the significant statutory guidance and policy documents relating to child protection that were issued during the sixty-five years covered by this book. I shall then go on to discuss the role of parents in protecting their children and what happened when parental care broke down. This is followed by a discussion of the ways parents exercised their authority, especially by smacking. I shall go on to discuss the various forms of abuse experienced by children, including physical abuse, neglect, emotional abuse, criminal exploitation and various types of sexual abuse. The chapter will conclude with a description of positive changes in relation to the protection of children that occurred over this period.

Changes in legislation and statutory guidance

A little over a decade before the sixty-five years covered by this book had started, the 1948 Children Act had focused on the steps that needed to be taken when parental care broke down. It had given local authorities the responsibility for providing alternative forms of care, especially in children's homes and in foster care when this happened. In 1960, the Indecency against Children Act was passed. The Act made it an offence to commit an act of 'gross indecency' with or towards any child under the age of fourteen, or to incite a child to such an act. It did not protect those over fourteen but under the age of sixteen, the age of sexual consent. In 1963, the Children and Young Persons Act changed the emphasis in cases of concern about parental competence from the provision of alternative care to providing support for families in difficulty so that such alternative arrangements would not be necessary. From that time, legislation fluctuated from putting the emphasis on supporting families to the performance of their protective functions to ensuring that, if children were not adequately protected, they were removed from the family.

The next major piece of legislation relating to child protection was the 1989 Children Act. This emphasized that in situations where there was a conflict of interest, for example, between what might be best for a mother's mental health and what might be best for a child, the child's welfare must be seen as paramount. The Act changed the emphasis on parental rights to parental responsibilities, these being the responsibility not just of the mother, but of both parents. In contrast, children had rights that must be respected. Wherever possible, support for the family should be provided *within* the family. Responsibility for the provision of appropriate services was once again placed firmly on local authorities. From this time onwards it became the responsibility of the education authority (in relation to school staff), health authorities (in relation to child health services) and social services (in relation to social workers), to ensure that all staff were trained to identify early signs of child maltreatment and abuse, and to have a clear understanding of who to inform if they suspected a child was being harmed.

In 1997, Part V of the Police Act established a centralized criminal register system across the UK. This made possible the Protection of Children Act 1999 which aimed to prevent individuals with unsuitable backgrounds, especially those who had been convicted of an offence against children, from working with them. Subsequently all organizations in contact with children had a duty to check, as part of their recruitment practice, whether a candidate for a post had a criminal record, making them unsuitable to work with children. In 2012, the Disclosure and Barring Service (DBS) was established to help employers make safer recruitment decisions. The role of OSTED in child safeguarding is described in Chapter 5.

The 2004 Children Act directed local authorities to appoint Directors of Children's Services who would be responsible both for education and for the child elements of Social Services Departments. The 2014 Children and Families Act made relatively minor changes to adoption, the administration of family justice and the education of children with special needs. The Children and Social Work Act 2017 made it mandatory for local authorities to inform a new Child Safeguarding Practice Review Panel of all abusive incidents resulting in death or serious harm to a child under eighteen. From 2018, such notification occurred, and Annual Reports were published by the Serious Incident Notification Panel providing information derived from such notification. The Act also improved support for looked-after children and care leavers. The 2017 Digital Economy Act extended protection to children from online pornography. The Online Safety Act, 2023, specifically introduced penalties for transmitting intimate imagery of children on the internet as well as protecting them from other harmful material transmitted on social media.

Alongside the legislative changes, government departments also periodically published statutory guidance and policy documents to assist local authorities to implement legislation. Two of these were particularly important for child protection. In 1999, *Working Together to Safeguard Children* outlined how various agencies and professionals should cooperate to protect children from harm and promote their welfare. In 2003, a government policy document, the Green Paper, *Every Child Matters*, reinforced the need for agencies to work together so that children could be safe, healthy, enjoy life and achieve, make a positive contribution and ultimately achieve economic well-being. In 2018 and again in 2023, the Working Together guidelines were updated.

As well as legal changes to protect children against various forms of personal harm, there were also new relevant laws directed towards the general population, specifically the 1965 Race Relations Act and the 2000 Race Relations Amendment Act (see Chapter 1) which aimed to protect children belonging to ethnic minority groups, as well as adults, from racist abuse and discrimination.

The role of parents in child protection

Over the whole period covered by this book, parents were seen as the main source of protection against the various harms children faced. As the years went by, there were significant changes in the social context in which families lived and in the family structures which affected the way parents were able to fulfil their protective responsibilities (Connelly et al. 2014). As we saw in Chapter 2, in the 1960s, 90 per cent of children lived with their two biological parents who were married and living together. The rest were living with a single parent, in nine out of ten cases the mother. Gradually, this situation changed. By 2021, less than two-thirds of children were living with parents who were married. Of the remainder, about one in five was living with a single parent, mostly the mother. About 9 per cent of children were living in stepfamilies nearly always with a new father but very occasionally with two women (or, even more occasionally, with two men) as parents. This change occurred gradually over the years but was accelerated by the passing of the Matrimonial Causes Act in 1973. This Act made it much easier and cheaper to obtain a divorce. From then on, if both members of a couple lived apart and wanted a divorce, this could be obtained after two years and if only one of the couple wanted a divorce, this was possible after five years separation. Following the passage of the Act, there was a slow but strong decline in the number of people getting married, so that by 2021, there had been a 78 per cent drop in marriage among men and a 73 per cent drop among women (Benson 2023). The trend was particularly strong in the lower socioeconomic groups so that in 2015, 87 per cent of children were living with their married parents in the highest income quartile, compared to 24 per cent in the lowest income quartile. The lower income groups had been particularly affected probably because of the financial disincentives (loss of income from benefits) involved in couples moving in together rather than maintaining single households (Benson 2025).

The trend over time therefore was for fewer children to be living with their biological fathers though a somewhat larger number were living with stepfathers. This trend was important in considering the way children were disciplined. In the 1960s, when a child was disobedient during the daytime, this was most commonly with the mother, who, if her own punishments failed, would threaten to tell the child's father when he came home. The threat of a severe telling off or a smack on the bottom (see below) from the father was regarded as a major deterrent to bad behaviour. Over the decades, responsibility for all aspects of childcare, including discipline, was more evenly balanced between the two parents. Indeed, over the fifty years from the early 1960s, there was a considerable increase in the share of childcare shouldered by fathers. In the 1960s, fathers spent on average eighteen minutes a day on childcare. By 2015, this had increased fourfold to one hour and eleven minutes though this was still less than half the amount of time spent by mothers (Viagni 2024). This meant that, by the twenty-first century, mothers were more likely than had been the case to deal with disobedient behaviour without recourse to the child's father.

A further change relevant to child protection was the gradually increasing move away from the belief that children would be harmed by any separation from their parents, especially their mothers. This belief, which had been fuelled particularly by the child psychiatrist and psychoanalyst, John Bowlby (1969), had a major effect not just on the behaviour of parents but also on public policy. For example, during the 1960s and early 1970s, local authorities, on the grounds that they would be harmful to young children, were reluctant to open day nurseries for the children of mothers who, increasingly, were taking up opportunities for part-time or full-time employment (see Chapter 2).

This belief was particularly relevant to social workers and other professionals involved in cases when maternal care was grossly inadequate or seriously neglectful. While recognizing that the quality of care at home was harmful to the children in question, social workers were reluctant to take children into the care of local authorities and place them in alternative accommodation, for example, with foster parents or in children's homes because of this belief in the harmful effects of separation. It should be added that the awareness of social workers that the quality of care in children's homes was often questionable was a further factor in discouraging any attempt to remove the child from home. It was not until the publication of Michael Rutter's *Maternal Deprivation Reassessed* (1972) that it was realized that harmful effects attributed to separation were, in fact, usually the result of the accompanying neglect and ill-treatment rather than the separation. This new knowledge only gradually changed the minds of those making social policy and training social workers and other professionals.

When parental care broke down

As explained in the introduction to this chapter, the presumption made by the laws safeguarding children is that the family and particularly the parents have responsibility for looking after and providing a good, safe home for their children. However, for one reason or another, family care does sometimes break down or is not possible even immediately after a baby is born. In this section, I describe the alternative arrangements that were then made during our period.

a) Adoption. In the early 1960s, adoption, giving the adoptive parents legal rights over the child and the child a permanent family home, was regulated by the 1939 Adoption Act which laid down that adoption societies had to register with local authorities and banned any sort of financial transactions around adoption. During the 1960s it was very difficult for unmarried mothers to keep their babies as stigma around 'illegitimacy' was strong and benefits to support the mother and baby were inadequate. Thereafter stigma reduced and the size of benefits increased so that more unmarried mothers were better able to keep their babies.

   The 1976 Adoption Act aimed to professionalize adoption further with local authorities taking a larger role in adoptions not involving other family members. However, the decline in the number of available babies meant that there was a sharp reduction in adoption to 4,800 in 1998. Further, fewer and fewer adoptions involved babies (by 2011, only 2 per cent), but more children aged one to four years were being adopted (62 per cent compared to 34 per cent in 1998). Children adopted in the first six months of life showed no more behaviour problems than children living with their two biological parents from birth. The older the child at the time of adoption, the more likely was the child to show problematic behaviour later on, usually as a result of changes of care and caregivers before the adoption. Children from an ethnic minority background were more difficult to adopt partly because of a belief they were more likely to show behaviour problems. Further, there was opposition to the idea of white families adopting children of colour because of the largely mistaken idea this would create identity confusion in the mind of the adopted child (Tizard and Phoenix 1989). All this meant that it was not possible to find adoptive parents for many older children from ethnic minorities or of mixed race who thus were more likely to remain throughout their childhoods without permanent families in local authority residential or foster care.

b) Foster care. Regulation of foster care, the placement of children in the care of local authorities with families who are paid to look after them, was laid down in the 1948 Children Act. In the 1960s and 1970s, there was a significant increase in the number of children in foster care as a result of the belief that it was better for children to live in families than in children's homes. This trend continued during the 1980s and 1990s. By 2022, there were more than 82,000 children living in foster care with 44,000 families providing foster care. At this point 70 per cent of children in the care of local authorities were in foster care. Various forms of foster care were recognized: long term, short term, kinship, emergency, short breaks, remand, fostering for adoption and specialist therapeutic. Over the whole of this period, although much foster care had been loving and conscientious, the supervision of foster care by financially stretched local authorities had been variable with the result that a number of scandals relating to abusive foster parents had been exposed. In the 2000s, the need for training of foster carers looking after children with severe mental health problems was increasingly recognized. This issue had been made more complicated by the fact that, by the twenty-first century, much foster care was arranged by private providers.

c) Residential care. There were very considerable changes in all aspects of residential care in the UK over this entire period. The number of children in the care of local authorities increased slightly from around 70,000 in the 1960s to around 75,000 in the 2020s though this was largely accounted for by the rise in the size of the child population. In general, the number of children in care has varied not just because of changes in the size of the child population but also because of variability in attitudes to removal of children from their homes, with changes in how risk-averse local authorities were. Most children in care were in foster care (see above), but many were in children's homes or in residential special schools. From the 1980s onwards, children's homes gradually reduced in size from an average of about six or seven children to about three places. Increasingly, the children placed in such homes tended to be male and in their teens, where previously, there had been a roughly equal gender balance with more children in their pre-teens. From the late 1980s, residential childcare was largely privatized so that by the mid-2020s, 80 per cent of children's homes were run for profit, around 15 per cent were run by local authorities and 5 per cent by voluntary organizations. A minority of places, around 250 were in secure accommodation for young offenders. Staff of children's homes were largely poorly paid and there was a significant turnover, meaning the residents had little continuity of care. About half the homes were located outside the boundaries of the local authorities responsible for them, which meant that resident children were often living some distance away from their homes. The experience of children living in residential care was often inadequate by any standards and it was from among their number that some victims of 'grooming gangs' were drawn (see below).

How parents exercised their authority

Over this period, a number of studies established four different types of parenting (authoritative, authoritarian, permissive and uninvolved), and the outcomes likely to be associated with each of them (Baumrind 1966). These styles were categorized based on levels of demandingness (expectations and control) and responsiveness (warmth and support) from the parent. Authoritarian parenting involved generally high and inflexible expectations, with limited nurturance and the use of punishment rather than reward to enforce discipline. Authoritative parenting, which was the most desirable in terms of outcome, involved providing a supportive and nurturant environment. With this type of parenting, discipline was exercised by setting clear rules and boundaries, with avoidance of conflict and the use of rewards rather than punishment to set children on the right path. During the 1960s and 1970s, there was a gradual move away from authoritarian to an authoritative style of parenting.

Alongside the changing patterns of enforcing discipline within families was a gradually increasing concern about the use of physical punishment by parents. This arose in the 1960s for a variety of reasons. First was the question whether it was effective. Whereas there was general agreement that a smack on the bottom would put an immediate stop to disobedient behaviour, there was increasing evidence that it was an ineffective deterrent to further disobedience. It became clear that rewarding good behaviour was a more effective method of changing behaviour than punishing naughtiness. Second, there was increasing evidence that parents of juvenile delinquents more commonly used physical punishment than parents of non-delinquent children. So, a question arose as to whether the use of physical punishment made subsequent criminal behaviour more rather than less likely as had been believed. Third were concerns that hitting children provided an undesirable role model for children themselves. Children who were hit were more likely to hit and bully other children. When they became parents, they were more likely to hit their own children. Such arguments persuaded the authorities first in Scandinavian countries to make it a legal offence for parents to punish their children physically. In 1979, Sweden became the first country to pass such a law and in 1982, the Nordic Council agreed on a recommendation which urged its five member countries to do the same.

In the early 1960s, a representative survey carried out by John and Elizabeth Newson in the city of Nottingham revealed that the use of physical punishment to discipline children was widely prevalent there and therefore almost certainly more widely in the UK. In a summary of their findings (Newell 1989), it was stated that 'the first general finding is that smacking is, in general, used for dealing with four-year-olds to a very considerable extent, three quarters of all mothers smacking on average at least once a week'. By seven years of age, the 75 per cent of mothers who smacked at least once a week at age three years was only reduced to 41 per cent.

Over the rest of the century, there was a very slow and inconsistent reduction in the use of physical punishment by parents. In the early years of the twenty-first century, findings from the Millennial Cohort obtained between 2004 and 2008 provide the best-available evidence (Department of Epidemiology and Public Health 2024). The figures are not readily comparable with the 1960s study, but, at three years of age, 70 per cent of boys and 64 per cent of girls were being physically punished. At five years, 58 per cent of boys and 52 per cent of girls and at seven years, 49 per cent of boys and 47 per cent of girls were 'at least occasionally' smacked. These figures suggest a very small, if any, reduction in the use of physical punishment over the fifty years from the early 1960s. There was a further slight decline in the use of physical punishment in the first two decades of the twenty-first century but, even so, in 2021–2, among children aged ten years, one in five had experienced it. There is some suggestion that relying on parents for information on the use of physical punishment may result in under-reporting. In Scotland, the only UK country where children were also asked about smacking, they reported about 10 per cent more use than did their parents. Its use was slightly more common in low-income families, but social class differences were relatively small (ibid.). By 2024, the use of physical punishment by parents was no longer lawful in Wales or Scotland. It was still legally permissible in England and Northern Ireland though there were moves to change the law in this respect.

Most of the smacking that went on in both the early 1960s and in the twenty-first century fell well short of what most people would think of as abusive behaviour. But this was not the case for a significant minority of children. In the 1960s, working-class mothers (and this was only rarely the case for middle-class mothers) 'often referred to the use, or threat, of strap or stick or belt, and to "good hidings", in the punishment of older but still pre-school children' (Newson and Newson, p.206). This could involve the infliction of bruising. One cycle-assembler's wife reported about a child with temper tantrums, 'His Dad hits him to mark him sometimes, but it doesn't do any good' (ibid., p.207).

Physical abuse

The line between physical punishment and physical abuse is necessarily ill-defined. The NSPCC defines physical abuse as 'hurting or harming a child on purpose'. The father of the child whose mother is quoted above would fall into this category of abuse. Over this whole period, physical abuse of this type, if one calls it that, was widespread. Other types of physical punishment (more readily classed as physical abuse) included kicking, shaking, throwing across the room, burning (with lighted cigarettes) and scalding (with boiling water), poisoning, biting and scratching, breaking bones and poisoning (often very difficult to diagnose).

The most extreme form of physical abuse to which children were exposed resulted in their death. Throughout the sixty-five years from the late 1950s, there were periodic reports in the media of horrific murders by parents of their children. Those reported were however only the tip of the iceberg. In 2024, the NSPCC reported that in the previous five years, an average of fifty-two child deaths by assault or undetermined intent a year in the UK. Child homicides were most commonly caused by the child's parent or stepparent. It was much less common for children to be killed by strangers, people previously unknown to them. Children under the age of one were the most likely age group to be killed by another person, again most frequently a parent or stepparent. These were followed by children aged sixteen to seventeen, the victims of murder, usually by stabbing.

The murders that were publicized in the press were often followed by legal enquiries which provided very full information on the circumstances leading up to the death of the child. These descriptions were highly informative and a number of conclusions could be drawn from them. The first such enquiry was chaired by a barrister, Sir Walter Monckton, and considered the death of a Welsh boy, Dennis O'Neill, born in 1932, who died in January 1945 following a brutal beating by his foster-father, Reginald Gough, who was convicted of his murder. Gough had a previous conviction for assault. When he died, Dennis was malnourished and covered in bruises. The enquiry, which lasted six months, was thought to be important in the moves that led to the 1948 Children Act.

Maria Colwell was born in 1965 and shortly afterwards her father died, and she was placed in foster care where she was happy and well looked after. At the age of six, she was returned to her biological mother and her new husband. He already had children by a previous relationship whom he favoured over Maria. She was brutally punished for minor misdemeanours, her stepfather kicking her and leaving her with severe internal and external injuries as well as a broken rib and black eyes. She died at the age of seven in a state of malnourishment and her stepfather was found guilty of her murder.

As a result of public campaigning, a public enquiry was set up. This was therefore the second time an enquiry of this sort had been established following the death of a child to investigate what had happened in order to see what might be learned to prevent similar events in the future. It involved a three-person tribunal and took forty-one days. The enquiry was held in public and attracted much media attention, not always helpful. The social worker who had been most involved was threatened and had to be given police protection. The Report that emerged from the enquiry focused on inter-agency and inter-professional working (Department of Social Services 1974). As a result of its conclusions, child protection became the first priority of social services departments, taking priority over family support, though such support remained an important part of such work. A new system of responding to serious concerns about child protection was developed, involving case reviews, case conferences, child abuse (or child protection) plans and area review committees (now called local safeguarding partnerships).

In 1984, a four-year-old child, Jasmine Beckford, living in the London Borough of Brent, was murdered by her stepfather in remarkably similar circumstances. She also had had spells in care but was then sent back again to her mother. She was battered to death by her stepfather. At the inquiry following her death, it transpired that Jasmine had been locked in a small bedroom with body-building weights tied to her broken legs to stop her moving. Emaciated and deformed, she weighed just 23 pounds. She had forty injuries to her face and body – her ribs were also broken, and she had ulcers, burns and cuts to her leg. Her social worker, believing that the child was loved by the family, only visited once in ten months before her death. The Report of the Beckford inquiry called for greater cooperation between social service and health departments while criticizing the social workers for 'regarding the parents of children in care as the clients rather than the children in their own right' (London Borough of Brent 1985).

Faced with a clearly unsatisfactory child protection system, in the mid-1980s, the Law Commission set up an enquiry of its own. This made recommendations (Law Commission 1988) which was partly responsible for the passage of the 1989 Children Act. This Act established the primacy of helping families with children in need, working in partnership with parents and across agency boundaries, whilst also protecting and caring for children when necessary (see above). The Act introduced the term 'looked after', or in the care of a Local Authority. This term was subsequently very widely used to refer to children and young people under the age of eighteen who lived away from their parents or family and were supervised by a social worker from the local council children's services department. A 'looked-after child' might either be accommodated which meant that the council was looking after them with the agreement (at the request or in the absence, of their parents) or subject to an order made by the family courts.

Under the Thatcher government in 1983, a businessman, Roy Griffiths, who had been tasked with recommending how social care should be funded, advocated handing over budgets from the social security budget to local authorities who would commission services from private providers. The Blair administration, which came into power in 1997, continued this arrangement. It also brought more emphasis on performance management and audit of children's services. This added significantly to the paperwork required of social workers, which many of them saw as unhelpful. It also, however, tackled child poverty and had some success – child poverty fell from 26 per cent to 18 per cent from 1998 to 2010, as a result of increased spending on benefits and tax credits. The early years of the Blair government also saw the introduction in 1999 of the early years intervention, SureStart, described in Chapter 2.

The next major child protection scandal occurred in 2000 and concerned a child, Victoria Climbié, born in November 1991in the Côte d'Ivoire but arriving in England via France with her great aunt in 1999. This great aunt, and the great aunt's boyfriend, treated her with almost unmentionable cruelty. She was forced to sleep bound in a black bin-liner filled with her own excrement in an unheated bathroom. They burned her with cigarettes and scalded her with hot water, starved her, tied her up for periods longer than twenty-four hours, and hit her with bike chains, hammers, wires, shoes, belt buckles, coat hangers, wooden spoons, and their bare hands and inevitably, she died. Up to her death, the police, the social services department of four local authorities, the National Health Service, the National Society for the Prevention of Cruelty to Children (NSPCC) and local churches all had contact with her and noted signs of abuse. However, in what the judge in the trial following Victoria's death described as 'blinding incompetence', all failed to properly investigate the case and little action was taken. Both the great aunt and her boyfriend were convicted of murder and sentenced to life imprisonment.

After Victoria's death, all the agencies involved in her case were widely criticized. A public inquiry, headed by Lord Laming, was ordered. It discovered numerous instances where Victoria could have been saved, noted that many of the organizations involved in her care were badly run, and discussed the racial aspects surrounding the case, arising from the fact that many of the families were Black and there had been concern among professionals about accusations of racism being made against them. The subsequent report by Laming (2003) made numerous recommendations related to child protection in England and was largely responsible for the 'Every Child Matters' initiative, Labour's agenda to join up services in order to improve the health, safety and well-being of children (see above). This laid the ground for the 2004 Children Act which merged children's social services with education departments to form Children's Services Departments. This Act changed the focus onto the achievement of desirable outcomes for children and families. These outcomes – safety, health, enjoyment and achievement, making a positive contribution and experiencing economic well-being – were intended to provide the basis for all government departments concerned with children. These were mandated to work together more effectively to achieve these outcomes. A national inspectorate was established to ensure that child protection work was recognized to be the responsibility of every police force in England and Wales.

The need for these recommendations to be implemented rapidly became apparent in 2007 when a further enquiry chaired by Lord Laming was set up to consider lessons to be learned from the death of Peter Connelly, known as Baby P. He was born in March 2006, his biological father leaving the home shortly afterwards. His mother's new boyfriend and this boyfriend's brother then became responsible with his mother for Peter's care. Over the next year, he was noted to be suffering from serious injuries and, at the age of sixteen months, was admitted to hospital with a broken back and broken ribs. He died the day after he was discharged from hospital. His mother, her boyfriend and the boyfriend's brother were all imprisoned for their part in contributing to Peter's death. Lord Laming's report (Department of Children, Schools and Families 2009) noted that many local authorities had failed to adopt the reforms recommended in his previous report. (It should be added that the furore surrounding the death of baby P led to a considerable rise in the number of children taken into care and subject to care plans.)

The murders of these four children, Maria Colwell, Jasmine Beckford, Victoria Climbié and Peter Connelly, have been described in some detail because they share a number of features reflecting social aspects of the entire historical period under review. In all four cases, the biological parents had split up not long after the child's birth. All the families involved were on low incomes and struggling to make ends meet. The mothers or mother substitutes of the children had formed new partnerships and all the children had been partly looked after by men with aggressive personalities. In all cases, the injuries from which the children suffered had come to the attention of social workers and health professionals, but all of these had been poorly trained in under-funded organizations that were too stretched to meet adequately the demands made of them. Massive media attention was given to all these cases, and this contributed to the pressure to set up enquiries into the circumstances leading up to the deaths. The recommendations made in the reports of the enquiries led to governments introducing further protective legislation. For example, the separation of children's from adult services laid the ground for the 2004 Children Act which merged children's social services with education departments to form Children's Services Departments (see above). It is unclear whether these changes in the law resulted in any measurable change in the rates of abuse suffered by children.

Indeed, more generally, it is impossible to know with any degree of accuracy whether the prevalence of physical abuse increased or decreased over the sixty-five-year period covered by this book. Certainly, the extent of such abuse at the end of this period was deeply concerning. In 2018 and subsequently, following the 2017 Children and Social Work Act, when a child had died or been seriously harmed as a result of abuse or neglect, it became the duty of the local authority to notify the Child Safeguarding Practice Review Panel (England) and the Department of Education. There were 393 SINs (serious incident notifications) and rapid reviews submitted for serious incidents where abuse and/or neglect were known or suspected between April 2022 and March 2023. Around two-fifths of these notifications were due to the death of a child and around three-fifths due to serious harm (Child Safeguarding Practice Review Panel 2022–2023). However, these figures do not include incidents that local authorities failed to notify or those that were less serious but nevertheless significant.

Child neglect

This involves failure to meet a child's basic needs. As examples of neglect, a child might be starved of food, dirty and lacking proper clothing. The child might be left uncovered in freezing weather. A child might not be taken to a health professional when obviously physically ill or might be exposed to dangerous situations such as unprotected open fires. The exact prevalence of child neglect in the UK is unknown, but according to the NSPCC, it is the most common form of abuse. It is also the most common form of abuse mentioned by adults contacting the NSPCC helpline (NSPCC Learning 2024). There is evidence that unfortunately neglect is taken less seriously by social workers and other professionals than are other forms of abuse. A survey of 242 social workers revealed that '60% said they felt pressure to "downgrade" neglect cases and 59% said that it was "quite" or "very" unlikely that children's social care would respond swiftly to children suffering neglect' (Community Care 2013).

Although not all neglected children come from low-income families, the data on poverty in the UK are relevant to the prevalence of neglect. While clearly some children living in families on very low incomes did have their basic needs met by unusually competent parents, those parents living in financially impoverished circumstances had particular difficulties in ensuring this was the case. There is a meaningful sense in which, when the State accepts the existence of child poverty, it is condemning children to neglect. From the 1950s to the 1970s, levels of poverty were relatively flat. After the election of the Thatcher government in 1979, as a result of high-income growth with much greater income inequality, there was an unprecedented rise in levels of poverty. This was not reversed until the early 2000s, when levels of poverty were 50 per cent higher than they were in the 1970s. When

New Labour took office in 1997, income inequalities and levels of child poverty were higher than they had been for decades. The new government introduced policies which significantly reduced levels of child poverty but, if anything, income inequality increased somewhat.

In response to the financial crisis of 2008, the coalition government elected in 2010 chose to follow a path of austerity with cuts particularly targeted towards poor people and public services. This led to the pauperization of the welfare state with diversion of public money to the private sector and increasingly prevalent and intense poverty. The number of homeless households living in temporary accommodation in England rose from 49,680 in September 2010 to 117,450 in March 2024. Particularly badly hit were larger families. As many as 43 per cent of children in families with three or more children were in poverty in 2021/2. These were drawn mainly from families where parents had childcare responsibilities that limited their ability to work, especially lone parent families (Joseph Rowntree Trust 2024). In all four devolved administrations, levels of poverty have been shown to be linked to the number of children in local authority care (Mason 2017).

Emotional abuse

According to the NSPCC, this is any type of abuse which involves the emotional mistreatment of a child and is sometimes called psychological abuse. It often forms part of other types of abuse. It might involve deliberately trying to scare, humiliate, isolate or ignore a child. It may involve threatening, shouting at a child or calling the child names, making the child the subject of jokes, blaming and scapegoating, making a child perform degrading acts, failing to recognize a child's individuality and exercising excessive control, pushing a child too hard academically, exposing a child to upsetting events like domestic abuse, stopping a child from having friends, persistently ignoring a child, not being physically present for a child and manipulating a child.

Most emotional abuse is directed towards children by their own parents or stepparents, but teachers are also sometimes responsible. It is most likely to occur when there is a combination of social and financial problems, such as relationship difficulties and family arguments, made worse by money problems or unemployment. Additional stresses include mental health issues, addiction to drugs or alcohol or domestic abuse. It is impossible to know the extent of emotional abuse because children are too frightened to report it and, in many cases, would not realize what was being done to them or have the language to describe it. There is no doubt, however, that it was widely prevalent.

Criminal exploitation of children

From the 1980s until the 2020s, children and young people have been recruited, especially by drug-dealers, to assist in criminal activities. Typically, children in their early teens (but those as young as nine or ten have been involved) were identified as vulnerable usually because they came from poor families or had some form of disability and offered money to distribute illegal drugs. They were offered a smartphone to make contact with customers, arrange to meet with them often in some town or city distant from where they lived and hand over quantities of drugs in exchange for large sums of money which was then passed back to the drug dealer. The child was given money as an inducement to cooperate. Once children have cooperated, they were then blackmailed by threats of exposure if they were reluctant to continue to assist. If they refused, they might be beaten up or even killed as a warning to others who might refuse to cooperate. The police referred to the systems set up by dealers with children making journeys to points of delivery as 'County Lines'. Criminal exploitation of children was widespread with many police forces having set up County Lines programmes to identify victims. Data from 2023 showed 14,420 children in need assessments in England because of criminal exploitation putting them at risk of harm.

Child sexual abuse

This is defined as occurring when a young person is forced, tricked or manipulated into sexual activity to which he or she has not given consent. This may be 'contact' or 'non-contact' abuse, such as exposing or flashing or showing pornography. Sexual exploitation, to be described in more detail below, is a form of child sexual abuse identified in the later years of our period, though prevalent well beforehand, in which a person takes advantage of a power imbalance to force or entice a child into engaging in sexual activity in return for something received by the child and/or those perpetrating or facilitating the abuse. In the later years of our period, this form of abuse came to be linked to so-called 'grooming gangs', groups of men who joined together to sexually exploit deprived teenage girls, handing them from one to the other.

After physical abuse and neglect, sexual abuse was the next form of trauma to children to come to public attention. Both contact and non-contact sexual abuse had existed to an unknown extent for hundreds of years. Police statistics reveal the number of prosecutions for sexual offences against children. These remained at a low level (under two thousand a year for England and Wales) until 1940 after which there was a rise to over 12,000 in 1970. In fact, only a tiny proportion of offences against children led to prosecutions and, when there was a prosecution, many offenders were acquitted. In 1951 magistrates in Clitheroe, Lancashire, dismissed a charge of indecent assault on a nine-year-old girl, because they said she had willingly accepted an invitation to touch an adult man who approached her when she was walking along a riverbank. This led to much concern about the unsatisfactory state of the law, resulting in the Indecency Against Children Act 1960 (see above). The passing of this Act did not lead to any significant increase in prosecutions (Jackson 2015).

The low level of prosecutions arose mainly because of the reluctance of children to report to their parents or, if they were in care, to the authorities in charge of children's homes or foster care, when they had been abused. This reluctance arose because most abuse was by family members and abused children were frightened of being disbelieved or of creating disturbance in family relationships. Even when they did disclose that they had been abused, they were likely to be disbelieved (Delap 2018). Such disbelief was reinforced by some professionals. For example, as late as 1963, a pamphlet *Child Victims of Sex Offenders* by criminologist Joyce Prince and forensic psychiatrist Trevor Gibbens claimed that 'the most elaborate and circumstantial accusations are sometimes made without any basis in fact'. They elaborated on the psychoanalytic view that children were sexual beings who might seek out sexual encounters with adults. 'Many little girls know a great deal about sex behaviour from observation from an early age, and it holds no great surprises. They may not participate emotionally in offences, but they certainly precipitate them; and, if supported by another child of the same age, will blackmail adults to pay them weekly for the repetition of the same indecent act' (Prince and Gibbens 1963, quoted in Delap 2015). Evidence given to the Wolfenden Committee (Home Office 1957) brought sexual offences against under-age boys to attention for the first time, but the final Report of the Committee made no mention of this information.

The 1970s and 1980s brought a dramatic increase in awareness, public discussion and concern about child sexual abuse. The impetus came mainly from the United States. Although Henry Kempe, an American paediatrician, had published an article on the physical abuse of children in 1962, it was not until the publication of his article on child sexual abuse in 1978 that it became recognized in the UK (as well as in the United States), that children were so frequently the victims of such abuse (Kempe 1978). Kempe was invited to lecture in London, where he proposed an understanding of sexual abuse that involved family interaction rather than just the attack on a child, usually a female child by a violent male member of the family. He suggested that a mother might collude in her partner's sexually abusive behaviour to 'hold on to her man for her own needs', particularly if she was 'frigid, rejected sexually, or herself promiscuous'. This chimed well with the understanding of individual disturbance as a reflection of a disturbance of family relationships which was current in the UK at the time (Mrazek et al. 1983), though it would later be seen as inappropriately removing responsibility from the abusing parent. A study group at the CIBA Foundation met from 1981 resulting in a book whose content was along these lines (CIBA Foundation 1984). This publication, authored by influential child psychiatrists and paediatricians, helped to break down the barriers of silence which had prevented children from disclosing abuse and prevented professionals from listening to them and taking them seriously if they did. Referrals to paediatricians rapidly increased, especially in areas where paediatricians were open to hearing and believing such accounts (Wild 1986).

The medical approach to child sexual abuse, pioneered as they saw it largely by white male doctors, angered a number of feminists who had become aware of the extent of child sexual abuse through their work in rape crisis centres and sheltered accommodation for victims of domestic violence. Women attending these facilities often reported that they had been abused during their childhoods by fathers or stepfathers. Feminists saw the problem of sexual abuse, not as one requiring 'assessment', 'diagnosis' and 'treatment', but as a matter for political and social action to counter patriarchal, male-dominated attitudes regarding the rights of men to treat girls and women as objects available for their own pleasure (Beecher 2023). Although the medical view prevailed in clinical practice, the feminist perspective was influential in changing public attitudes to the problem.

The number of referrals for sexual abuse in the county of Cleveland, especially in Middlesborough, raised particular public concern. There, in 1987, 121 children were taken into care for reasons of suspected sexual abuse over a period of five months. A number of parents who believed that their children had been wrongfully removed complained to their MP who made violent accusations of incompetence against the paediatricians involved. Politicians and civil servants at the Department of Health were anxious that this stream of referrals, if generalized to the rest of the country, would overwhelm the paediatric services and reduce their availability for other conditions. They were also preoccupied with rising costs of both social and health care. As a result of the furore created, in 1987, the responsible Secretary of State for Social Services set up a Committee of Inquiry chaired by an eminent judge, Dame Elizabeth Butler-Sloss, to report on the situation and to make recommendations.

The matter was made more complicated by the fact that the paediatricians, who had been responsible for most of the diagnoses, had developed a specific clinical finding, the reflex anal dilatation test, for determining whether sexual abuse had or had not occurred. A number of their colleagues did not believe that the investigation was either valid or reliable and this controversy fed into public concerns. The enquiry, which sat over several weeks, did not attempt to confirm or refute individual diagnoses of sexual abuse. It concentrated on the processes involved in deciding to take children into care. The final Report concluded by severely criticizing the paediatricians involved as well as the social workers, the police and police doctors for failing to work together. The Report made recommendations as to how services should work better in the future, concentrating on parent and child involvement, and cooperation between the various professional services. Most important, however, from the view of public perception was the fact that, as a result of the inquiry, ninety-eight of the children were returned home (Editorial 1988).

It was thus assumed that most of the diagnoses of sexual abuse had been wrong. This was a misperception. As Beatrix Campbell has pointed out (2023) the Inquiry did not concern itself with the accuracy of the diagnoses, but with the fallibility of the process. It was this last that resulted in so many children being returned to their families. Indeed, a largely concealed report by the Northern Regional Health Authority stated that an investigation into individual children strongly suggested that 75 per cent of the diagnoses were correct. Naturally, for financial reasons, central government was very happy for the assumption to be made that there had been faulty diagnoses and complied with the degrading and humiliating subsequent treatment of the two paediatricians and lead social workers involved.

Child sexual abuse post-Cleveland

Since 1987, while the identification and reporting of child sexual abuse, in the light of Cleveland-induced scepticism, declined, the prevalence of sexual abuse almost certainly did not. A National Society for the Prevention of Cruelty to Children (NSPCC) study carried out by Radford et al. (2011) asked over 6,000 adults, children and parents about their experiences of child maltreatment and sexual abuse. The findings were reported under three headings: parents of the under eleven years of age; children aged eleven to seventeen; adults aged eighteen to twenty-four. The investigators asked 2,275 children aged eleven to seventeen about their experiences of abuse. As many as 4.8 per cent of eleven- to seventeen-year-olds (7.0 per cent of girls and 2.6 per cent of boys) reported experiencing contact sexual abuse, as defined by the criminal law, at some point in their lives. The NSPCC divided sexual abuse into contact and non-contact. The figure above did not include non-contact sexual abuse (such as flashing or saying sexual things). The proportion of children who reported experiencing any form of sexual abuse, including non-contact abuse, was much higher. As many as 16.5 per cent of eleven- to seventeen-year-olds had experienced any form of sexual abuse, including non-contact abuse, at some point in their lives. Only a tiny minority of these even with contact abuse would have been identified by the authorities with appropriate protective action taken. It was possible to compare the rates of maltreatment and abuse found in this NSPCC study with those identified twelve years earlier in another study carried out in

1998. The comparison revealed that there had been a decline in neglect and physical violence, but rates of coercive sexual acts had been very similar.

A little earlier, Gallagher et al. (2002), in a questionnaire study of nine- to sixteen-year-old children of stranger-perpetrated abuse, found that 19 per cent had been the victim of any attempted or completed sexual abuse or abduction incident away from home at some point in their lives. Indecent exposure, touching and attempted abduction had been the most common types of abuse. In all these studies of abuse, girls had been two to three times more likely to be victims than boys and, overwhelmingly, the perpetrators were more likely to be male than female.

There were strong elements of continuity between the twentieth and the twenty-first century in the approach to understanding child sexual abuse. Even in the early 2020s, there was a systemic failure to identify, respond to and prevent child sexual abuse within the family. Practitioners were ill-equipped to deal with a culture of fear and abuse. Children were not given the opportunity to speak and, if they did, were not listened to. Practitioners were not clear about the need for joint social work and police investigation. Race issues, including fears of taking appropriate action because of anxieties about accusations of racism, were poorly addressed. There was inadequate recognition of the needs of parents, especially those suffering from coercive relationships (Child Practice Review Panel 2024). Judgemental attitudes persisted and the advantages of forgetting and 'moving on' were often stressed by those in authority. The terminology sometimes changed but the basic message remained the same – 'don't rock the boat'.

It has to be added that, in some respects at least, this response was understandable. An allegation or disclosure by a child was indeed likely to lead to major disturbances in family relationships. The involvement of social services, so feared by parents, might well have led to the child being taken away and having to provide evidence for criminal or family court procedures. Then, for those placed in children's homes, there was the additional hazard of being abused in the home, perhaps by staff (see later) or by other young people in care. The child and parents might well have felt that covering up the abuse had advantages, particularly if some, at least partial, solution, such as a father being persuaded to leave home, could be made. Responsible professionals will not have been able to express this thought, but many will have felt it.

This is not to suggest that the UK responded less adequately than other countries to the menace of child sexual abuse. Indeed, the reverse was the case. In 2019, the UK was ranked first on most indices among forty countries for its response to the threat of sexual violence against children. The index used to make this judgement, drew on quantitative as well as qualitative data, including input from thirty-six international experts. It took into account the environment, legal framework, government commitment and capacity, and engagement of industry, civil society and media (Economist Intelligence Unit 2019).

Nevertheless, the extent to which responsible authorities could turn a blind eye to the victimization of children and younger teenagers was sometimes almost unbelievable. This is nowhere better illustrated than in the case of Jimmy Savile, the media celebrity, who sexually abused children and adolescents from the beginning of our period in the late 1950s almost until his death in 2012 (Davies 2014). His sexual misconduct was by no means confined to children; he also abused hundreds, if not thousands, of adults. Savile's charity work gave him unimpeded access to hospitals. For example, at Leeds General Infirmary, sixty people, including both staff and patients, stated that they had been abused by Savile, their ages ranging from five to seventy-five. There, it was reported that a number of organizational failures had allowed him to continue unchallenged. At Stoke Mandeville Hospital, it was found that he had sexually abused more than fifty people, including staff, patients and visitors. One was an eight-year-old child. He had full access to all parts of the hospital.

Sexual exploitation and the internet

A newly recognized, though not a new form of child sexual abuse, sexual exploitation, was described in the early years of the twenty-first century. As described above, this involved a form of child sexual abuse in which a person(s) of any age takes advantage of a power imbalance to force or entice a child into engaging in sexual activity in return for something received by the child and/or those perpetrating or facilitating the abuse which sometimes involved the trafficking of children. As with other forms of child sexual abuse, the presence of perceived consent does not negate the abusive nature of the act.

Sexual exploitation had existed for many years, but, from the late 1990s, was greatly facilitated and expanded by the internet. It involved forcing young people into selling sex and, later, using them to create indecent images to sell on the internet. The internet was also used by paedophiles to make contact with vulnerable children and young people. Contact might continue solely on the internet with the passing of increasingly intimate information and then indecent images. However, it might also progress to arrangements to meet face to face. The young person would then usually receive gifts which would be used to induce a sexual relationship. Such contact might involve violent behaviour, in the worst cases leading to the murder of the victim. The Internet Watch Foundation (IWF) was set up in 1996 in response to increasing concern about internet-facilitated abuse. Its 2024 Annual Report recorded that 291,273 reports were confirmed to either contain criminal imagery of child sexual abuse, link to this criminal imagery or were found advertising it. All the most successful social media platforms (Facebook, Twitter (X), Snapchat and Instagram) were used for these purposes. The

Online Safety Act, 2023, specifically introduced penalties for transmitting intimate imagery of children.

The first major indication of the widespread nature of groups engaged in sexual exploitation came in the Jay Report (2014). This revealed that a minimum of 1,400 children had been sexually exploited in Rotherham in northern England between 1997 and 2013. The appalling abuse these children had suffered included having been

> raped by multiple perpetrators, trafficked to other towns and cities in the north of England, abducted, beaten, and intimidated. There were examples of children who had been doused in petrol and threatened with being set alight, threatened with guns, made to witness brutally violent rapes and threatened they would be next if they told anyone. Girls as young as 11 were raped by large numbers of male perpetrators.

The victimized girls were largely highly vulnerable girls, often 'looked after' in the care of local authorities. The majority of the perpetrators were British Pakistani men.

This involvement of Pakistani men led to problems for the children's services whose staff were concerned about appearing racist. In sentencing four men found guilty of sexual offences at Liverpool Crown Court in 2012, the judge, Gerald Clifton, raised this issue. He said of the defendants and their attitude to their victims:

> All of you treated them as though they were worthless and beyond all respect. I believe that one of the factors that led to that was that they were not of your community or religion. Indeed [A], said in the course of the trial that he did not wish to be seen with young white girls in his community in Oldham. Some of you raised in the trial the suggestion that this prosecution was triggered by racial factors. That is so much nonsense. As I have said, what triggered this prosecution was your lust and greed. I wish to emphasize that the sentences I am about to pass on to you all are sentences which would apply to all defendants be they white or Asian.

It is certainly not the case that all perpetrators were Asian, but in certain places, men from Pakistan were considerably over-represented among them.

However, a national audit of sexual exploitation conducted by Baroness Casey suggested that the predominance of ethnic minority groups among perpetrators might be confined to certain towns and cities (Home Office 2025). It remained clear that most of the victims were girls aged eleven to fifteen and that the great majority of the perpetrators were men. Certain groups of children, those in care and those with disabilities, have been regarded as particularly vulnerable, but the audit makes clear that these were by no means the only groups to suffer sexual exploitation. When children in care were identified as being sexually exploited, they were not infrequently placed in other institutions where they had the same experience. A common feature of victims of sexual exploitation was that they were brought up in low-income families, often suffering neglect (see above). The first sign that a child might be being exploited was when he or she went missing from home or from an institution. Policing sexual exploitation presented major difficulties, despite it having been a priority on a par with terrorism since 2015. In particular, the police found it virtually impossible to penetrate networks or groups of perpetrators (Home Office 2025).

Alexis Jay was then asked to chair a national much more comprehensive enquiry into sexual abuse in institutions which reported seven years later (Home Office 2022). This concluded that child sexual exploitation was a widespread problem throughout the country. There was no evidence that the prevalence was decreasing and, indeed, it was probably becoming more prevalent. It is likely that the vast increase in the amount children and young people looked at social media from the beginning of the twenty-first century onwards was at least partly responsible. An explosion in online-facilitated child sexual abuse underlines the extent to which the problem was endemic within England and Wales.

Sexual abuse in institutions

During the twenty-first century, aspects of child sexual abuse which had been prevalent for many decades were first fully revealed. In particular, the Final Report of the Independent Inquiry into child sexual abuse revealed the degree to which religious institutions had been involved (ibid.). There was widespread abuse by priests and members of religious orders in the Roman Catholic Church in England and Wales. Much of the abuse took place in Catholic boarding schools, such as Ampleforth and Downside Abbey. Between 1970 and 2015, the Church received more than 3,000 complaints against more than 900 individuals connected to the Church. In the same period, there were 177 prosecutions, resulting in 133 convictions. Many millions of pounds had been paid by the Catholic Church to victims and survivors in civil proceedings. Since 2016, there had been more than 100 reported allegations of recent and non-recent child sexual abuse every year. The true scale of abuse over a fifty-year period was likely to be much greater. Responses to disclosures about child sexual abuse had been characterized by a failure to support victims and survivors. This was in sharp contrast to the vigorous action often taken to protect perpetrators and the reputation of the Church.

Investigation into the institutions linked to the Anglican Church also revealed major deficiencies. Safeguarding arrangements were under-resourced until 2015 when there was significant improvement. A total of 390 people associated with the Church of England from the 1940s to 2018 were convicted of sexual offences against children. In 2018, 449 concerns were reported to the Church about recent child sexual abuse, of which more than half related to Church officers. Much abuse was related to the downloading and possession of indecent images of children. The Inquiry found that the Church of England failed to respond consistently to victims and survivors with sympathy and compassion, accompanied by practical and appropriate support. This often added to the trauma of those who had experienced child sexual abuse by individuals connected to the Church. An inadequate response to a finding that a member of the Anglican clergy had been found guilty of sexual abuse led to the resignation of the Archbishop of Canterbury in November 2024.

The Inquiry also considered the extent to which local authorities failed to fulfil its responsibilities led to sexual abuse occurring in a variety of settings. Nottinghamshire County Council was a particular focus of attention. This Council was chosen because of the high levels of allegations of child sexual abuse made by individuals in its care but there is every reason to think that such abuse occurred frequently in other local authorities. The Inquiry, which looked at the Nottinghamshire Local Authority's record from 1960 to 2000, found poor recruitment practices in residential care, few qualified staff and little in-service training. These problems were compounded by overcrowding and low staffing ratios in the homes for which it was responsible. The Authority behaved, in its recruitment of foster parents, as if anyone could carry out the important work of being a substitute parent to damaged children. In some instances, a sexualized culture existed in residential homes, with staff behaving wholly inappropriately towards children, paving the way for sexual abuse. As a result, it is not surprising that, between the late 1970s and 2019, sixteen residential staff were convicted of sexual abuse of children in residential care and ten foster carers were convicted of sexual abuse of their foster children. In this one Authority, there were also twelve convictions relating to the harmful sexual behaviour of children against other children in care.

However, Nottinghamshire County Council was far from the only local authority that failed to protect children it its care. The Independent Inquiry (2021, ibid.) stated: 'It is hard to comprehend the cruelty and sexual abuse inflicted on children in the care of Lambeth Council over many years, by staff, by foster carers and their families, and by "volunteers" in residential settings.' Members of this Authority were distracted over many years from their duty to care properly for 'looked after' children by political activities attempting to frustrate the aims of the current government.

Residents in custodial institutions which were the responsibility of the Home Office were also at considerable risk of being abused. The Independent Inquiry (2021) found that complaints of sexual abuse in Youth Offender Institutions (YOIs) and Secure Treatment Centres (STCs) were rarely investigated properly, with little evidence of involvement of the statutory authorities. Local authority residential homes were rather better supervised for the presence of abuse but were not infrequently inadequate in this respect.

The voices of survivors of child sexual abuse

An important component of the Report of the Independent Inquiry into Child Sexual Abuse chaired by Alexis Jay (2014) was that devoted to the voices of victims and survivors of abuse. A total of 5,862 of these consented to provide information to the Inquiry. These were adults of all ages, recalling what had happened to them in their childhood. As many as 70 per cent were women and 30 per cent male. Ninety per cent were white, the remainder from different ethnic minority groups. A high proportion, 45 per cent, had a current disability, reflecting the level of vulnerability to abuse of children with disability.

Nearly half were abused by a family member and 12 per cent by another child and about the same percentage by educational staff. Others were abused by religious staff, foster parents, residential care staff, health professionals, sports staff, custody home staff and defence forces personnel (ibid., Table D1). As many as 79 per cent were sexually abused when they were only eleven years old or younger, many much younger (ibid., D4 para 29).

Sam attended a religious boarding school during the 1970s. He explained how he was one of several boys who were sexually abused by a teacher. This man was not a priest, but a lay member of staff. Very soon after he joined the school, he started abusing Sam. He would invite Sam to his personal quarters on the pretext of helping him with his studies. The abuse followed a regular routine. Sam would go to this man's room each day at the same time, as did other boys. The abuse began with him touching Sam's upper body, then his penis and bottom. He penetrated Sam with his fingers. Sam says that at the time he knew that it was 'a secret', but he didn't know that it was wrong.

Some survivors were sexually groomed from a young age. Alyssa was sexually groomed online from the age of ten. She said that the men who sexually abused her flattered her and made her feel good: 'I was getting the attention online that I never got elsewhere'. She added: 'I didn't realise what happened to me online was sexual abuse until I was 18 years old' (ibid., para 17). Some survivors were made to believe that the abuse was part of a game. 'Macy was sexually abused by two girls at school during "truth or dare" type games. She was forced to perform oral sex and was penetrated by various objects. Macy was seven years old at the time. She sometimes bled as a result' (ibid., para 22). Perpetrators commonly lied about their age. For example, 'when Amy was a child she began chatting online to a male she thought was 18 years old. He turned out to be a much older teacher and he sexually abused her multiple times' (ibid., para 24). Many victims tried to stop the abuse but were prevented from doing so. Ciar reported, 'When I tried to disengage, he threatened to screenshot our messages and show everyone how disgusting I was for seeing the things he'd sent ... I was terrified and felt trapped' (ibid., para 26).

Perpetrators often began with non-contact abuse and then gradually progressed to more severe acts. For example, 'Maddy was sexually abused by a school caretaker from the age of eight. The caretaker befriended Maddy by giving her sweets and praising her schoolwork. Initially, he forced her to touch and kiss his penis. The caretaker then began to orally and vaginally rape Maddy' (ibid., D5, para 34). Most survivors who had shared their experience with the Independent Inquiry investigators felt positive about their experience. One said:

> Since my meeting with IICSA it was a heavy burden taken off my shoulders. The people there were kind and patient, and I felt that at last someone is actually believing in what I endured. After my meeting I felt fine but a day later I became very tearful and felt I had lost my strength to carry on facing people, wondering was it worth it unloading my past to strangers and what good will come out of it. Five days later I realised I had done the right thing. Sharing my experiences would help other children.
>
> (ibid., 2.1)

Positive changes around child abuse

Although it is extremely disappointing that one cannot point to any definite evidence that any form of abuse declined in prevalence over these sixty-five years, a number of positive changes did occur over this period. There were improvements in public policy. As recorded elsewhere, corporal punishment in state schools was made illegal in 1986 and in independent schools in 1996. While one cannot say that all corporal punishment administered by teachers could necessarily be regarded as abusive, some of it certainly was. Not only was it stopped but it was clear that teachers did not want their right to punish children in this way restored. By 2024 it was illegal for a parent or other relative to smack or otherwise physically punish children no matter how naughty they had been, in Scotland or Wales. There were also significant moves to make physical punishment by parents illegal in England and Northern Ireland.

Many parents, denied the right to smack their children, were at a loss to know what to do when their children have disobeyed them. To fill this gap, from the 1980s onwards, a large number of parenting programmes were developed. Some of these, such as Triple P, have been imported from abroad;

others, such as Mellow Parenting, were developed in the UK. A number have been subjected to controlled trials and shown to be effective (Stewart-Brown et al. 2019).

During the early 2000s a number of social media sites began to propagate a highly male macho attitude towards women, encouraging boys and young men to believe that, for example, if a girl agreed to go out on a date, this gave the boy or young man she went out with the right to think she had agreed to have sex with him. One such site had attracted 9 million followers by mid-2024. To counter this message, a number of programmes designed to help boys and young men accept that it was not permissible to touch someone of the opposite sex unless she clearly showed her consent. For example, a programme called Expect Respect was funded by the Home Office and was widely used in schools. Its effectiveness in countering the messages on popular social media was unknown.

The establishment of Children's Commissioners in all four principalities must also be seen as a positive development. The stated aim of the Commissioners was to promote and protect the rights of all children in England in accordance with the United Nations Convention on the Rights of the Child (UNCRC). This certainly included protection against the dangers posed by all forms of abuse, especially to vulnerable groups such as the disabled and those with special educational needs. The Commissioners offices provided advice and representation to children and young people who were encouraged to make direct contact with them. Similarly, the young were encouraged to make contact directly with the various helplines, such as ChildLine and Young Minds, set up for this purpose.

Finally, this period saw a change in the degree to which children and young people were given control over their own bodies as far as health care was concerned. In 1984, Victoria Gillick, a Roman Catholic mother of ten children, brought an action against her Health Authority which had ruled that a family doctor need not inform parents before prescribing oral contraceptives to a minor under the age of sixteen. It was up to the doctor's clinical judgement to decide whether or not to inform parents. Lower courts differed as to whether or not to support the Health Authority and eventually, in 1985, the case was taken to the House of Lords. This gave a majority verdict in favour of the Health Authority with Lord Scarman pronouncing that 'children could consent if they fully understood the medical treatment that was proposed'. Since that time, young people who meet this criterion have been termed 'Gillick competent'. This principle was upheld on a number of occasions. In particular, in late 2021, an appeal against a decision of a judicial review to uphold a case brought by an appellant against the Tavistock Clinic Gender Identity Service was rejected on the grounds that the initial judicial review had not sufficiently taken into account whether the appellant had been 'Gillick competent' at the time he/she had been treated with puberty blockers (Bell and another 2021).

Conclusion

Over the sixty-five years covered by this book, the types of danger to which children have been exposed have been increasingly recognized as physical abuse, neglect, emotional abuse, criminal exploitation and sexual abuse (including in the latter years, sexual exploitation). The most extreme form of physical abuse, child murder and the media attention given to particularly horrific cases has resulted in the setting up of statutory enquiries making recommendations how such abuse can be prevented or, if not prevented, identified and appropriately dealt with. Better training of professionals with improved collaboration between statutory and voluntary services was consistently recommended. There is no evidence that these recommendations have led to any reduction in child maltreatment; indeed, judging by the number of children taken into local authority care, the prevalence of various forms of abuse may have increased. A consistent research finding has been a strong link between child maltreatment and family poverty, particularly strong when examining children taken into local authority care and suffering from neglect. However, there have been a number of positive developments. The banning of corporal punishment in schools and changes to the law in some devolved administrations to make physical punishment by parents illegal must count as one such improvement. The development of centres children can call if they want help to escape abuse is another. The establishment of Children's Commissioners to protect children's welfare was a further positive development.

Throughout this period of sixty-five years though the predominant principle has been the need to keep children from harm, different, sometimes conflicting approaches have influenced the approaches used. In the 1960s and 1970s, as physical abuse emerged into the public consciousness as a significant issue, it was seen as a medico-social problem in which the expertise of doctors was seen as focal (Parton 1996). In the 1980s and 1990s, concern that the rights of parents were being ignored led to more legalistic approaches with an emphasis on ensuring that appropriate legal procedures were respected. Following the 1989 Children Act, welfarism, or the principle that a child's welfare is the paramount consideration in decisions about their upbringing, became dominant. This meant that the best interests of the child took precedence as the primary factors determining custody, care arrangements and other decisions affecting their well-being. The 2000s saw the establishment of the Children's Commissioners as well as Local Safeguarding Children's Boards. The new century also saw the launch of the influential Every Child Matters initiative with its holistic emphasis on the interconnectedness of children's lives and the consequent need for improved collaboration between the various services promoting child welfare and protecting vulnerable children. Sadly, while arguments continued over which forms of intervention were preferable, the primary influences of damage to vulnerable children, namely absolute and relative poverty, while showing some degree of fluctuation, remained largely unchanged with the result that, unsurprisingly, levels of abuse remained unacceptably high.

8

Special Groups

Introduction

The other chapters in this book are relevant to over 90 per cent of children in the UK. But there are a number of groups who, for one reason or another, have led different, sometimes very different, lives over the sixty-five years in question. Some of the children in these groups were special because they were limited by their capacities or by where they lived or by the financial resources of their families; others were different because they arrived as immigrants with their parents or are descended from immigrant families. All these special groups were at risk of exposure to negative discrimination. This chapter describes these special groups and the attitudes they faced over the years.

Children with disabilities

During the 1950s and 1960s, the term 'handicap' was used to describe the incapacity of children who were unable to undertake normal activities on a long-term basis. This was gradually replaced by the term 'disability'. In the 1960s, for the first time in the UK, prevalence studies were carried out to determine the numbers of children with disabilities. The first such study was carried out on the Isle of Wight (Rutter, Tizard and Whitmore 1970). It produced the striking and unexpected finding that one in six of the nine- to eleven-year-old children were suffering from a disability. In 2022/3, it was estimated that 11 per cent of children had a disability (Wade, Stiebahl and Wong 2024). These figures are, of course, meaningless without some idea of what was meant by 'disability'. While most people might think of physical handicaps being the most common form of disability, in fact this was the least common. Most common were children with so-called educational retardation, defined in terms of their reading ability being well below that expected given their general intelligence. Although in fact such children were excluded by their illiteracy from meaningful participation in society, not being able to read newspapers, for example, many people would not have thought of them as handicapped. The next most common group were the intellectually retarded, or those with an IQ below 70. The most retarded of these would not be expected to be economically independent once they had left school. This group needs sub-division into those with mild or moderate learning difficulties and those with profound retardation, with IQs below 50. The latter were the most severely impaired in the population, often unable to feed or dress themselves, thus requiring help in all everyday tasks. This group is described further in Chapter 4.

Those with emotional and behaviour disorders formed the most problematic group to define as clearly their problems fell on a continuum. These ranged from those unable to function in a normal school because they were autistic, or too anxious, depressed or aggressive and those whose difficulties were present and impairing but fell far short of this level. Finally, there was the least numerous group, those with physical disorder alone. Paradoxically, these were usually the least impaired. Even a child with inability to move his or her legs, if of normal intelligence and given aids to mobility such as a wheelchair and lifts to go to all classrooms, was able to participate in most, if not all, lessons and social activities.

The Isle of Wight Study was carried out in a semi-rural community. When the survey was repeated in an inner-city area, it became clear that some of these disabilities, particularly the rates of behaviour and emotional or psychiatric disorders, occurred at twice the frequency of those on the Isle of Wight (see Chapter 4). As most children in the UK live in cities and towns rather than in rural areas, national figures must be assumed to be higher than those found on the Isle of Wight.

In 1970, the Chronically Sick and Disabled Persons Act 1970 was the first UK legislation to recognize and give rights to disabled people, obliging local authorities to provide welfare services, housing, assistance and adaptations to homes, and to ensure equal access to recreational and educational facilities. It also required local authorities to provide services to disabled children, including practical assistance, home adaptations and help with recreational and educational activities, and also to assess and record the needs of disabled children in their area. The next most relevant piece of legislation was the Equality Bill 2010 which largely reinforced previous legislation, particularly as far as the duties of teachers to ensure the absence of discrimination against children with disabilities. However, it will be apparent from Chapter 5 that often during the 2010s and afterwards, children with special needs suffered from a reduction of resources in a manner that goes against the principles of the legislation.

The prevalence of disability over the years probably remained reasonably steady with around 7 per cent of children being classifiable as disabled. However, patterns of disability differed between the sexes with boys having a higher rate overall and more likely than girls to experience difficulties with physical coordination, memory, concentration and learning, and communication. Further, disabled children lived in different personal situations from their non-disabled counterparts and were more likely to live in families with low-income, deprivation, debt and poor housing. This was particularly the case for disabled children from Black/minority ethnic/mixed parentage groups and lone-parent households. Childhood disability was associated with lone parenthood and parental disability and these associations persisted when social disadvantage was taken into account.

Between 2012–13 and 2022–3, there was a sharp rise in the number of children for whom Disability Living Allowance (DLA) was claimed. This might have been due to greatly increasing pressure on family finances over this period but there is strong evidence that there was also a sharp rise over that period in the prevalence of poor health and disability among British children. Between 2012–13 and 2022–3, the number of disabled children in Great Britain increased by almost half a million (440,000), rising from 780,000 to 1.2 million.

There have also been remarkable changes in attitude towards children with disability in the UK during the sixty-five years covered by this account. This is reflected in the legislation described above. The most striking changes have occurred in attitudes towards individuals with learning disabilities. These have become distinctly more positive, with a focus on inclusion and respect rather than stigma and misunderstanding. Changes in special education, described in Chapter 5, with much greater emphasis on integration of children with learning disabilities into mainstream schooling are particularly notable and reflect changes in wider society. It was only shortly before our historical period started that parents who gave birth to a child with Down syndrome were encouraged to place the baby in an institution so as to be 'kind' to the child. By the mid-1960s, parents who institutionalized a child with Down syndrome were regarded with puzzlement and criticism.

Over the sixty-five years covered by this book, a number of advocacy organizations were active on behalf of children with disabilities. MENCAP was originally founded in 1946 as the National Association of Parents of Backward Children and was later known as the Royal Mencap Society before simply being called Mencap. It supported all people with learning disabilities. The Council for Disabled Children, which formed part of the family of organizations under the umbrella of the National Children's Bureau, advocated for all children with disabilities. Most genetic disorders causing disability in childhood are rare and Genetic Alliance UK advocated for all of these. PHAB (Physical Health/Able Bodied) was an organization that brought together physically disabled and non-disabled children and young people for joint activities.

Children from poor families

Increasingly during the 1960s, it was recognized that children living in low-income families were at particular risk for the development of learning problems, behavioural difficulties and subsequent unemployment. However, it took until 2010 for a Child Poverty Act to be passed which laid down targets for the reduction of child poverty that must be met by subsequent governments.

There are two main ways of defining poverty: absolute and relative. Absolute poverty refers to a situation where individuals lack the basic necessities for survival, while relative poverty defines poverty in relation to the average standard of living within a society. Though this has not been without controversy, most government agencies have preferred to use relative poverty as their criterion and have defined it as 60 per cent or below of median income. I shall discuss poverty using both definitions as appropriate.

Relative poverty was relatively stable in the UK during the 1960s and 1970s at around 13 per cent (Joyce and Ziliaki 2019). Coinciding with the dominance of free market economics, it then rose rapidly during the 1980s to a peak of 29 per cent in 1992. By 1994/5, child poverty rates had reached 25 per cent, meaning that one in four children in the country was living in poverty (Platt 2024).

Relative child poverty rates have been consistently higher than overall rates for the total population in the UK, though this is not a universal pattern, with many countries seeing lower rates for children. Poverty rates are largely determined by policy decisions about the organization of the social security system. The rates of absolute poverty fell quite sharply during the ten years following the mid-1990s, largely as a result of the introduction of tax credits for working families. Children at greatest risk of living in both absolute and relative poverty were those living in large families, many of whom were from minority ethnic (particularly Pakistani and Bangladeshi) groups. By 2022/3 the government estimated that 4.3 million children, or 30 per cent of all children in the UK, were living in relative poverty. As has been seen in previous chapters describing physical health, mental health, education and child protection, in every respect, children living in poverty have been at greatest risk of disadvantage compared to the general population.

Alongside the rise in the relative poverty rate during the 2020s, the use of food banks by families with children was high, suggesting a similar rise in absolute poverty occurred. In 2022, 800,000 children under the age of eighteen (about 6 per cent of the total population of children of this age) were living in families that used food banks. Many parents preferred not to use food banks even though this meant they or their children went hungry because of fear of stigmatization. The charity Barnardo's (2024) estimated that about one in four parents claimed they didn't have enough money to buy sufficient food for their children. The cost of living crisis in the 2020s meant that many families did not have enough money to buy clothes for their children. One mother explained:

> 'At one point, we didn't have the internet turned on for three weeks because I just couldn't afford to pay the bill. Things like the internet are becoming a luxury for us. But when you have two kids in secondary school, you need the internet on for them to do their homework and access education. It often feels like I have to choose between paying for the essentials and paying for things for the kids. I've had to rely on food banks, especially towards the end of the month when money is running low, the food bank is all I have.'

Children living in rural areas

The great majority of children and young people in the UK live in large towns or cities. 83.1 per cent if the population live in towns with more than 10,000 population. The remainder (16.9 per cent) of the population are classed as rural. However, most of the rural population live in close proximity to others. Only 2 per cent (and probably less as far as children are concerned) live in such remote places that a town with at least 10,000 cannot be reached with a thirty-minute drive or less. All the same, there were, for example, areas such as West Dorset, where nearly half the population were living in villages of less than 500 people in the late 1970s. Over the twentieth century, there was a significant move away from rural into urban areas especially for employment. However, in the twenty-first century, a desire for less pollution and noise with the availability of online employment has led to a reverse trend.

What does living in the country mean for children? From the 1950s onwards, the opportunities that had previously existed to roam the fields safely and explore the nearby countryside gradually diminished as landowners increasingly kept people off their land. Marion Shoard (1980), in *The Theft of the Countryside*, complained, 'Already a quarter of our hedgerows, 24 million hedgerow trees, thousands of acres of down and heathland, a third of our woods and hundreds upon hundreds of ponds, streams, marshes and flower-rich meadows have disappeared.' These would have been exciting places for the young to play in and explore. Some did find trees to climb, ponds to fish in, woods to hide in, but these were a declining minority.

It is not just the shrinking of the countryside, but the attractions of the media, first radio, then the television, then the mass media, streaming and the iPad, that distract children from being out and about in their neighbourhood. Many local schools shut, following a 1986 circular from the Department of Education and Science that schools with less than sixty pupils should not be retained. Though the circular was later withdrawn, the tone had been set. This meant that more and more children had to be bussed to school. Now the school bus could be an educational experience. A boy from East Yorkshire was quoted as saying:

> I often think that the bus is the real educator. There's an endless chatter and babble that drives the driver mad, but it is part of the process of self-education through obligatory conversation with other children. They talk and talk and pick up an incidental education, just like the rest of us do, through exchanging information with their peers. Even the aristocracy on the back seat, the comprehensive kids, exchanging smokes and homework, prepare the primary kids for the wider world.
>
> (Ward 1988, p.85)

Small country towns and villages were not the sort of places where rural teenagers could live the adolescent lives they watched on the television, and many felt isolated and lonely as a result. But most managed to find transport to larger local towns and, in any case, most wanted to continue to live in their neighbourhoods even if, on leaving school, they were inevitably drawn to urban areas to find employment. Typically, young people in their teens were ambivalent about where they really wanted to live.

Children arriving with or descended from migrant families

While there have always been immigrants into Great Britain, the hundred years before 1960 and the sixty-five years covered by this book saw particularly large numbers of migrants enter the country. Their heritage and often their religion have influenced their children's lifestyle to a sufficient degree to make it necessary to provide separate descriptions. Despite numerous attempts to limit migration, openness to migration from Commonwealth countries and UK membership of the European Community between 1975 and 2020 meant that migration levels (mainly legal but with a small proportion illegal) have been high throughout this historical period.

A description is given below of the main groups of children whose lifestyle differed to the greatest extent from the general population. These are given in the order of their arrival in large numbers in the UK.

Jewish children and young people

This group is included here, as, although Jewish migration had virtually ceased by the onset of our historical period in 1959, there was a sizeable number of Jewish children living in families who had migrated previously with lifestyles distinctive from the general population.

The origins of the Jewish people are told in the Old Testament, the first part of the Bible that tells the story of the world before the birth of Jesus

Christ. The second part of the Bible, the New Testament, tells the story after Christ's birth. In fact, the Old Testament is based on little or no historical evidence. It is not until about 1000 BCE (before the Christian era) that there is good evidence for the existence of the Jewish people and what happened to them subsequently.

The Jewish religion was probably founded in Mesopotamia, a highly fertile part of the Middle East between the rivers Tigris and Euphrates. From the start Jews developed their own distinctive beliefs and religious practices. In particular, they believed they had been chosen by God to follow his Law or Torah which had been handed by God to their prophet, Moses, on Mount Sinai, as they journeyed out of slavery in Egypt. This Law contained 613 commandments their descendants are meant to follow.

Once they settled in land on the eastern end of the Mediterranean, they had a chequered history, sometimes prospering, sometimes defeated by their enemies. After the birth of Jesus Christ, many Jews converted to Christianity and soon there were far more Christians than Jews. In AD 70, their Second Temple in Jerusalem, their most important place of worship, was destroyed and they were comprehensively defeated by the Romans. Although some Jews remained in their original land, most dispersed north, south, east and west to all different parts of the world to what was known as the Diaspora. However, they never gave up their feeling of attachment to their original land, despite the fact that many other peoples lived there and regarded it as theirs after they largely departed.

While there have been small numbers of Jews living in the UK since the eleventh century, as a result of expulsions, there has only been a continuous presence of Jews since the seventeenth century. During the late nineteenth century, Britain acquired a reputation for religious tolerance and immigration from Eastern Europe, Russia and Germany greatly increased. The need to emigrate from these countries arose as a result of discrimination against Jews and not infrequently pogroms or murderous attacks on their populations.

There was a further significant wave of immigration of refugees in the 1930s as a result of the Nazi persecution of Jews. Most of the Jews who did not escape, six million of them, were murdered in the Holocaust, carried out by the Nazis between 1939 and 1945.

By 2021, Jews represented about 0.5 per cent of the total British population, the fourth largest religious group after Christians, Muslim and Hindus, including Sikhs. The main concentrations of Jews were in London (Golders Green and Stamford Hill) and Manchester. There were five groups who might be considered to be Jewish: the ultra-orthodox who adhered strictly to the Torah, the Law as handed down over millennia; the orthodox (observant but less strict in their practice); those who belonged to Liberal or Reform synagogues adhering to a relaxed form of Judaism; secular Jews who did not belong to any synagogue but considered themselves to be Jews; and those who were of Jewish or partly Jewish descent but did not think of themselves as Jewish (lapsed Jews). Some of this last group did not even know of their Jewish ancestry.

It is only the ultra-orthodox and the orthodox whose religion meant they had a significantly different lifestyle to the general population. Children from ultra-orthodox families attended Jewish schools. In 2021, there were 133 ultra-orthodox Jewish schools in the UK and 89 orthodox ones. Children from ultra-orthodox families are not allowed to watch television or go onto other screens though they are permitted to use mobile phones with limited functionality. They have to attend the synagogue daily and observe all the dietary rituals and prohibitions concerning, for example, the use of public transport or motorized vehicles on the Sabbath. Other, less observant Jews live lives indistinguishable from the general population. Young people from ultra-orthodox families were expected to study the Torah (Law) full time at Yeshivas (religious schools) for some time after they left school.

As far as their schooling is concerned, the only children affected by their religion were those who came from ultra-orthodox, orthodox, Liberal or Reform families. In most schools, these children were excused from attendance from religious parts of school assembly and many attended Jewish prayers if there were any. They were absent from school on Saturdays and on Jewish holy days, which usually comprised the Jewish New Year (two days), the Day of Atonement (one day) and the Passover (two days). Children from ultra-orthodox and orthodox families were excused school on other days. In general, children attending orthodox Jewish schools felt secure in their identity and generally well-adjusted (Miller and Pomson 2024).

Among the religious groups, Jews had the highest rates of university education and working in professional and managerial occupations and were over-represented in senior positions. They were most likely to own their own houses.

In the last year of the period covered by this book, 2023–4, there was a rise in antisemitism stimulated by the war in Gaza following the Hamas attack in October 2023 and the Israeli response. The rise in antisemitism was largely but not entirely confined to those areas with a high population density of ultra-orthodox Jews, conspicuous by their appearance and dress.

West Indian children and young people

Although a few migrants from the Caribbean had entered the UK for centuries beforehand, numbers increased significantly during the Second World War when many men came over to volunteer to serve in the armed forces. These and subsequent migrants from the Caribbean were descendants of slaves who had been captured in Africa and forcibly deported to work as slaves on sugar plantations and in other labouring occupations. Slavery had been abolished in the Caribbean in 1834 but was followed by a short-lived forced apprenticeship scheme until 1838 when slaves became fully free. After they were freed, most remained in the West Indies as labourers or in other low-skill occupations, though a significant number prospered in trade. There continued to be social separation with lighter-skinned people, so-called 'white Jamaicans' enjoying less discrimination and a higher standard of living. The effects of slavery on family life persisted often with women bearing children by different fathers, only cohabiting and settling down with the last of their partners (Clarke 2002).

Most of the early migrants who came during the Second World War went back after the war but, from 1948 to 1971, much larger numbers migrated from Jamaica, Trinidad and Tobago and from all the smaller islands, to find work. These were known as the Windrush generation, named after the ship carrying West Indian migrants and docking in London in June 1948. They mainly settled in particular areas of London, such as Brixton, and in Birmingham but also, in smaller numbers, in many other parts of the UK. There was a distinctive migration family pattern with first men arriving to find work. They then brought over their wives and partners, followed a year or two later by any children they had had at home who had meantime been looked after by their grandmothers. This meant that West Indian children often had several breaks of parental care in their early lives (Graham and Meadows 1967). These migrants were given full British citizenship but many years later, in 2017–18, an attempt was made to deport a significant number on the erroneous grounds that they had not been granted such citizenship.

West Indian migrants, both men and women, filled important gaps in the British labour market in the 1950s and 1960s but, after the 1960s, the demand greatly diminished, and migration greatly reduced. The size of the population stabilized, and by 2021, it comprised about 1 per cent if the total British population (Office of National Statistics 2022). Early migrants faced severe discrimination and stigmatization; it was common to see notices in the windows of flats to rent which read: 'No coloureds or dogs'. Anti-coloured feelings turned violent during the Notting Hill riots in the late 1950s and 1970s, spurred on by far-right groups such as the Union Movement. Despite laws, such as the 1965 Race Relations Act, discrimination against people of colour continued over the decades. In 1993, the murder by white youths of Stephen Lawrence, a teenager of Afro-Caribbean origin, triggered an enquiry which found evidence of institutional racism in the Metropolitan police force.

The educational achievement and behaviour of children of Afro-Caribbean origin caused concern over the years. Triggered by false ideas of genetic inferiority, a number were wrongly categorized as 'educationally subnormal' and sent to special schools. The rates of school exclusion for disciplinary reasons were ten times higher in Afro-Caribbean children than in children of Indian origin and three times higher than in indigenous white

British children. Afro-Caribbean children did show high rates of educational retardation but, by the early 2000s, white British boys were performing still less well (Cassen and Kingdon 2007).

There was also concern that children from the Caribbean showed high rates of behaviour and emotional problems. These were systematically investigated by Rutter et al. (1974), who found that this population of ten-year-old children living in London did not differ from indigenous children in rates of behaviour problems at home but did show higher rates of conduct disorder in school. This difference was probably explicable in terms of the number of adverse experiences, especially separation from parents, affecting the lives of the West Indian children.

West Indian migrants made significant contributions to many aspects of British social and cultural life, especially in music and sport. In music, reggae music permeated the British popular music scene from the 1950s onwards (see Chapter 7). In sport, boxers such as Frank Bruno, British heavyweight boxing champion and athletes, such as Linford Christie, multiple Olympic champion, provided role models for Afro-Caribbean children.

Hindu children and young people

Although the term 'Hindu' is a nineteenth-century Western invention, the Hindu religion has existed for at least three or four hundred years before the birth of Christ and has been the major religion practised on the Indian sub-continent since that time. Western Sikhism grew out of Hinduism in the sixteenth century. Sikhs, who are also numerous in the UK, share many concepts with Hindus, including karma and dharma.

The size of the Hindu population in the UK gradually increased from 1960, when it formed only 0.06 per cent of the total population. By 1981 it formed 0.56 and by 2011 1.4 per cent of the total population of England and Wales. By the mid-1980s, there were 360,000 Hindus in the UK.

Although there were very small numbers of Hindus in Britain earlier, the first significant influx of Hindus into the UK occurred in the 1950s with men moving into the industrial cities to find employment. They were joined by their wives and children in the mid- to late 1960s. Most of these migrants came from Gujarat and the Punjab. The second wave of migration came from eastern and central African states from the descendants of indentured labourers who had migrated from India, again in search of employment. In 1972, a large number of Ugandan Asians, mostly middle-class, arrived in the UK having been expelled from Uganda by Idi Amin (Jackson and Nesbitt 1993).

Hinduism was the third largest religious group after Christianity and Islam. Hindus had higher levels of material wealth than any other religious group, but they also had higher levels of poverty than the general population. After Jews, they had the highest level of property ownership and were least likely to live in council-rented accommodation. However, they were 7 per cent more at risk of poverty than Anglicans.

Most Hindu children attended state and a smaller number of independent schools. There were seven Hindu faith schools in the country. Academic achievement is not recorded by religion, but British Indians had higher levels of attainment in public examinations than other immigrant groups or the indigenous population. As many as 28 per cent of Hindu males and 24 per cent of Hindu females had a university degree compared to 18 per cent and 15 per cent in the general population. Hindus were more likely to be in professional and managerial occupations than other religious groups. Although the vast majority of Hindus descended from immigrant groups, intense interest in Yoga and Meditation in the indigenous population meant there were a significant number of converts.

Religious practice varied widely in the Hindu population. About half the Hindu population attended a temple once a week, but many more worshipped at home. Caste, or affiliation to a hereditary social group within which marriage must take place, operated to a very variable and diminishing extent in the British Hindu population. In general, apart from their religious practices, the lifestyle of Hindu children and young people was very similar to that of the general population with a stronger emphasis on the importance of education and educational achievement. However, although Hindu children and young people were often rather ignorant of their religious heritage, for many their Hindu identity was important to them (ibid.).

Muslim children and young people

Islam, at the beginning of the twenty-first century, was the second-largest religion in the UK, with just under four million Muslims. Islam was founded by the prophet Mohammed, who, in 610 CE, had his first revelation that he was the last of the true prophets and that the Quran which he wrote was the word of God. In that he believed that Abraham was the father of both Judaism and Christianity. Islam became the third of the so-called Abrahamic religions. It rapidly acquired large numbers of followers, and its armies conquered the countries on the south of the Mediterranean, reaching and taking most of Spain. It then spread to many other parts of the world, including Southeast Asia and much of Africa. Shortly after Mohammed's death, there was dispute about his succession which led to a split with the formation of two major groups, the Sunnis and the Shiites. There are differences between these two groups in doctrine and ritual, often rather minor but of great importance to those who belong to them.

They were only 0.8 per cent of the UK population in 1960 but by the beginning of the twenty-first century, they were 6 per cent of the population. Between 1940 and 1975, Muslims began to arrive in Britain in large numbers, mainly from East Africa and South Asia. The partition of India in 1947 with racial conflicts in and around Kashmir brought large numbers of people, especially Muslims from that area as well as from the Sylheti area in Bangladesh. The expulsion of Asians from Uganda in 1972 produced a further wave of Muslim immigration. By 2021, over half the Muslim population was born in the UK. Throughout the second half of the twentieth century and during the first quarter of the twenty-first, the Muslim population was relatively young with a high proportion of children and young people. A total of 33 per cent of the Muslim population was under fifteen years of age, compared to 19 per cent in the general population. Muslims were by no means evenly spread throughout the UK. The highest proportion (15 per cent) lived in London but there were high concentrations in Manchester, Bradford, Luton, Birmingham, Blackburn and Dewsbury, with Shiites living in London, Birmingham and Manchester. In these areas, some of the schools were almost exclusively Muslim. Most UK Muslims (90–95 per cent) were Sunni, the remainder were Shias. Relationships between these two groups were generally good but, as a result of small numbers of Wahhabis among the Sunni population, some divisions did occur, especially in universities.

Most Muslim children attended State non-denominational or Church of England or Catholic Schools. There were under thirty state-funded Muslim schools in England and Wales, and about 180 private Muslim schools. Muslim children were high achievers. In 2008, 86.5 per cent of pupils attending Muslim schools achieved five GCS, compared to a figure of 72.8 per cent of Roman Catholic schools and 64.5 per cent of secular schools. Such high achievement was achieved despite the fact that the poverty rate among Muslims was over twice the rate in the general population and, generally, academic achievement was linked to low income. In 2019, four Islamic schools were in the top ten ranking for secondary schools in England, including Tauheedul Islam Girls High School, Blackburn in first place. A study of fourteen- to sixteen-year-old young people in two large comprehensive schools in suburban London found that, compared to all other religious groups, Muslim students had a lower level of psychological distress. The lowest levels of psychological distress were found in Muslim students who lived with both biological parents and were doing more than nine GCSEs. Muslim students who were more Westernized identified themselves as British, perceived less discrimination and reported lower levels of psychological distress (Dabbagh et al. 2011).

It may seem surprising that a Muslim girls' school in Blackburn, in a relatively deprived area of the north of England, should be so high-ranking academically. The reasons probably lie in the cultural origins of these girls. In the parts of Kashmir and Bangladesh from which their parents came, the education system was under-developed even in relation to other parts of the countries from which they came. But from the ages of four or five many were compelled to learn the roughly five hundred pages of the Quran in Arabic. This meant that although their knowledge of other aspects of the Arabic language was minimal, their memories were developed to an extraordinary degree. This served them well when they came over to the UK and had to learn English. Further, the fact that the educational qualifications up to GCSE became increasingly one large memory test meant that they were at a distinct advantage compared to indigenous children. It was further to their benefit in some areas of higher education which might explain why so many of them became doctors, success in the biological sciences and medical degree depending similarly on having an extremely good memory.

Generally, apart from concessions made to girls' dress (see below) there were few other ways in which Muslim children's schooling was affected by their religion. It was noted by their teachers, however, that there was often a change in the personality of girls at ten or eleven years of age as they moved towards puberty. This was particularly the case for girls who had been outgoing and enjoyed playing with boys. These became quieter, less boisterous and more modest in their behaviour in order to conform to cultural norms in relation to gender.

Some Muslim homes had separate spaces for men and women, especially when visitors who were not close family relatives were present. Muslim children were allowed one day off for the Eid festivals, either Eid Ul Adha or Eid Ul Fitra. The home was often considered to be the domain of women and children, as opposed to public space which was male territory. The UK saw a rise in Halal tourism, with major cities like London, Cardiff, Glasgow and Liverpool home to significant Muslim communities. The country had a thriving Halal food scene, and some high-end establishments offering Halal options upon request.

There was controversy about the degree to which girls should be allowed to cover all parts of their bodies between the neck and their ankles as their religion demands, but most state schools permitted such dress. Only a small minority of girls wished to wear the niqab or full face covering and schools were permitted to forbid such veils if it was thought they hindered communication. In general, schools permitted the covering of the hair or hijab. In areas with even a small Muslim population, most schools provided halal meals which conformed to religious dietary demands.

The degree of religious observance among Muslim children and families varied considerably. It is not known what percentage of children attended a mosque once a week, but it was probably around half and depended on whether parents attended. There is very wide variation in the numbers of Muslim children who attend madrasas or religious schools, with estimates varying from between 5 per cent and 80 per cent depending on the location. One might have expected that, as went on, as had been the case with other immigrant groups, such as Jews (see above), that, as contact with the indigenous population increased and intermarriage occurred, the degree of affiliation to the original identity would gradually reduce, but in fact, the reverse was often the case. It was more difficult for immigrant

Muslims to assimilate than it was for Jews. First, Jews could easily change their names to local-sounding ones; this was much harder for Muslims for whom their names were an important part of their identity. Second, because of their lighter skin colour, Jews could much more easily 'pass' for native British citizens. Darker skin colour, beards (in the case of men) and veiled dress (in the case of women) meant that Muslims could not 'pass' in this way. Further, many Muslims had, some generations back, converted from Hinduism. Like many converts, they wished to show closer adherence to their religion. As a consequence, second-generation Muslim migrants unlike Jews were often more and not less religious than their parents. The number of mosques increased, and they made sure there were sufficient madrasas, or religious schools for their often numerous children, with large families often being a feature of their culture.

Patterns of child migration in the twenty-first century

During the twentieth century, patterns of migration largely involved homogeneous groups of Jews, West Indians, Hindus, Muslims, etc., arriving over relatively few years. Towards the end of the twentieth century, this pattern changed for a variety of reasons. Instead, migrants arrived from many different countries at the same time. In the first two decades of the twenty-first century, the majority of migrants to the UK were from other parts of Europe, especially Poland and Romania but also Hungary, Portugal, Spain and Italy. The Brexit referendum meant that from 2021, the numbers from Europe declined sharply. Earlier, most migrants from Europe were initially men who came looking for work and, if they found it, as they usually did, they brought their wives and children over to settle permanently. Other major contributors to the number of migrants were former Commonwealth countries such as India, Pakistan and Bangladesh.

The 2021/2 revealed that, among migrants to the UK at that time, India, Poland, Pakistan, Romania, Ireland and Nigeria were the most common countries of origin in that order at that time. Migration numbers varied considerably in the late 2010s and 2020s. There was a considerable drop in migration in 2020 and 2021 due to COVID-19 and Brexit, followed by a sharp rise in 2022 and 2023, followed by a further fall. Although only about a third of migrants arrived illegally in the 2020s in small boats across the English Channel, this was a considerable number and caused much public concern (Migration Observatory 2021).

About 6 per cent of children in the UK in 2021 were born abroad. Compared to indigenous children these showed somewhat higher rates of deprivation (41 per cent vs 32 per cent) compared to those in the general population, and they had lower levels of achievement. They largely came from Europe, India, the Middle East and North Africa. Of those who arrived as children, about 40 per cent were children under the age of three at the time of their arrival. These generally integrated well into state schools (Migration Observatory 2022), though they not infrequently faced racism and discrimination in their neighbourhoods, depending on where they lived. Children who arrived under the age of eighteen unaccompanied, of which there were relatively slow numbers, were taken into the care of local authorities and fostered or placed in residential care.

Lesbian, gay, bisexual, trans, queer (LGBTQ) children

Homosexual children and young people

Over the sixty-five years covered by this book, there were major changes in public attitudes to children sexually attracted to others of the same sex, in understanding same-sex attraction and in the law relating to same-sex behaviour. Sexual arousal in relation to others is first experienced at adrenarche, around the age of nine to eleven years when the adrenal glands start secreting small quantities of sex hormones. It is experienced in much greater intensity with the onset of puberty, at eleven to fourteen years. At this point, most young people experience such attraction in relation to those of the opposite sex, but about 10 per cent experience it to those of the same sex or those of both sexes. Sexual arousal is often accompanied by feelings of some degree of confusion both in those with heterosexual and homosexual experience but, once those with heterosexual feelings realize their experience is shared by most other young people, their confusion rapidly diminishes. This is not the case for those with homosexual feelings who continue to feel 'different'.

From the 1950s to the 1980s, if their sexual orientation was suspected or recognized at school, gay boys were very often teased and/or bullied, called names like 'poofter', 'queer' and 'pansy'. Other young people often did not want to have anything to do with them, so that they were likely to experience loneliness and depression. Over this time, there were often no appropriate role models for them to take after (Williams 2021). Until 1967, homosexual behaviour was criminalized, and those caught engaging in it could be sent to prison and sometimes were. It was not until the passage of the Sexual Offences Act in that year that private, consensual homosexual acts between men were decriminalized in England and Wales and then only if the men were over the age of twenty-one. The law was only changed in this direction in Scotland in 1980 and in Northern Ireland in 1982.

The lack of provision for those aged sixteen (the age of consent to heterosexual behaviour) to twenty-one years resulted in protest, but for some years, no change in the law. Indeed in 1968 a group of teenagers were sent for Borstal training when caught in homosexual behaviour. In the 1970s, the first counselling services for gay teenagers were established in

Liverpool. The Gay Liberation Front Youth Group was set up and in 1971 demanded abolition of the age of consent, unbiased sex education, an end to aversion therapy (behavioural treatment to change sexual orientation) and the decriminalization of young homosexuals. Nevertheless, teasing and bullying of young gay boys remained common though gay girls were less commonly recognized and so often escaped ostracism. In 1982, the first part-time youth workers for gay teenagers were appointed, though with much resistance from religious groups.

The 1980s brought public concern for gay teenagers on three counts. A Paedophile Information Exchange (PIE) consisting of young men providing information to each other about boys, often quite young boys who were available for sexual purposes. This was stopped in 1984 after ten years. Related to this was the fact that a number of teenage boys running away from home, especially to London, got caught up in selling sex to earn money and survive financially. Finally, the mid-1980s saw the beginning of the AIDS epidemic, which, although mainly affecting older men, also resulted in the deaths of a number of younger men who had contracted the condition in their teenage years. The AIDS epidemic provided an excuse for a further wave of homophobia with, for example, James Anderton, the Chief Constable of Manchester, declaiming that we were 'swirling around in a human cesspit of our own making'.

Gay and lesbian sexual attraction continued to be stigmatized at least to some degree after the passage of the 1967 Sexual Offences Act but to a more limited degree. In 1994, the age of consent to gay sex was lowered to eighteen years, and in 2000, the Sexual Offences Act finally reduced it to sixteen years, the same as the age of consent to heterosexual behaviour.

A major controversy arose in 1988 when, under the premiership of Margaret Thatcher, the Local Government Act 1988 was passed. This stated that local authorities in England, Scotland and Wales 'shall not intentionally promote homosexuality or publish material with the intention of promoting homosexuality' or 'promote the teaching in any maintained school of the acceptability of homosexuality as a pretended family relationship' (Section 28). This section of the Act was only repealed in England and Wales in 2003.

Transsexual children and young people

In this section, gender identity is considered. Gender identity, the experience of being male or female, is normally established earlier than most people imagine in the third and fourth year of life (Graham 2017, pp.35–8). At this age, depending largely on the presence or absence of a penis, young children identified as boys or girls. However, a tiny number of young children saw themselves as the opposite of their biological gender. The great majority of children, from then on, until they were in their early or mid-teens, largely socialized with children of the same gender. They played gender-stereotypical games: doll play for girls, and football, construction and other competitive games for boys. As the decades went by, anecdotal evidence suggests such strict gender segregation gradually diminished so that by the end of the century there was much more mixed-gender and less stereotyped play though same-gender play remained more common. Gender stereotyping remained common throughout this period. For example, six-year-old children saw boys as more intelligent and girls as nicer. Teachers differently rewarded boys' and girls' behaviour, and representations in children's stories were often stereotyped while many parents with new babies and young children inadvertently reinforced gender stereotypes creating a 'gendered world' through toys, play, language and environment.

From the 1980s onwards, a group of Dutch psychologists and psychiatrists based in Amsterdam pioneered medical and psychological interventions for that small minority of children suffering from gender dysphoria or discomfort with their assigned biological gender (Cohen-Kettenis et al. 2011). After full psychological assessment, these children were, around the age of twelve, if they and their parents consented, put on puberty blockers so that, in girls, breast development and periods did not occur and, in boys, the external signs of puberty did not appear. As puberty ended, if the wish to change gender persisted, at around the ages of sixteen and seventeen, the young people were put on sex hormones, testosterone and oestrogens, to conform to their desired sexual identity. Then, in their early twenties, if, as was virtually always the case, the desire to change gender persisted, appropriate surgery was undertaken to achieve the desired appearance.

In the UK, a gender identity clinic was eventually established at the Tavistock Clinic in London that provided a similar set of interventions for a relatively small number of children with roughly equal numbers of boys and girls. However, from 2009 to 2016, the number of referrals to this clinic increased considerably so that the waiting list for assessment and intervention rose to the thousands. This new wave differed from earlier referrals in three ways. Firstly, the children had presented with gender dysphoria usually in early adolescence rather than in the pre-school period. Secondly, while previously, there were roughly equal numbers of children who had been biologically identified as boys and girls, now there were far larger numbers of children identified as biological girls at birth. Finally, this new wave of referrals were much more likely to have mental health problems, including autistic traits. There is some indication that most of these new referrals were confused teenagers, for whom gender confusion was but one feature of more general identity confusion, and that they had been influenced by social media (Graham 2022). Further, subsequent studies showing high rates of same-sex attraction, e.g. trans women who had been born biologically male being sexually attracted to women, it may be that the desire to change sex was, at least to some degree, motivated by a need to justify already experienced sexual orientation.

In December 2020, a Judicial Review was held at the request of a patient of the Tavistock Gender Identity Clinic who claimed he/she had not been adequately assessed before being put on puberty blockers. The Review upheld the patient's complaint, but this decision was reversed on appeal. The Department of Health then commissioned an independent review under the chairmanship of Professor Hilary Cass (Department of Health 2024). This recommended banning the use of puberty blockers except for those patients who were already receiving treatment and for those entered into clinical trials. The government accordingly issued a ban on the prescription of puberty blockers, though this was contested.

Conclusion

The population of children and young people during the years 1959–2024 changed significantly with the influx of a number of new migrant groups. In some parts of the country, this greatly changed the composition of the population so that, for example, between 40 and 50 per cent of those living in London in the 2020s had both parents born outside the country. In addition, there were a number of groups of children, such as those with disability and those living in families with low incomes, who were not able to participate as fully as the rest of the population in, for example, schooling and leisure activities. Variations in sexual orientation and/or in gender identity characterized other groups. Overall, the population was much more diverse at the end of this period than it had been at the beginning.

9

The Impact of COVID 2020–4

Introduction

The COVID-19 epidemic had a devastating effect on children while in its active phase from March 2020 to the end of 2021. But its effects did not end there. Its aftermath continued until the end of the period covered by this book at the end of 2024. Lady Hallett, the Chair of the UK COVID-19 Inquiry, said in her introductory remarks to the public hearing of Module 8 on Children and Young People (29 September 2025): 'Children and young people lost educational opportunities, they lost social interaction, they lost the protection from abuse they needed, they lost loved ones. Some suffered and are still suffering the debilitating consequences of Long Covid. Mental health issues in children and young people have increased significantly.' She did not mention the loss of often the only proper meal of the day by those children on free school meals. All these effects are confirmed by the accounts given by the several hundred children and young people who were interviewed in the preparation of the Report of the Children and Young People's Project (2025) carried out for the Inquiry. Because of this massive and long-lasting effect, a separate chapter is taken up with an account of the epidemic and its impact on the lives of children and young people.

Background

There will probably always be controversy regarding the origins of the UK 2020/1 COVID-19 epidemic. Did it begin in a market in Wuhan City, Hubei, China, or as a leak from a laboratory there? We may never know. What we do know is that the virus spread throughout the world and that British children suffered as much, if not more than, children elsewhere. While the fatality rate among the young was negligible, the disruption to children's lives was immense. The long-term effects were still present at the end of our period in 2024.

By the time the virus had spread from China to Italy and then to the UK in the early weeks of 2020, the opportunity to contain it had already been lost. When Boris Johnson, the prime minister, announced on 16 March 2020 that all non-essential contact and travel should be stopped, there had already been a number of widely attended events, such as the Cheltenham race meeting, at which considerable spread had occurred.

School lockdowns

On 18 March 2020 the prime minister announced the first lockdown with partial closure of all schools, which remained open only for children of essential workers and some children with special needs. This first lockdown partially ended at the end of May 2020 with regional variations. In fact, schools in England largely remained closed until September 2020, though a few primary and secondary schools opened in June, Welsh schools in late June and schools in Northern Ireland in August and September 2020. Scottish schools largely reopened in August 2020. Schools only remained open from September until 4 January 2021 when, as a result of a second wave of infection caused by a new variant of the virus, English schools were instructed to close again except for the children of key workers and vulnerable children. Primary schools largely reopened on 8 March 2021 after two months with secondary schools opening more gradually. School closures in the devolved administrations followed roughly the same pattern. In summary, with relatively minor variations, UK schools were largely closed for three months in the spring of 2020 and for six weeks in early 2021.

Subsequently, there was much criticism of the lack of preparation for the lockdown of schools, though this was denied by Boris Johnson. In fact, the public hearings of the Covid Inquiry held in 2025 revealed that both the then Permanent Secretary of the Department for Education, Jonathan Edwards, and the then Secretary of State for Education, Gavin Williamson, recalled that 'there was a discombobulating 24-hour sea change from keeping schools open, on 16 March, to discussions about closing schools on 17 March', the day before the announcement was made. The speed of the decision was such that no consultation was made with any of the groups most immediately affected, particularly parents, teachers and children themselves. The then Children's Commissioner, Anne Longfield, recalled (Covid Inquiry Public Hearing, 2 October 2025) that failure to consult with her organization meant that the children's interests were not considered when the lockdown decision was made. She indicated that, had she been consulted, some of the problems that arose, particularly over the impact on vulnerable children, might well have been avoided.

Much educational disruption in 2021 was also caused by teacher absence due to the COVID-19 omicron infection, and in December 2021 a request went out to retired teachers to return as there were so many staff absences.

From the beginning of 2022, the decision whether schools should remain open was delegated to individual local authorities. In January 2022 face masks were made obligatory in secondary schools but later that month the requirement was dropped, first in classrooms and then in communal areas.

Secondary school public examinations normally held in May and June were cancelled for that year in March 2020 and results calculated on the basis of predicted grades. Predicted grades were used to determine results both in 2020 and in 2021 but normal examinations were reinstated for 2022, with some modifications based on allowances for disrupted education. An attempt in 2020 to make an algorithmic correction to teacher predictions created protests and was dropped. Using teacher predictions resulted in generally inflated grades and increased discrepancies between state and private schools with inflated achievement greatest in private schools. OFSTED inspections were also suspended in March 2020, but there was a phased return in 2021.

Home learning was encouraged during the lockdown periods. Teachers were asked to remain in touch with students as much as possible and to set work online. The Department of Education funded an online website called the Oak National Academy which provided free lessons for teachers to use which many did. However, nearly 10 per cent of students did not have access to a computer at home and so missed out entirely on online learning. On average, students spent about eleven hours a week learning online but there were wide discrepancies with some socially disadvantaged students doing no online learning at all.

While the changes described above directly affected children, at the same time, there were significant changes to the lives of the adult population, many of which indirectly affected children. For fifteen months from March 2020, those people who could work at home rather than go to work were instructed to do so, so many parents were also at home while their children were at home from school, leading to tensions over space and access to computers. Social distancing with its limitations on social gatherings lasted from March 2020 until the end of 2021 (with respite in the summer of 2021), which meant children could not go out to visit friends or other members of the family over that prolonged period. The closure of cafés, restaurants, swimming pools and other places where children usually met others similarly restricted their lives. When in August 2021, it was decided for a relatively brief period to relax the restrictions in order to boost the economy, especially in the hospitality industry, by the Eat Out to Help Out scheme, children joined their parents in going out more, but this probably spread the infection unnecessarily.

Children's lives were also affected by the UK vaccination programme which began to be rolled out in December 2020. This greatly lowered the risk of spread of the disease. To begin with, vaccination was limited to the over-80s and vulnerable members of the population, but it was rapidly extended to the entire adult population. Because children were only rarely infected, children were initially not given the vaccine but in September 2020, twelve- to fifteen-year-olds entered the vaccination programme, mainly to limit the spread of the condition rather than because they were at risk themselves.

Impact on post-natal services and pre-school children

Throughout the UK, for several weeks after a birth, mothers are normally given support and babies regularly monitored by community midwives. The baby is checked over by a doctor at six to eight weeks after birth to ensure its development is progressing well. The result of the lockdown in March 2020 meant that most mothers with new babies faced significant reductions in support. Health visitors were instructed to make visits to new births over the phone and to stop visits to older babies and toddlers unless the families had been identified as vulnerable. There was reduced contact with family, friends and informal support networks, so that the usual help new mothers got, for example, from their own mothers, was no longer available (Children's Commissioner, September, 2020). Many children's centres stopped offering in-person support and attendance at childcare and early years settings was much reduced. Social work support had to be provided virtually. The reduction of face-to-face contact with professionals meant that many developmental problems were not identified so that appropriate advice could not be given. The many babies and toddlers living in stressed families with parents with mental health difficulties, with drug and alcohol problems or where there was domestic abuse were deprived of appropriate support, even though such problems increased in frequency during the pandemic (see below).

The restrictions on movement outside the home meant that the great majority of mothers of young children could not leave home over a prolonged period, except very occasionally to shop or to take exercise. Women friends were not allowed to visit and this meant that often mothers were left alone with their babies in an anxious and depressed state. Normal bonding with their babies was made more difficult (Singh et al. 2021). There was little help with common feeding problems. Understandably, many mothers of newborns developed stress symptoms. Mothers of pre-school children, especially those living in flats, are at particular risk of developing depressive disorders (Brown and Harris 1984). Such disorders, often characterized by frequent spells of crying, feelings of worthlessness and suicidal ideas, make effective parenting difficult if not impossible. A supportive partner living in the home makes depression less likely but, as we have seen in Chapter 2, by 2020, many mothers, either as a result of divorce or separation or because the father of their children had never lived with the family, were living alone.

In line with policies regarding the closure of schools, nursery schools were closed for three months or longer in the spring of 2020 and for six weeks in early 2021. This meant that children entering infant schools in September 2021 had had either very little or no nursery school experience before they transitioned. Results of an investigation (Bakapoulou 2022) revealed that support for the transition of young children from nursery to school was significantly negatively affected by the lockdown. This was particularly disadvantageous for those children with special educational needs, many of whom arrived in infant school without their special needs having been identified. Some children were still not toilet trained on arrival and infant schoolteachers found themselves changing nappies rather than teaching.

Impact on primary schools: Attendance, achievement

a) Attendance. The absence rate of primary school students before the pandemic was in the region of 4.3 per cent. In the last three months of 2020, after the first lockdown when, in theory, all children should have been back at school, it was 14.8 per cent. In the summer of 2021, after the second lockdown, it was 12.9 per cent (Gibbons et al 2024). It then declined to 7.4 per cent the following year. However, and more seriously, in 2023/4, 21.2 per cent of primary school pupils were classified as persistently absent, which is defined as missing 10 per cent or more of possible school sessions. This was significantly up from 13.1 per cent before the pandemic. The absenteeism rate was highest in 2024 in those areas where restrictions on attendance had been greatest during and around the lockdown periods.

b) Achievement. There were immediate negative effects of school closure, but these were not uniformly distributed across the age range. There was some evidence that in primary schools, younger age groups (Key Stage 1 pupils) were the most significantly affected with lower attainment than previous cohorts in all subjects (Weidman et al. 2022). Other research showed that there were particularly negative impacts for pupils in key stage 3 and that, on average, pupils were not performing as well in both maths and reading as pre-pandemic cohorts. Socially disadvantaged students were particularly badly affected (ibid.). For example, the disadvantage gap widened to a degree that represented an increase of between 4 per cent and 17 per cent from before COVID-19. This widening happened particularly during the first lockdown (see below).

By the academic year 2023/2024, much recovery had been made, but again this was uneven. For example, on average, for Years 4 and 5 (children aged nine and ten years), the COVID-19 gap seemed to have closed (Rose, Lord,

Ager et al. 2024). In Year 4 Mathematics and Year 5 reading, there was no significant difference in pupils' performance compared with the 2017 pre-pandemic levels. Indeed, in both reading and mathematics, there was a constant improvement between spring 2021 and spring 2024. However, the social disadvantage gap remained wide. For both reading and maths, disadvantaged pupils in Year 4 were on average seven months behind their non-disadvantaged peers. Disadvantaged pupils in Year 5 were, on average, six and seven months behind their peers for reading and mathematics, respectively.

By 2024, the disadvantage gaps in both reading and mathematics had generally not widened but remained sizeable, still equivalent to about seven months progress. Both student and staff absences remained the main impediments to progress. Parents continued to provide significant support to their children, and nearly all schools made additional support available for very low-attaining pupils. There did not seem to be any difference in the social maturity of pupils compared to pre-pandemic levels, although again socially disadvantaged students had lower social skills than others (Weidman et al. 2023/2024).

Quotations from a survey carried out by the Children' Commissioner (September, 2020) give a flavour of the problems caused by the school lockdowns:

> There are massive arguments within the family as home schooling is tough & they are just wanting to play & watch all day. (Survey respondent).
>
> My eight-year-old, she'll do studying some days, and another day, she loses interest. I say to her, 'You need to constantly do maths and English, and then you can go to colouring in, and then reading, because it's keeping the brain active.'

Impact on secondary schools: Attendance, achievement

a) Attendance. Before the lockdown, in the Autumn of 2019, the average absence rate in secondary schools was 7 per cent. In the last three months of 2020, it was 17.5 per cent even though all children were meant to be in school. In the summer of 2021, after the second lockdown, it was 21 per cent (Gibbons et al. 2024). The persistent absence rate before the pandemic in secondary schools was 10.9 per cent. After the pandemic in 2024, it was 20.1 per cent, a massive increase. It was predicted that it would be another four years before absence rates declined to their pre-pandemic levels. In 2024, the absenteeism rate was highest in those areas where restrictions on attendance had been greatest during and around the lockdown periods.

b) Achievement. This can best be assessed by looking at examination results and this is problematic because 'A' level examinations that would have been taken in the summer were cancelled in 2020 and 2021. In 2020, grades were decided on the basis of teacher-assessed grades (TAGs), initially with some correction using an algorithm designed to correct teacher bias. However, as already stated, the use of this algorithm caused protest and was dropped. Teaching was once again disrupted in 2020/1, and the 2021 exams were again cancelled but this time results were based only on centre-assessed grades. These continued a trend of grade inflation, with 44.8 per cent of students getting an A* or A grades, compared with 38.5 per cent in 2020. This compared with 25.2 per cent in 2019 and 26.2 per cent in 2018. Yet, the trend of grade inflation did not play out evenly across the board, with private schools showing the biggest jumps in grades, and the largest jump in state schools being likewise weighted towards grammar and selective schools.

In 2022, grades were given based on a mixture of coursework and exams (LSE 2022). 'A' and GCSE examinations went ahead as normal in 2023 and 2024. However, there was concern that there would be learning loss due to COVID-19 lasting several more years (Major et al. 2024). The 'A' levels and GCSE results in 2024 were slightly higher than was the case pre pandemic but nothing can be deduced from this finding as the grades had been manipulated to arrive at this or a very similar result.

Again, quotations from surveys carried out by the Children's Commissioner (September, 2020) illustrate the problems at secondary school level.

> I think my 16-year-old is worried about what his results are going to be, so until he gets that, he's all over the place as well.
>
> (Ann-Marie)

Other parents reported that their children were struggling with online learning because they could not afford the technology or the technology they had was broken:

> 'And now my daughter, she can't even do her schoolwork on the laptop because the laptop's broken. So, I know she's going to get in trouble over that because she hasn't got the laptop now. There's nothing else I can do. I can't go and afford one or even afford to get it fixed.'
>
> (Clare)

> Due to coronavirus and school and college not open it's affecting them very badly as it's mostly online live learning but as we're on low income benefits, I can't afford an up to date laptop so their education is suffering.
>
> (Survey respondent)

One mother regretted:

> He's had six months of the best education and that's gone, he lost it ... he can't go back to do year 6 again, which is what he wants. He's got to go to year 7 ... he's not accessed any academic work for about three or four years ... There are fundamental packages of learning missing. That means I know for a fact later on in life there'll be big gaps in his abilities. It won't be because he's stupid and it won't be because he's autistic, it will simply be because he was let down.

Impact on children with special educational needs

As noted in Chapter 5, educational provision for children with special educational needs (SEND) had been declining for ten years before the COVID-19 epidemic began. It is not surprising therefore that both children with such needs and their parents were especially affected by the onset of the pandemic. A study of 402 children and adults with special needs (especially autism and Down syndrome) revealed that most of them (about 80 per cent) had to be kept at home during the lockdown period. Compared to their 'typically developing' siblings, they had a marked increase in anxiety (Sideropoulos et al. 2022). This is notable as children who did not have special needs also had increased levels of anxiety during the pandemic. Another study of 241 children with special educational needs (Asbury et al. 2021) reported that both parents and children appeared to be experiencing loss, worry and alterations in mood and behaviour as a result of the rapid social changes that had occurred. Some parents reported feeling overwhelmed. Waiting times for assessment, especially for possible autistic spectrum disorder, were particularly affected.

One mother reported:

> I have 2 children with ASD (autistic spectrum disorder) and one has OCD (obsessive compulsive disorder) – my eldest son. He's beside himself constantly washing. This child was off school the week before we were told to as he was sure he was going to die. Was using a hand sanitiser a day. Irrational thinking. Has become even more aggressive and curls up repeating I'm scared I'm just scared. He will not leave his room, he's worried the family has it and will give it to him.

Another reported:

> He only eats a limited amount of very specific things which means we have to shop almost daily, putting ourselves at risk more than we would if we didn't have to. Unlike other children, my boy will NOT eat if he's hungry enough. He will starve!

The lack of usual support from others as a result of COVID-19 restrictions was also found incredibly stressful. A mother related:

> Our entire support network has been taken away from us, including family. I am a single parent of twins, both who have complex learning difficulties and the thought of having to manage alone fills me with dread … his world has been turned upside down, no school, no church, no music lessons, no karate, no seeing friends and family, and he doesn't understand why.

A minority of parents of children with special educational needs reported, however, that COVID-19 had had little impact on mental health in their family or had even led to improvements.

Impact on physical health

The main impact of the pandemic on physical health was a reduction in physical activity. This was by no means the case for all children and young people; a number spent at least some of the time they were not in school during the lockdowns in parks and other green spaces. However, most stayed indoors and spent more time on their screens than would otherwise have been the case. The degree of rise in obesity levels that might be expected will not be known for several years.

There was a massive fall (88 per cent) in face-to-face contacts children had with primary care professionals (Foley et al. 2022). This was considerably made up for by online consultations. It should also be remembered that almost certainly the need for consultations fell as the lack of contact with others meant that children had fewer respiratory and other infections. Hospital care was also affected. Attendance at Accident and Emergency Departments increased significantly with longer waiting time. Waiting lists for hospital appointments for children and young people grew by 22 per cent in 2021. There is no information about the impact on chronic physical conditions in the young.

Impact on mental health problems

At the time of the onset of the pandemic in March 2020, probably at least partly because of the austerity policies of the Coalition and then the Conservative governments, the mental health of certain sections of the UK population of children and young people had been deteriorating for some years (see Chapter 4). In particular, there had been an increase in the prevalence of emotional disorders and eating control problems among older girls.

Newlove-Delgado and Cresswell (2025) suggest a variety of reasons for the increase in mental health problems during the pandemic. In their view, the negative impact was 'due in large part to the disruption on a population level of many protective factors, such as in-person connection, learning, play and socialising, and to a greater exposure to risk factors, such as unstable home environments, parental stress, isolation, and financial strain, as well as reduced opportunities to identify and address emerging problems early through support in home, school, community or service settings'. Perhaps the most significant stress was being physically cut off from friends. Most children of school age, when they look forward to going to school, which many do, are excited at the prospect of talking to their friends, sharing gossip they have picked up on social media, exchanging ideas about what they have seen on their screens, talking about their family members and, once they have reached their teens, about the beginnings of romantic relationships, their own and others. Of course, children and young people were able to exchange such chat on their mobile phones and by texting, but the lack of personal, physical contact was felt as a deprivation, giving rise to frequent feelings of loneliness. A number of children of all ages suffered from disrupted sleep often caused by anxieties about ways in which their family members might be affected by the epidemic. The high rate of severe illness and death among the elderly meant that many children had grandparents who were taken ill and sometimes died prematurely and unexpectedly. Because of visiting restrictions, it was not possible for their parents to visit grandparents who were admitted to hospital, giving rise to further stress. The overall rate of mental health problems in five- to sixteen-year-olds went up from 11 per cent in 2017 to 16 per cent in July 2020 during the first lockdown, though, as we shall see, studies on changes in the rates of mental health problems more generally produced inconsistent results.

In the early months of the epidemic, there was particular deterioration in the mental health symptoms among preadolescent children, with a 10 per cent increase in emotional symptoms, a 20 per cent increase in hyperactivity/inattention and a 35 per cent increase in conduct problems. In contrast, changes among adolescents were smaller (4 per cent and 8 per cent increase for hyperactivity/inattention and conduct problems, respectively) with a small reduction in emotional symptoms. Children and young people in low-income households and those with special educational needs and/or neurodevelopmental disorders were more affected than others (Waite et al. 2021). There was also considerable concern about the impact of the pandemic among pre-school children. Newlove-Delgado and Cresswell (2025) note that reasons for us to be particularly concerned about pre-school children include the fact that the majority of children experienced extended absence from early years settings and minimal opportunities for play and interaction with peers in typical settings (e.g. playgrounds, parent and toddler groups), while many parents attempted to work from home while caring for pre-schoolers who would have high support and care needs.

Deterioration in symptomatology was particularly marked with some symptoms. There was sufficient evidence to suggest a marked rise in eating difficulties and disorders during the pandemic period. The pandemic is likely to have disrupted established eating and exercise routines and coping behaviours, and at the same time, increased the use of restrictive behaviours to maintain a sense of control at a time of heightened anxiety and uncertainty (Newlove-Delgado and Cresswell 2025). In one study (Jack et al. 2023), the incidence of tics in children and young people increased across all age and sex groups during the COVID-19 pandemic, with a differentially large effect in teenage girls (a greater than fourfold increase).

There was a strong association between low income and mental health problems, not surprising as many parents, having been made unemployed because of the pandemic and with inadequate income subsidy were in debt with increasing numbers having to resort to food banks in order to have enough food to put on the table. The negative mental health impact was 'particularly prominent among adolescents in one-parent, one-child, and low-income households' (ibid.).

The impact of the pandemic on children and young people with pre-existing mental health conditions and developmental conditions was highly variable with outcomes determined by individual variabilities and social situations rather than by diagnosis. There were no consistent changes in either internalizing or externalizing disorders (Ching et al. in the press). However, some quotations from a survey carried out by the Children's Commissioner (September, 2020) make it clear that COVID-19 had had a serious effect on a significant number of vulnerable children and their parents. For example:

> My daughter started self-harming again and very depressed she's 16 and myself I've always had mental health issues and managed them ok up until covid-19 and I'm now suffering with depression ...
>
> Having to change benefits and wait five weeks for a payment has meant struggling to buy food, keep the children's mental health up. Keep our mental health up. It's been horrendous!
>
> My mental health has declined and I'm feeling like each day is a battle. My child's mental health has been affected too with the whole situation. It's definitely impacted our lives and I certainly hope there is light at the end of the tunnel.
>
> My child is very sad, she isn't herself anymore the Covid-19 has crushed her and she believes she has no friends which I have been trying my hardest to [reassure] her isn't true – everyone loves her we just can't go there it destroys me hearing this ...

There were marked effects on referrals to child mental health services. Initially, as a result of problems of access, referrals declined, and then, in April 2020, general practices in England saw a substantial decline in new diagnoses of anxiety and depression, antidepressant prescribing and self-harm presentations across all age groups, including young adults (Carr et al. 2021). Probably at least partly as a consequence, this was rapidly followed by a sharp rise in referrals and crisis presentations in other settings, with increasing pressure on all levels of the NHS, especially CAMHS. This extended into 2021 beyond the end of the second UK lockdown (Newlove-Delgado and Cresswell 2025, p.44).

Impact on free time

As would be assumed from the content of Chapter 6, the impact of COVID-19 with its lockdowns and restriction of the opportunities to mix with others was variable and depended heavily on the types of leisure activity and the range of activities enjoyed before the pandemic. The opportunities to engage in some activities, such as looking at screens and listening to music, both highly popular with teenagers and younger children, were enhanced. Non-academic children and young people who either hated going to school or found it boring were pleased to have more opportunities to do things they really enjoyed. Some children who missed out on activities during lockdown learned to appreciate them more when lockdown stopped. One thirteen-year-old girl remarked: '*There was a point where I would only really come [windsurfing] in the summer because of the cold. I have now got more into it even though it's still pretty cold, but I like coming here whereas during lockdown I couldn't, and I realised how much I missed it*'. On the other hand, lockdown meant that some young people missed out on never to be repeated opportunities. A sixteen-year-old girl's mother reported: '*She has missed out on her opportunity to go to the Youth Championships because that has been delayed. Her goal has always been to go and compete there and now she will never be able to do that because she will be too old. So she has just missed out*' (ibid.). But, for many children, the lockdown meant that life without friends was monotonous. One thirteen-year-old boy said: '*I couldn't see the friends I have here. I couldn't see any friends in general or even just like have fun*' (ibid.)

For children from low-income families who relied on state or local authority provision for their leisure activities, the lockdown was a time of particular deprivation (Howes et al. 2020). Nearly all UK spaces outside the home closed with opportunities for leisure involving physical proximity, essentially stopped. Such facilities had already been cut during the austerity years from 2010 to 2020 and then, those that had remained available, were shut down too. This gave rise to feelings of a lack of freedom and entrapment at home. Woodrow et al. (2021) reported that the effects of such restriction among the socially disadvantaged were beginning to result in increased criminalization, social exclusion and stigmatization which might well outlast the pandemic.

Children in young offender institutions, whose free time was, in any case, severely restricted, were subject to much greater limitations of time they could spend outside their cells. Charlie Taylor, HM Inspector of Prisons, in his evidence at the public hearing of Module 8 of the Covid Inquiry described how the pandemic led to children in prison being locked up in isolation, unnecessarily for very long periods, in one case up to forty-eight hours with no human contact (Covid Inquiry, 2 October 2025)

Impact on child protection: Maltreatment, abuse, neglect

As might be expected, the COVID-19 epidemic had a major effect both on the stress factors increasing the likelihood of maltreatment, abuse and neglect, and on the child protection services (Affolter et al. 2025). Economic hardship inevitably affected low-income families, including many families fostering children. The pandemic resulted in a decline in income as a result of many parents losing their often low-paid jobs, especially in the hospitality industries. Benefits were often slow to arrive and, when they did, failed to make up for lost income. The cost of food went up, often almost doubling. Further, during lockdown, those children getting free school meals did not get them, though some schools made efforts to keep them fed, both at breakfast and lunch. Nearly nine in ten families who responded to an online survey said they faced additional costs as a result of coronavirus, and were spending substantially more than before on food, electricity and other essentials (Children's Commissioner, September, 2020). Such financial stress was felt by mothers trying to keep putting food on the table and by fathers, often made to feel even more inadequate because of the experience of failure in their role as breadwinners. Emotionally, this led to irritability and anger which was sometimes taken out in aggression between parents and towards the children. The restrictions on visiting made life particularly difficult for separated parents who, up to the time of the pandemic, had visitation arrangements that worked well.

School closures with the accompanying demand for online learning also selectively affected the poor. There was often a lack of availability of computers, with perhaps only one computer to share between several members of the family. Poor quality of the internet connection meant some children were unable to access the lessons they were given, and some schools were not as good at making learning opportunities available as were others. Some parents, especially if in the low-income bracket, were less able to help their children with online learning. Many parents found it difficult to get their children to spend time on their schoolwork when their screens were an attractive, easily accessible alternative. The impact of school closures continued after they reopened. For example, one parent, Laura, seen in a survey carried out by the Children's Commissioner (August 2020), reported:

> 'When my son finally stayed out at my parents' house, he didn't want to stay there, because obviously he'd been with me for the whole time under lockdown. So I think it really affected him as well, and he didn't want to go back to nursery school, he doesn't like going to his nursery, because he wants to stay with me'
>
> (Laura)

Children and young people living in low-income families were far more likely to be overcrowded with little opportunity for privacy, especially with the children at home all the day during lockdown periods. The restrictions regarding social contacts meant that teenagers were unable to see their friends, were at home much more of the time and more liable to have frictional relationships with their parents and sibs.

As well as the increase in stresses, leading almost inevitably to more violence within the family, there was a reduction in the availability of child protection services (Carsley et al. 2024). Due to the restrictions on working outside the home, social workers were unable to make visits and contacts had to be online. There was a marked reduction in attendances for child maltreatment in Accident and Emergency Departments but, almost certainly this resulted from restrictions in travelling rather than any reduction in the rates of abuse and maltreatment.

Impact on low-income families

Even among those low-income families whose employment had not been disrupted – including those who were not working prior to the pandemic, the majority reported a worsening in their financial situation (Howes et al. 2020; Woodrow and Moore 2021). This had a major impact on their ability to provide for their children. For single parents, in particular, the drop in income if they lost their jobs due to the pandemic made a massive difference to their childcare. A report by the Children's Commissioner (August, 2020) carried this example:

> I am a single mother with depression and anxiety. I lost my job at the beginning of March and been unable to find a new job as my son's nursery closed to the pandemic. My health has deteriorated, and I have become very lonely and suicidal. I am in more debt and struggling to pay bills and feed my son and myself.
>
> (Single mother with one child, Yorkshire and the Humber)

Another mother reported:

> I lost my job in a cafe at the beginning of lockdown. I was not offered furlough as the business was closing. My benefits have also decreased [due to benefit cap]. After bills have been taken out, I am left with under

> £50 a week for food or other essential items for myself and 3 children. Struggling to see how I will be able to afford new school uniforms. Especially for my oldest who is moving into senior school.
>
> (Single mother with three children, East Midlands)

Nearly nine in ten families who responded to our online survey said they faced additional costs as a result of coronavirus, and were spending substantially more than before on food, electricity and other essentials. For non-working families, this was the main financial impact of coronavirus.

COVID-19 made the situation more difficult for other low-income families already living in highly unsatisfactory accommodation. For example:

> After finally saying we can move ... nothing is being done and everything is on hold ... my house is yet again infested with bugs due to broken windows which the council and the landlady refuse to know about ... We currently live in a two-bed flat but only have the full use of the living room – everywhere else is damaged and we can't even leave and go to our friends or families to get away from this due to Covid-19.
>
> (Survey respondent)

Other children's perspectives

The Children's Commissioner produced several reports about the impact of the epidemic on children. The quotations below are drawn from a report issued only a month after the first school lockdown (Children's Commissioner, April 2020). The following are quotations from children asked to explain how COVID-19 has affected their lives:

Michael, aged five, explains what lockdown means to him

> 'We have to stay at home because of the virus. It's home learning every day. I see my friends on Zoom, like daddy has his work meetings. I like being at home because I can play with my cat.'

Indie, aged fourteen, talks about his experiences of lockdown

> 'At first it was annoying, because all my friends are at school. But I have to stay at home, it's not a choice. I'm sharing a room with my younger brother.'

'My school uses Google classrooms, it's alright because they put videos to explain it. We can email teachers. Hopefully it doesn't affect GCSEs next year.'

'Sometimes it worries me. Seeing people in masks, it's a bit weird and people need to stop sitting in the park. There's loads of people with picnic blankets and that's not allowed.'

'I exercise on my bike and there was a bunch of police officers that passed me and one of them stopped and shouted at me for being selfish for being on my bike. It was embarrassing because there were other people watching.'

'I miss playing cricket and football, but I still talk to my friends but over the phone.'

Laura, aged eleven, wrote about her feelings on schools closing

'I would just like to express my feelings on schools closing. Due to school closing I'm missing out on a huge chunk of education that can prepare me for secondary school and later life.

That makes me feel unprepared and not ready for the journey ahead.

Moreover, I will be missing out on end of year events, some I've been waiting for since nursery.'

Despite doing the same subjects, I miss a sense of structure in my life. I miss socialising with my friends and laughing with them. Fortunately for me I am able to see them on FaceTime but not all children are lucky enough to be able to FaceTime their friends.

Although I do enjoy the time with my family, I miss my school life as well.

Nic, also aged eleven, wrote about what she's been up to, what she likes and doesn't like and how her views have changed

I first went into lockdown the Tuesday before schools closed. I felt happy because I didn't have to do school stuff, but I hate learning from home because it's boring and we have already done lots of it at school.

Some of the things I've been doing while I've been off school are watching the whole of Netflix and every tiktok that lives. I have learnt new skills like cooking, but I'm not keeping very active (right now I'm on spring break though).

I really wanted to do SATs because my whole time at primary school was leading up to that. I do miss things about school, like my friends, my teacher and my counsellor at school. The best things about the lockdown are I can eat as much as I want, I get to see my mum and dad and I can stay in bed longer.

The worst things about the lockdown are no friends, not having siblings so I'm lonely and having to hear my dog bark all day.

I'm getting on good with my parents I guess, but sometimes we argue. I'm staying in touch with my friends with texts, WhatsApp and FT (FaceTime). I am spending more time than normal on my phone and on screen-time.

I think schools should go back soon. If they do go back then I'll be most excited about the Year Six Leavers Party!

Conclusions

There are certain definite conclusions that can be reached about the impact on children and young people of the lockdown both on the general population and on schools. There was a massive impact on the quality of life of the young in all areas of their lives. These included: relationships within the family, physical contact with friends, opportunities to take physical exercise, situations leading to mental health problems, loss of education, cancelling of public examinations, changes in the way free time was used and increases in stresses leading to maltreatment. Very occasionally, COVID-19 led to an improvement in the quality of life, but, much more commonly, there was a deterioration. Further, in all the areas of life impacted by COVID-19, children and young people in low-income families were more seriously, often much more seriously affected.

Given the negative effects, there is a serious question as to whether schools should have been locked down at all. It should be remembered that the main purpose of locking down schools was not to protect children who, for reasons not fully understood, rarely contracted the condition and virtually never died from it. Instead, the purpose was to reduce the likelihood of the spread of infection. Thus, the quality of children's lives was quite significantly impaired to protect the adult population. A small number of other countries, particularly Sweden, used lockdown very sparingly even, as far as schools were concerned, not at all, and do not seem to have suffered higher rates of infection or mortality.

There is a small number of lessons for the future (Children's Commissioner, August 2020). First, the interests of children and young people should be taken into account when lockdowns are contemplated. There is evidence that children's interests were low down on the priority list of factors to be taken into consideration and even older teens were not (Bjorkman et al. 2023) consulted at all for their views. Teachers were consulted for their views on the best way to conduct online learning but not on the severity of lockdown measures. When lockdown is not in place, and individual children are found to be infected, rapid testing and isolation should be seen as preferable to sending whole classes home and facilities should be available in all schools to ensure as much rapid testing is possible.

10

Conclusions

Introduction

In this concluding chapter, three questions will be addressed. First, what were the main changes occurring in the lives of children over the sixty-five years from 1959 to 2024 that this book covers? Second, were the lives of children and young people better or worse at the end of the period than they were at the beginning? Third, how could the lives of children and young people at the end of the period have been made better than they were?

The main changes

The period from 1959 to 2024 saw very considerable changes in the lives of all British children. The following were the main but by no means the only changes.

Leisure pursuits and communication

This was the area in which perhaps the most marked changes took place. In the 1950s and 1960s, listening to the radio and playing gramophone records were the most popular entertainments but, by the mid-1960s, nearly all homes either owned or rented a television set. *Watch with Mother* for very young children and *Blue Peter* for the slightly older continued to be very widely viewed until they were partly replaced in 2002 by CBeebies for those aged under six, and CBBC for those aged six to twelve, though *Blue Peter* continued until after 2024. Viewing on own screens then gradually overtook watching television.

The development of the cordless phone in the early 1980s and the arrival of the internet in the mid-1980s greatly increased the ease of communication with friends. Boys especially then began to spend and continued to spend large amounts of time playing video games. By the early 2000s, digital streaming made possible much greater variety of both television and streamed channels such as YouTube and Netflix. The first social networking site, Facebook, was launched in 2004, and this was followed by large numbers of social media platforms, each with its own claim to uniqueness, including Twitter (later X), WhatsApp, Snapchat and TikTok. These technical advances made massive differences to the way children and young people communicated and spent their free time. They also exposed children to new harms from their peers and from strangers.

Listening to and, to a lesser extent, playing music were favourite leisure occupations throughout, but each generation developed its own brand of youth music, beginning, in our period, with rock in the 1950s and the massively popular Beatles and Rolling Stones in the 1960s and thereafter, Means of access to music changed too, beginning with the radio and gramophone and continuing with the development of cassettes in the 1960s and the Sony Walkman in the late 1970s. A big advance came at the turn of the century with streaming media and then dedicated music sites such as Spotify. Social networking sites like Facebook and MySpace created the possibility of shared lists of popular music.

In the 1960s and 1970s, the Saturday morning cinema shows run by all the major chains for children were the great cultural experience of the week for many children. The British Board of Film Classification rated films as X, if they were thought unsuitable for children under the age of 16, later raised to 18. Although the average amount of time spent reading for pleasure was very small (only 5–10 minutes a day for eight- to eleven-year-olds and about the same for twelve- to sixteen-year-olds), some children read a great deal more than this.

In the 1960s and 1970s, many children in their teens attended youth clubs of various types, including Boy Scouts, Girl Guides and youth clubs run by local authorities. Many youth clubs were closed during the austerity years following the financial crash in 2008 and never reopened. There was also a great change over the years in the way holidays were spent. In the 1960s and 1970s, holidays away from home, if they occurred at all, usually involved a week or a fortnight in a hotel or boarding house in a British seaside resort or in a holiday camp. Holidays abroad, usually in Spain, France or Greece became more common in the 1980s and much more common with the advent of cheap air travel in the 1990s. Wealthier families now bought second homes in the UK but also abroad, especially in Spain. Of course, many children from poor families never went on holiday at all.

Child poverty

This was an area of variable change. In the 1960s, the relative child poverty rate in the UK was in the region of 15 per cent or slightly over two million children. It went up in the 1980s after the election of the Thatcher government. The 1980s and 1990s were very difficult times financially for many of those living in areas in the Midlands, north of England and Scotland where de-industrialization resulted in very high rates of unemployment. In the late 1990s, however, there was a significant reduction in the prevalence of low-income families as a result of the targeted policies of the prime minister, Tony Blair and the chancellor of the exchequer, Gordon Brown. Then in the 2010s after the 2008 financial crash and the election of the Coalition government, there was a further rise in the numbers of children living in relative poverty throughout the country with a marked rise in the cost of living, accompanied by cuts in benefits. The COVID-19 epidemic and the war in Ukraine worsened the national financial situation with further rises in the rates of poverty in the 2020s. Indeed, in 2022/3, it was estimated that 4.3 million children, or 30 per cent of all children in the UK, were living in relative poverty. The use of food banks rose sharply during this twenty-first century, strongly indicating a rise in absolute poverty.

Family structure

During the 1950s and 1960s, only one in ten children in their mid-childhood was not living with their two biological parents. By the end of the period, over two in five children of this age did not live with their biological parents. In 1970, only 8 per cent of families were headed by a single parent, whereas by 2024, it was 24 per cent. The size of families diminished considerably. At the beginning of our period, only about one in ten children was an only child, whereas this was the case for four in ten in the 2020s.

Parental divorce and separation

This was unusual at the beginning of our period but by the end, over two in five parents had separated or divorced, and of those who were still together, many more were cohabiting rather than married, a more unstable form of relationship, more likely to break up. Linked to the changes in family structure but also made possible by the development of labour-saving devices, there was a considerable rise in the employment of mothers, meaning many more children came home to empty houses after school and family meals became more irregular.

Physical health

There were very significant improvements in the outcome of nearly all types of physical illness. Effective treatments became available for virtually all forms of disease, in some cases achieving a good outcome for conditions which previously had been almost always fatal. Unfortunately, this improvement in the outcome of most diseases was accompanied by an increase in obesity with many more cases of diabetes in older children and adolescents.

Mental health

There were major improvements in our capacity to measure the prevalence of mental ill-health. Although the public perception of rates of mental disorder was that there was a very considerable rise, in fact, apart from mid- and late teenage girls who more frequently suffered from depression and eating control problems, rates of mental ill health remained relatively steady. An apparently enormous rise in the rate of autism was probably largely or entirely due to a change in the definition of this condition.

There were, however, significant changes in the way mental ill health was perceived. In the 1960s and 1970s, parents were very reluctant to see quite serious depression and anxiety as a mental health problem because of both lack of knowledge and fears of stigmatization, but by the 2000s they were much less negative about having their children referred for psychiatric help. Consequently, there was a sharp rise in the numbers on waiting lists for psychiatric care and a great deal of dissatisfaction with the long periods between referral and first assessment.

Mixed and same-sex gender relationships

Attitudes towards mixed gender sexual relationships in unmarried couples in their late and sometimes even mid-teens became much more relaxed from 1960 to 1990, during which time the average age of first intercourse went down three years from twenty for young men and nineteen for young women. Teenage pregnancies increased over this period but then declined again in the twenty-first century with improved contraceptive advice and the availability of the morning-after pill. Attitudes towards same-sex relationships moved from almost universal condemnation and stigmatization at the beginning of our period to a much more tolerant attitude by the 1980s and 1990s, helped by the decriminalization of homosexuality for those under twenty-one in 1967.

Anti-social use of free time

The number of crimes committed by teenagers rose after the Second World War until the 1980s when it fell sharply, but by the 1990s it had plateaued and remained fairly steady subsequently. The reasons for both the rise and the decline were unclear. Changing rates of family disharmony, child poverty and the increasing absorption in video games might all have been relevant. Self-reported offences were always much more common than convictions with some studies reporting that the great majority of young people had committed undetected crimes.

Before 2007, with the advent of Pornhub, most children in their later teens certainly did watch pornographic images but generally only occasionally and for short periods of time. By 2020, the average age of first exposure to porn was thirteen and 10 per cent of ten-year-olds had seen it. A fifth of teenage boys and one in fifteen teenage girls watched porn at least once a day. A significant amount of pornographic content viewed by young people contained violent images and consequently, it is not surprising that a number of teenage girls came to believe that aggressive behaviour was part of normal sexual activity. The average amount of time spent watching porn is not known, but at least a small number of young people become addicted and, against their will, could not stop watching it for hours at a time.

Other uses of the internet

From the 1990s, the internet, especially through search engines such as Google, made access to information by children and young people immensely easier. Print encyclopaedias and dictionaries became largely redundant. Similarly, shopping was transformed. Window-shopping was replaced by internet browsing and purchases of clothes and tickets for entertainment were mainly carried out online.

The COVID-19 epidemic

There was a massive change in the lives of children and young people as a result of the COVID-19 epidemic. This began in March 2020, largely as a result of the school lockdowns, but its effects continued until the end of our period in 2024 (see Chapter 9).

Were the lives of children and young people better or worse in 2024 than they had been in 1959?

Not surprisingly, there is no simple answer to this question. In some respects, the quality of life of children and young people was unquestionably better in 2024 than it had been in 1959. In others, it was probably but not certainly worse. Mostly, while life had clearly changed, often considerably, it was difficult to say whether there had been an improvement or deterioration. I shall discuss changes in the quality of life under a number of different headings relating to the most significant changes that took place.

Child poverty

It is never a good time to be poor, but if one compares the quality of life of children living in low-income families in 1959 compared to that in 2024, it seems clear that children in the 2020s fared worse. Those living in the earlier period were benefitting from the period of food rationing which had only ended a few years earlier. This had ensured that all the child population, including the poor, had a well-balanced, adequate diet. In the 2020s, a significant number of poor children, especially those living in families with three or more children, were suffering from inadequate diets, their parents having to attend food banks which had only existed from the beginning of the twenty-first century. Poor children were distinctly less likely to benefit from the changes in leisure and communication described above.

As described above, during the sixty-five years from 1959 to 2024, the number of children living in poverty fluctuated considerably, often upwards. At the same time, there was a considerable improvement in the understanding of poverty as a result of a new distinction between absolute poverty, the lack of the basic essentials for a life of reasonable quality and relative poverty, or income below a certain percentage (usually 60 per cent) of the median income in a given country or region. A further improvement occurred as a result of the studies carried out by the social scientists Brian Abel-Smith and Peter Townsend (1965) which established the level of child poverty in the population. Their work led to the creation of the Child Poverty Action Group and the recognition of child poverty as a major societal problem. The 1997 Labour government pledged to reduce the level of child poverty and did indeed make significant progress in this direction. Although, as described above, there was a distinct worsening to the rate after 2010, the problem retained a high profile which it retained until the end of our period. Indeed, fourteen years after he stopped being prime minister, Gordon Brown (2024) was still advocating for measures to reduce child poverty. There can be no doubt, however, that during the period 1959 to 2024, there was a worsening in the situation regarding children living in low-income families, both in the numbers affected and in the quality of lives they led in relation to the rest of the child population.

Family relationships

It is widely assumed that because many more parental relationships broke down in the twenty-first century than was the case in the 1950s and 1960s, this inevitably meant that the quality of children's lives worsened over this period. This is not an unreasonable assumption. When children see their parents, most likely the two people they love most in the world, argue violently and make each other unhappy, they themselves are often made deeply distressed. But parental separation by no means always occurs following a period of violent disharmony; situations are often a great deal more complicated than this and the consequences for children when they no longer live with their two biological parents are correspondingly varied.

Many studies over this period showed with some certainty that the major trauma for children and young people as far as their family relationships were concerned lay in a poor quality of parental marriage or cohabitation. A frequently asked question was whether, if parents found each other at worst detestable and, at best unlikeable, it was better for their children if they split up or stayed together. Unfortunately, there was no clear answer. However, it would be surprising if the instability of parental marriages and, even more, of parental cohabitation, did not cause much anxiety and heartache in their children. Although among parents who split up, remarriage was the rule rather than the exception, step-parent relationships were often problematic, even occasionally abusive.

Another, potentially traumatic aspect of parental break-up was father absence. In many cases of separation, although fathers often remained in contact for the first year or so, very commonly they then dropped out of the picture completely. The presence of only one parent is inevitably anxiety-provoking, as it always raises the possibility of absent parental care if that one parent develops an illness or dies.

However, fortunately, many parents, certainly over half, did stay together during their children's childhood and among those who didn't many parted amicably causing no or very little distress to their children. Further, at time went on, separating parents much more commonly, in deciding what to do, took their children into account and, indeed, more often, especially as far as older children were concerned, considered their views seriously.

The impact of the internet

The arrival of the internet in the mid-1990s radically changed the lives of children and young people. It transformed the use of mobile phones and personal computers, introducing laptops and eventually iPads. Communication with others, including especially friends and new contacts, was greatly facilitated. It made possible access to enormous amounts of information both for the purposes of education and for general interest. It introduced different forms of entertainment, including streamed films and videos, as well as a great variety of online games that could be played alone or with others. As described above, there were great changes in the use of free time. All these uses of the internet can be seen as enhancing the richness of the quality of the lives of children and young people.

Unfortunately, alongside these undoubted advantages, the internet brought very significant risk of harm. Children and young people were exposed for the first time to much harmful screen content. Some sites portrayed self-harm as a desirable and exciting way of dealing with loneliness and unhappiness. Porn, sometimes with violent sexual imagery, became easy to access. Children had always suffered from bullying by their peers, but a new form of harassment, cyberbullying, appeared, with girls, but not only girls, targeting girls with offensive material, accusing them, for example, of being slags or ugly.

Many children and young people spent hours on their phones, some becoming addicted, unable to detach themselves from their screens, thus having little or no time to interact with other children. Such sedentary behaviour, often associated with over-eating, led to high rates of obesity with its link to many poor health outcomes, including diabetes.

Girls particularly were exposed to images of unhealthily thin models and encouraged to think they were unattractive and would never have partners unless they lost weight and developed pole-shaped bodies. Dissatisfaction with bodily appearance made unhappy girls even unhappier. The images of thin models at least sometimes led them to dieting behaviour which developed into eating control disorders with a seriously adverse impact on health.

While the grooming of vulnerable children did not always start with online contact (perpetrators could meet vulnerable girls face to face outside school in the street or in parks), this was a frequently used means of getting to know victims. These might then be seduced into unwanted sexually intimate behaviour or recruited into working in 'county lines' as couriers for illegal drugs.

The switch from high street shopping to shopping online exposed children and young people to a variety of scams to separate them from their money. The young were particularly vulnerable to deceptively attractive-looking offers of deals, with very high rates of interest charged on sales for which the young person could not pay outright.

It should be noted that anxiety about these various harms led to major public concern. The 2023 Online Safety Act was a parliamentary response of uncertain effectiveness. At the same time, some schools banned their students from bringing their phones into school or, more commonly banned their use in school time. Parents were discouraged from allowing younger children, perhaps under fourteen years of age, from owning smartphones.

On balance, for most children, the positive effects of the internet greatly outweighed the harms it brought, but, for a significant minority, it had a seriously negative effect on the quality of their lives.

School experience

As far as primary school-aged children (5–11 years) were concerned, in the 1960s and 1979s, there was probably at least a small improvement from earlier times in the amount of freedom and relaxed classroom discipline. As far as academic achievement is concerned, there may have been some decline in certain aspects of number work (e.g. knowledge of times tables) with perhaps an improved level of understanding of mathematical concepts. In general, however, there was probably little change either in the level of enjoyment of primary school students or in their academic achievement.

Secondary schooling was a different matter. In the 1960s, the quality of the experience of students in secondary modern schools was often poor with many experiencing a sense of ingrained failure. The introduction of comprehensive schooling at least partly resolved this problem. The major change brought in by the introduction of the National Curriculum in 1988, followed by the highly prescriptive effects of the policies of Michael Gove in the 2010s led to what became widely regarded as a content-overloaded syllabus. By the 2020s, the lives of secondary school students were blighted by a plethora of public examinations. The almost exclusive emphasis on academic achievement meant that creative subjects, which, for many students were the most enjoyable and fulfilling elements, were squeezed out of the curriculum. There was a definite decline over the period in question, for example, in opportunities for music education and performance. The negative perceptions of many secondary school students of either relevance to their subsequent lives or of enjoyment and pleasure in their school experience suggest the quality of this phase of their school experience was poor, though whether it was better or worse in 2024 than it had been in 1959 is questionable.

Mixed and same-sex gender relationships

In that public and therefore parental attitudes to pre-marital sexual relationships as well as masturbation were much more relaxed in the 2020s than they were in the 1960s it is likely that teenage sexual frustration in male, and, to a lesser extent female adolescents was less prevalent at the end of our period than it had been at the beginning. However, the fact that sometimes emotionally immature girls became involved in intense, intimate relationships earlier on meant that when, as inevitably often happened, these relationships broke up, the girls involved more often suffered from feelings of loneliness and rejection. This probably partly accounts for the fact that emotional distress and disorders in older girls were more prevalent at the end of our period than they had been at the beginning (see below).

Mental health

Although precise comparisons are not possible, the chances of a child or young person having a mental health problem were probably greater in 2024 than they had been in 1959, and this is especially the case for older girls. Certainly, the new stresses faced by the young in 2024, especially those introduced by the internet (see above), were numerous and experienced by virtually all the population. Waiting lists for assessment and treatment were much longer at the end of the period, although the quality of care once this was received was distinctly more evidence based.

A more problematic issue relating to mental health is whether the increase in the medicalization of distressing emotional experience brought an enhancement or deterioration in the quality of life. For those children and young people with severe impairment arising from, for example, prolonged depressive or psychotic disorders, a formulation in psychiatric terms probably made it more likely that appropriate help would be available. For those with the much more common milder problems, the medicalization of what could be seen as 'normal' emotional reactions may well have reduced the likelihood of support and understanding from family and friends. These might have thought it inappropriate to intervene when 'expert' help was indicated.

Children with special needs

For children and young people with disabilities, especially those with moderate or severe learning difficulties (or mental retardation as it was known in the 1950s and 1960s), there was a definite improvement in the quality of life as time went on. New legislation meant that, instead of being denied education and spending the day in local authority-run training centres, children and young people with severe learning difficulties attended special schools with specialist teachers. Further, as a result of other legislation, children with special needs, whatever their nature, had their right to appropriate education safeguarded by the 1981 Education Act. This meant that the local authority had a duty to provide a type and level of special education laid down in a 'statement', later termed an 'education, care and health plan', prepared by a multi-disciplinary team of professionals. Further, children with mild learning difficulties were no longer placed in schools for the 'educationally subnormal' (a name inviting stigmatization) but integrated into mainstream schools.

Unfortunately, the situation of children with special needs was far from satisfactory as time went on. The demand for special education had greatly increased. Funding pressures together with lack of skilled staff meant that access to professional assessment was subject to prolonged delay. The availability of appropriate school places was no longer sufficient to meet the needs. However, on the positive side, public attitudes to disability changed considerably over the sixty-five years so that children and young people with disabilities were much less frequently excluded from public spaces, with disability legislation making it impossible for them to be denied access. On balance therefore the situation for children and young people with disability was distinctly more favourable than it had been in earlier years.

Opportunities for creativity and sport

The opportunities for non-academic activities were particularly important for those many children and young people who were not going to be academic high achievers. In the early part of our period, music was beginning to take its place as an important part of the curriculum, and many schools had their own orchestras. Individual tuition in the playing of a musical experiment was often available. Most schools had sports fields, either on site or nearby. At the end of the period, in 2024, much musical education had been cut. There were fewer music teachers and, if parents wanted their children to learn an instrument, this would most commonly have to be arranged privately, thus excluding children from low-income families. Under the Conservative government of the 1980s, many school sports fields had been sold off, so the opportunities for playing sport during school hours were reduced, though many children belonged to privately run sports clubs where they played at weekends.

Physical health

As the rates of mortality and morbidity demonstrated very clearly, the outcome for children who developed physical illnesses was far better in 2024 than it had been in 1959. Antibiotic treatment continued to transform the prognosis of infectious disease, with the pharmaceutical companies largely keeping ahead of increasingly antibiotic-resistant bacteria. Although some cancers remained lethal, many were now much more treatable, even curable.

However, there was one physical problem that had considerably increased in prevalence, namely obesity. As a group, being overweight meant that the children of 2024 were far less fit than those of 1959. This meant higher rates of diabetes and a propensity to a range of physical disorders for which obesity was a risk factor, including especially high blood pressure, heart problems and arthritis.

Child protection

While child protection was a cause for concern throughout the sixty-five years, there is no clear indication whether the situation was more or less problematic at the end of this period than it was at the beginning. The quality of assessments by social workers was probably better in 2024 than it had been in 1959, with greater appreciation of the variety of factors, especially abuse that might be affecting children's lives. However, the quality of the placements available to those working in Children's Departments remained highly variable and was certainly not clearly better than it had been. Further, the arrival of the internet in the early 2000s meant that subsequently children and young people were exposed to new types of danger which had not even been envisaged in previous times.

How could the lives of children in 2024 have been made better than they were?

Throughout our period, the responsibility for the welfare of their children was placed firmly with parents. This has been particularly the case for politicians in government who, whenever criticized for failing to take action over some contentious issue, always point the finger at parents who, they say, having brought children into the world, should make sure they are healthy, safe and well-looked after. Any suggestion of intervention by government was dismissed as meddling by a 'nanny state'. In contrast, social scientists contended that society makes it far more difficult than it needs for parents to fulfil their parenting responsibilities successfully. The rest of this section takes this perspective. How could society have made it easier for parents to ensure better lives for their children?

1 *By reducing the number of children living in poverty.*

   We have seen how, in all areas of their lives, children living in low-income families had a poorer quality of life than children in the rest of the population. Disagreements between parents are inevitable. Indeed, observing parents sort out their disagreements amicably helps children learn how to resolve their own problems with others. But chronic poverty puts parents in situations that are irresolvable. Throughout our period, far too many families have been in this situation. As international comparisons clearly show, high levels of poverty are by no means inevitable. The way the minimum wage and the tax and benefits system are managed during times when it is going through financial difficulty makes it possible for a country to ensure poverty levels are low or virtually non-existent (Platt 2024).

2 *By providing incentives for parental couples to be married.*

   Marriage, in itself, is by no means necessarily a desirable state for a couple. However, there are good reasons why governments should regard it as preferable for couples who are parents to be married rather than cohabiting or separated. The tax situation in 2024 meant that parental couples were better off financially if they were unmarried. Married parents are more likely to stay together than unmarried and parental separation is a major source of distress for children and young people.

3 *By ensuring that advances in technology improve the quality of the lives of the young.*

Billions of pounds/dollars of profit are made every year by tech companies selling advertisements linked to social media. With better regulation of the content and distribution of social media, very satisfactory profits could be made while the well-being of the population, especially the child population could be safeguarded (UNICEF 2014). While there may well be situations in which there is a conflict between freedom of expression and safeguarding the young, safety of children and young people must be seen as the priority when such conflict arises. Legislation with such severe sanctions for rule-breaking as to make rule-breaking unprofitable is required.

4 *By reorganizing the school system, especially the secondary school system, so that the school experience combines high academic achievement with enjoyment.*

At the moment, while most teachers are brilliant at their job, they are prevented from providing what students need by the curriculum they are forced to teach. This does not prepare students adequately for their subsequent lives. Further, for far too many students, the school experience is unnecessarily stressful and unenjoyable (Hyman 2020). The stress, which is experienced by teachers as well as students, relates particularly to an overloaded curriculum and the unnecessary GCSE examination. Every year, 30 per cent of students are labelled as failures. Further, the curriculum fails to take into account the need to give status to the acquisition of practical skills. A better balance needs to be found between head, heart and hand. Well-being and creativity should be seen as important goals. Inadequate advantage has been taken of new technology, including AI. Too often school leadership has been inappropriate with too much micro-management.

5 *By making a healthy diet affordable to families on the lowest incomes.*

In the early 2020s, about a quarter of UK children were either obese or severely obese. Obese children are at high risk of developing diabetes and, in the medium term, hypertension, heart disease, arthritis and a variety of other ailments. The causes of obesity have been identified with a great deal of certainty. The measures introduced by successive governments to counter the problem have been totally inadequate (National Food Strategy 2021). There is a need to introduce a sugar and salt tax, with some of the revenue raised used to get fresh fruit and vegetables to low-income families. The enormous inequalities in the healthiness of diets between those with low and high incomes should be tackled by funding holiday activities and food programmes. Healthy school lunches should be mandatory.

6 *By reversing the medicalization of mild and moderate unhappiness, sadness, anxiety and misery so that these negative emotions are seen and treated both by professionals and the general public as responses to loss and stress, requiring understanding and support rather than diagnosis and treatment.*

While it is imperative that children and young people with severe mental disorders are seen rapidly for assessment and then given appropriate treatment, the long waiting lists of children waiting to be seen by mental health services should be triaged to exclude those who have recently developed mild or moderately impairing problems as most of these will recover over a relatively short period of time. Such children should be regarded as being a cause for concern and in need of emotional support while they are suffering from family, friends and first-line professionals such as primary care nurses, doctors and primary care counsellors (Dowrick and Allen 2013).

7 *By making better preparations for a pandemic.*

As Chapter 9 reveals, the preparations for the 2020 COVID-19 pandemic were woefully inadequate. The effects of this lack of preparation were still apparent in 2024 with, for example, higher rates of mental health problems and a significant achievement gap between students from disadvantaged and better-off families.

If a pandemic were to occur in the future, and experts say it is inevitable that it will, then it would be inexcusable if better preparations were not made. In particular, there should be widespread consultation with parents, teachers and children's organizations before any decision on school lockdowns is made. Further, all students, including especially disadvantaged students, should have access to computers at home for online learning with stable Wi-Fi connections.

REFERENCES

Abbott, J., Hurley, M., Chadwick, H., et al. (2023) Ways of coping and survival in Cystic Fibrosis: A 20-year longitudinal study. *Journal of Cystic Fibrosis*, 22(1), 112–18.

Abel-Smith, B., and Townsend, P. (1965) *The Poor and the Poorest*. London: Polity Press.

Affolter, K. F., Tausendfreund, T., and Eicher, N. (2025) Child protection during COVID-19: A systematic meta-synthesis of empirical studies exploring perspectives of young people and caregivers. *Child Abuse & Neglect*, 167, 106645.

Alvarez-Díaz, F., Brito, J. M., Cordovilla, G., et al. (1973) Ascending aorta-right pulmonary artery anastomosis: Waterston's operation. *Thorax*, 28(2), 152–7.

Anderson, P. M., and Butcher, K. (2006) Childhood obesity: Trends and potential causes. *The Future of Children*, 16, 19–45.

Ariès, P. (1960) *Centuries of Childhood*. London: Penguin Press.

Armitage, J., et al. (2025) Characteristics of children with a psychiatric disorder in 1999, 2004 and 2017: Analysis of the national child mental health surveys of England. *Journal of Child Psychology and Psychiatry*, 66(2), 167–77.

Armitage, J., Kwong, A., Tseliou, F., et al. (2023) Cross-cohort change in parent-reported emotional problem trajectories across childhood and adolescence in the UK. *Lancet Psychiatry*, 10, 509–17.

Arnett, J. J., and Mitra, D. (2020) Are the features of emerging adulthood developmentally distinctive? A comparison of ages 18–60 in the United States. *Emerging Adulthood*, 8(5), 412–19.

Asbury, K., Fox, L., Deniz, E., et al. (2021) How is COVID-19 affecting the mental health of children with special educational needs and disabilities and their families? *Journal of Autism and Developmental Disorders*, 51, 1772–80.

Auty, J., Farrington, D., and Coid, J. (2015) The validity of self-reported convictions in a community sample. *European Journal of Criminology*, 12(5), 562–80.

Bailey, C. (2022) The origins of Type 2 diabetes medications. *British Journal of Diabetes*, 22, No.2.

Bailey, P. (2025) What is school for? The struggle for control of the curriculum is a fight for the soul of English education. *New Statesman*, 4–10 April 2025.

Bakopoulou, J. (2022) The impact of the COVID-19 pandemic on early years transition to school in the UK context Education 3-13. *International Journal of Primary, Elementary and Early Years Education*.

Barnardo's (2024) *A Quarter of Parents in Britain Struggle to Provide Enough Food for their Children*. London: Barnardo's.

Baron-Cohen, S., Scott, F. J., Allison, C., et al. (2009) Prevalence of autism-spectrum conditions: UK school-based population study. *British Journal of Psychiatry,* 194(6), 500–9.

Baron-Cohen, S., Wheelwright, S., Stott, C., et al. (1997) Is there a link between engineering and autism? *Autism*, 1(1), 101–9.

Bartels, A., and Zeki, S. (2004) The neural correlates of maternal and romantic love. *NeuroImage*, 21, 1155–66.

Bartram, J., Veys, P., and Vora, A. (2020) Improvements in outcome of childhood acute lymphoblastic leukaemia (ALL) in the UK – A success story of modern medicine through successive UKALL trials and international collaboration. *British Journal Haematology*, 191(4), 562–7.

Bateman, T. (2014) Where has all the youth crime gone? Youth justice in an age of austerity. *Children and Society*, 28, 416–24.

Bateman, T., and Hazel, N. (2014) *Beyond Youth Custody: Youth Justice Timeline*. Luton: University of Bedfordshire.

Baumrind, D. (1966) Effects of authoritative parental control on child behavior. *Child Development*, 37(4), 887–907.

Beecher, R. (2023) Rape revisited: Joanna Bourke reflects on historicizing sexual violence, in conversation with Ruth Beecher. *Women's History Review*, *32*(7), 1059–71.

Bell and another -v- The Tavistock and Portman NHS Foundation Trust and others". *www.judiciary.uk*. 17 September 2021.

Benson, H. (2023) *Sources of Family Breakdown in the UK*. London: The Marriage Foundation.

Benson, H. (2025) *The Marriage Gap*. London: The Marriage Foundation.

Bentovim, A. (2021) Changing generations, 1: Children, adolescents and young people. In Ikkos, G., and Bouras, N. (Eds), *Mind, State and Society: Psychiatry and Mental Health in Britain 1960–2010*. Cambridge: Cambridge University Press.

Beveridge, W. (1942) *Cmnd 6404. Social Insurance and Allied Services: Report by Sir William Beveridge*. London: HMSO.

Björkman, A., Gisslén, M., Gullberg, M., et al. (2023) The Swedish COVID-19 approach: A scientific dialogue on mitigation policies. *Front Public Health*, 11, 1206732.

Blakemore, S.-J. (2018) *Inventing Ourselves*. London: Penguin.

Blishen, E. (1969) *The School That I'd Like*. London: Penguin.

Bluebond-Langner, M. (2024) *Personal Communication*.

Bowlby, J. (1958) The nature of the child's tie to his mother. *International Journal of Psychoanalysis*, 39, 350–73.

Bowlby, J. (1969) *Attachment*. London: Penguin.

Bowlby, J. (2007) John Bowlby and ethology: An annotated interview with Robert Hinde. *Attachment Human Development*, 9(4), 321–35.

Brendon, V. (2009) *Prep School Children: A Class Apart over Two Centuries*. London: Continuum.

Brierley, P. W. (1993) *Reaching and Keeping Teenagers*. Tunbridge Wells: MARC.

Broadbent, P., Shen, Y., Pearce, A., Katikireddi, S. V. (2024) Trends in inequalities in childhood overweight and obesity prevalence: A repeat cross-sectional analysis of the Health Survey for England. *Archives of Disease in Childhood*, 109(3), 233–9.

Brown, G. and Harris, T. (1984) *Social Origins of Depression*. London: Tavistock Press.
Brown, G. (2024) Millions of British children born since 2010 have only known poverty. My £3bn plan would give them hope. *The Guardian*, 14 May 2024.
Bukowski, W. M., Motzoi, C., et al. (2009) Friendship as process, function, and outcome. In Rubin, K. H., Bukowski, W. M., and Laursen, B. (Eds), *Handbook of Peer Interactions, Relationships, and Groups* (pp. 217–31). New York: The Guilford Press.
Burke, C. and Grosvenor, I. (2015) *The School I'd Like: Revisited*. London: Routledge.
Burley, S. (2024) The impact of Govian reform has been unremittingly bad. *School Management Plus*, 15 February 2024.
Callaway, E., and Nadaf, M. (2023) Pioneers of mRNA Covid vaccines win medicine Nobel. *Nature*, 622, 228–9.
Campbell, B. (2023) *Secrets and Silence: Uncovering the Legacy of the Cleveland Child Sexual Abuse Case*. Bristol: Bristol University Press.
Carr, M. J., et al. (2021) Effects of the COVID-19 pandemic on primary care-recorded mental illness and self-harm episodes in the UK: A population-based cohort study. *The Lancet Public Health*, 6(2), e124–e135.
Carsley, S., Thomas, S., Oei, et al. (2024) Child abuse and neglect during the COVID-19 pandemic: An umbrella review. *Child Abuse & Neglect*, 149, 106645.
Cassen, R., and Kingdon, G. (2007) *Tackling Low Educational Achievement*. London: Joseph Rowntree Association.
Central Advisory Council for Education (1967) *Children and Their Primary Schools*. London: Her Majesty's Stationery Office.
Centre for Longitudinal Studies (2018) *The Millennium Cohort Studies*. London: UCL.
Chandler, D. (2023) *Free and Equal: What Would a Fair Society Look Like?* London: Penguin Books.
Charlton, A. (2001) Changing patterns of cigarette smoking among teenagers and young adults. *Paediatric Respiratory Reviews*, 2(3), 214–21.
Child Practice Review Panel (2024) *Child Sexual Abuse Within the Family Environment*. Child Safeguarding Child Practice Review Panel.
Child Safeguarding Practice Review Panel (2022–2023) *Annual Report*. London: Department of Education.
Children's Commissioner (2020a) *Childhood in the Time of Covid*, April, 2020.
Children's Commissioner (2020b) *Childhood in the Time of Covid*, September, 2020.
Children's Commissioner (2020c) *Putting Children First in Future Lockdowns*, August, 2020.
Children's Commissioner (2023) *Evidence on Pornography's Influence on Harmful Behaviour Among Children*. London: Department of Health.
Children's Commissioner for England (2021) *Child Poverty: The Crisis We Can't Keep Ignoring*. London: Children's Commissioner.
Children's Commissioner for England (2023a) *Family*. London: Children's Commissioner.
Children's Commissioner for England (2023b) *We All Have a Voice: Disabled Children's Vision for Change*. London: Children's Commissioner.

Children's Society (2024) *The Good Childhood Report 2024*. London.

Ching, B., Downs, J., Zhang, S., et al. (In the Press) The impact of the COVID-19 pandemic on the mental health of children and young people with pre-existing mental health and neurodevelopmental conditions: A systematic review and meta-analysis of longitudinal studies. *Journal of Child Psychology and Psychiatry*.

CIBA Foundation (1984) *Child Sexual Abuse Within the Family*. Cambridge: Tavistock Publications.

Clark, C. (2011) *Setting the Baseline: The National Literacy Trust's First Annual Survey into Young People's Reading*. London: National Literacy Trust.

Clark, C., Picton, and Cole, I., et al. (2024) *Children and Young People's Reading in 2024*. London: National Literacy Trust.

Clark, S. D. (2024) Spatial disparities in access to NHS dentistry: A neighbourhood-level analysis in England. *European Journal of Public Health*, 34(5), 854–9.

Clarke, E. (2002) *My Mother Who Fathered Me*. Kingston: University of the West Indies Press.

Cohen-Kettenis, P., Schagen, S., Steensma, T., de Vries, A., and Delemarre-van de Waal, H. (2011) Puberty suppression in a gender-dysphoric adolescent: A 22-year follow-up. *Archives of Sexual Behavior,* 40, 843–7.

Collishaw, S. (2015) Annual research review: Secular trends in child and adolescent mental health. *Journal of Child Psychology and Psychiatry*, 56(3), 370–93

Collishaw, S., Maughan, B., Goodman, R., and Pickles, A. (2004) Time trends in adolescent mental health. *Journal of Child Psychology and Psychiatry*, 45, 1350–62.

Community Care (2013) Social workers unlikely to act quickly on neglect cases. http://www.communitycare.co.uk/articles/27/09/2012/118548/

Connelly, R., Joshi, H. and Rosenberg, R. (2014) Family Structure. In Platt, L. (Ed.), *Millennium Cohort Study Age 11 Survey Initial Findings*. London: Centre for Longitudinal Studies.

Costello, E. J., Erkanli, A., and Angold, A. (2006) Is there an epidemic of child or adolescent depression? *Journal of Child Psychology and Psychiatry*, 47, 1263–71.

Court, J. P., and Kaplan, A. S. (2016) The disjointed historical trajectory of anorexia nervosa before 1970. *Current Psychiatry Reports*, 18(1), 10.

Covid Inquiry (2025) Report of the Children and Young People's Project, 15 September.

Covid Inquiry Public Hearing (2025a) Module 8, Children and Young People, 29 September.

Covid Inquiry Public Hearing (2025b) Module 8, Children and Young People, 2 October.

Crafts, N. (2024) The welfare state and inequality: Were the UK reforms of the 1940s a success? *Oxford Open Economics*, 3, i1191–i1200.

Dabbagh, N., Johnson, S., King, M., and Blizard, R. (2011) Muslim adolescent mental health in the UK: An exploratory cross-sectional school survey. *International Journal of Culture and Mental Health*, 5(3), 202–18. https://doi.org/10.1080/17542863.2011.594246

Davies, D. (2014) *In Plain Sight: The Life and Lies of Jimmy Savile*. London: Quercus.

Davis, A., and King, L. (2018) Gendered perspectives on Men's changing familial roles in postwar England, c.1950–1990. *Gender and History*, 30(1), 70–92.
Davis, J. (2002) The Inner London Education Authority and the William Tyndale Junior School affair, 1974–1976. *Oxford Review of Education*, 28(2–3), 275–98.
Delap, L. (2015) Child welfare, child protection and sexual abuse, 1918–1990. *History and Policy*.
Delap, L. (2018) 'Disgusting details which are best forgotten': Disclosures of child sexual abuse in twentieth century Britain. *Journal of British Studies*, 57, 79–107.
Department for Children, Schools and Families (2009) *The Protection of Children in England: A Progress Report*. London: HMSO.
Department for Education and Skills (2003) *Every Child Matters: Change for Children in Schools*. DES Publications: Department for Education.
Department of Culture, Media and Sport Select Committee (2011) *Taking Part Survey*. London: Hansard.
Department of Education (1978) *Report of the Committee of Enquiry into Special Educational Needs*. London: Department of Education.
Department of Education (2008) *Learning to Learn: A Framework for Early Years Education*. London: Department for Education.
Department of Epidemiology and Public Health: Research Briefing (2024) *Physical Punishment of Children in the UK*. London: UCL.
Department of Health (1976) *Fit for the Future. Report of the Committee on Child Health Services*. London: HMSO.
Department of Health (2024) *Independent Review of Gender Identity Services for Children and Young People*. Chair: Dr. Hilary Cass. London: Department of Health.
Department of Health and Social Security (1980) *Inequalities in Health*. London: Department of Health and Social Security.
Department of Social Services (1974) *Report of the Committee of Inquiry into the Care and Supervision Provided in Relation to Maria Colwell*. London: HMSO.
Department of Transport (2015) *Facts on Child Transport*. London: Department of Transport.
Desposito, F., McSheery, G., and Oleske, J. (2013) Blood product acquired HIV infection in children. *Pediatric Annals*, 17(5), 341–5.
Doll, R. and Hill, A. B. (1950) Smoking and Carcinoma of the Lung. *British Medical Journal*, 2, 739.
Donaldson, G. (2015) *Successful Futures: Independent Review of Curriculum and Assessment Arrangements in Wales*.
Donaldson, M. (1978) *Children's Minds*. London: Fontana.
Donoughue, B. (2003) *The Heat of the Kitchen*. London: Methuen.
Dowrick, C. and Allen, F. (2013) Medicalising and medicating unhappiness. *British Medical Journal*, 347, 14 December.
Eapen, V., and Graham, P. S. (2013) *Where There Is No Child Psychiatrist*. Cambridge: Cambridge University Press.
Economist Intelligence Unit (2019) *Shining Light on Child Sexual Abuse and Exploitation*. London: *The Economist*.
Editorial (1988) Report of the Cleveland enquiry. *British Medical Journal*, 297.
Erikson, E. (1950) *Childhood and Society*. New York: W W. Norton.

Evans, A. (2020) The taboo of love for children in care: Its emergence through the transference relationship and in the system around the child. *Journal of Child Psychotherapy*, 46(1), 72–89.
Evans, L. L., and Harrison, M. R. (2021) Modern fetal surgery – a historical review of the happenings that shaped modern fetal surgery and its practices. *Translational Pediatrics*, 10(5), 1401–17.
Farrington, D. P. (2011) Families and crime. In Wilson, J. Q., and Petersilia, J. (Eds), *Crime and Public Policy* (pp. 130–57). New York: Oxford University Press.
Feeney, P. (2010) *A 1960s Childhood*. Stroud: The History Press.
Fell, M., Davies, A., and Wren, Y. (2022) Current surgical practice for children born with a cleft lip and/or palate in the United Kingdom. *Cleft Palate Craniofacial Journal*, 60, 6. https://doi.org/10.1177/10556656221078151
Flynn, J. R. (1984) The mean IQ of Americans: Massive gains 1932–1978. *Psychological Bulletin*, 95(1), 29–51.
Foley, K., Maile, E., Bottle, A., et al. (2022) Impact of covid-19 on primary care contacts with children and young people aged 0–24 years in England; longitudinal trends study 2015–2020. *British Journal of General Practice*, 720, e464–e471.
Folstein, S., and Rutter, M. (1977) Infantile autism: A genetic study of 21 twin pairs. *Journal of Child Psychology and Psychiatry*, 18(4), 297–321.
Francis-Devine, B. (2024) *Income Inequality in the UK*. London: House of Commons Library.
Freedman, S. (2022) *The Gove Reforms a Decade On*. London: Institute for Government.
Frick, P. J., and Ellis, M. (1999) Callous-Unemotional traits and subtypes of conduct disorder. *Clinical Child Family Psychological Review*, 2, 149–68.
Gallagher, B., Bradford, M., and Pease, K. (2002) *The Sexual Abuse of Children by Strangers: Its Extent, Nature and Victims' Characteristics*. Huddersfield: University of Huddersfield.
Garralda, M., and Bailey, D. (1986) Children with psychiatric disorders in primary care. *Journal of Child Psychology and Psychiatry*, 27(5), 611–24
Garstang, J., and Pease, A. (2018) A United Kingdom perspective. In Duncan, J. and Byard, R. (Eds), *SIDS Sudden Infant and Early Childhood Death: The Past, the Present and the Future*, Chapter 18. Adelaide, AU: University of Adelaide Press.
Gennings, E., Brown, H., Hewlett, D., et al. (2023) Children and young people's perspectives from UK lockdown: Leisure-less experiences. *Leisure Studies*, 42(1), 147–55.
Gibbons, S., McNally, S., and Montebruno, P. (2024) *Pupil Absence and the Pandemic*. London: London School of Economics.
Giedd, J. N., Blumenthal, J., Jeffries, N. O., et al. (1999) Brain development during childhood and adolescence: A longitudinal MRI study. *Nature Neuroscience*, 10, 861–3.
Gopnik, A., Meltzoff, A., and Kuhl, P. (2000) *The Scientist in the Crib: What Early Learning Tells Us About the Mind*. New York: Harper Collins.
Graham, P. (1998) *Cognitive Behaviour Therapy for Children and Families*. Cambridge: Cambridge University Press.
Graham, P. (2004) *The End of Adolescence*. Oxford: University Press.
Graham, P. (2017) *Men and Sex*. Cambridge: Cambridge University Press.

Graham, P. (2019) Against the Stream: The teenage brain is not unique. *British Journal of Psychiatry Bulletin,* 43(6), 287–9.
Graham, P. (2021) *Mary Warnock: Ethics, Education and Public Policy in Post-War Britain.* Cambridge: Open Books Publisher.
Graham, P. (2022) Transgender children and young people: How the evidence can point the way forward. *British Journal of Psychiatry, Bulletin*, 47(2), 98–104.
Graham, P. (2023a) *Susan Isaacs: Freeing the Minds of Children*, 2nd Edition. Cambridge: Open Books Publishers.
Graham, P. (2023b) Transgender children and young people: How the evidence can point the way forward. *British Journal of Psychiatry*, *Bulletin*, 2, 98–104
Graham, P. and Maughan, B. (2025) Child mental health problems and poverty. *British Journal of Psychiatry Bulletin*, 22, 1–3. https://doi.org/10.1192/.
Graham, P., and Meadows, C. (1967) Psychiatric disorder in the children of West Indian immigrants. *Journal of Child Psychology and Psychiatry*, 8, 105–16.
Graham, P., and Midgley, N. (2020) *So Young, so Sad, so Listen*, 3rd Edition. Cambridge: Cambridge University Press.
Graham, P. and Rutter, M. (1968) Organic brain dysfunction and child psychiatric disorder. *British Medical Journal*, 3, 695–700.
Graham, P., and Rutter, M. (1973) Psychiatric disorder in the young adolescent: A follow-Up study. *Proceedings of the Royal Society of Medicine*, 66, 12.
Graham, P., Stevenson, J., and Flynn, D. (1997) A new measure of health-related quality of life for children: Preliminary findings, *Psychology and Health*, 12, 555–65.
Green, F. and Kynaston, D. (2019) *Engines of Privilege: Britain's Private School Problem*. London: Bloomsbury.
Greer, G. (1970) *The Female Eunuch*. London: McGibbon and Kee.
Guardian (2023) Number of adults living with parents in England and Wales rises by 700,000 in a decade. *The Guardian*, 10 May 2023.
Hagan, M. J., Sulik, M. J., and Lieberman, A. F. (2016) Traumatic life events and psychopathology in a high risk, ethnically diverse sample of young children: A person-centered approach. *Journal of Abnormal Child Psychology,* 44(5), 833–44.
Hakim, K. (2004) *Key Issues in Women's Work, Labour Force Survey*. London: Routledge.
Hansen, K. and Joshi, H. (Eds.) (2007) *The Millennium Cohort Study. Second Survey. A User's Guide to Initial Findings*. London: Centre for Longitudinal Studies.
Harris, J. (2024) Education's deepest crisis is being ignored by Westminster – and even harsher cuts are on the way. *Guardian*, 24 May 2024.
Hatzinger, M., Stastny, M., Grützmacher, P., and Sohn, M. (2016) The history of kidney transplantation. *Der Urologe, Ausgabe A, 55*(10), 1353–9.
Hawton, K., Saunders, K., and O'Connor, K. (2012) Self-harm and suicide in adolescents. *Lancet*, 379, 9834.
Henz, U. (2019) Fathers' involvement with their children in the United Kingdom: Recent trends and class differences. *Demographic Research*, 40, 30.
Himmerich, H., Keeler, J., Davies, et al. (2024) The evolving profile of eating disorders and their treatment in a changing and globalised world. *Lancet*, 403(10445), 2671–5.

HM Courts and Tribunals Service (2024) *Guide for Separated Parents and the Family Courts*. London: Ministry of Justice.

Holland, A. J., Sicotta, N., and Treasure, J. (1988) Anorexia nervosa: Evidence for a genetic basis. *Journal of Psychosomatic Research*, 32(6), 561–71.

Holland, J., Hall, N., Yeates, D. et al. (2016) Trends in hospital admission rates for anorexia nervosa in Oxford (1968–2011) and England (1990–2011): Database studies. *Journal of the Royal Society of Medicine,* 109(2), 59–66.

Home Office (1957) *The Wolfenden Report: Report of the Committee on Homosexual Offenses and Prostitution*. London: HMSO.

Home Office (2015) *Children's Views, Wishes, and Feelings Standard, Children's Homes (England) Regulations*. London: Home Office.

Home Office (2022) *Independent Inquiry into Child Sexual Abuse in Residential Settings* (Chair: Professor Alexis Jay). London: Home Office.

Home Office (2025) *National Audit on Group-Based Child Sexual Exploitation and Abuse*. London: Baroness Casey of Blackstock.

Howes S., Monk-Winstanley, Sefton, R. T., et al. (2020) *Poverty in the Pandemic: The Impact of Coronavirus on Low Income Families and Children*. London: Child Poverty Action Group.

Huttenlocher, P. R. (1979) Synaptic density in human frontal cortex – developmental changes and effects of aging. *Brain Research*, 163(2), 195–205.

Hyman, P. (2020) The way the school system creates student stress and disregards the need for student enjoyment. *Guardian*, 5 July.

Independent Inquiry into Child Sexual Abuse (2021) *Truth Project. Experiences Shared*. London: Home Office.

Isaacs, S. (1930) *Intellectual Growth in Young Children*. London: Routledge and Kegan Paul.

Isaacs, S. (1946) *Social Development in Young Children*. London: George Routledge and Sons.

Jack, R. H., Joseph, R. M., Coupland, C. A. C., et al. (2023) Impact of the COVID-19 pandemic on incidence of tics in children and young people: a population-based cohort study. *EClinicalMedicine*, 57, 101857. https://doi.org/10.1016/j.eclinm.2023.101857.

Jackson, L. (2015) Child sexual abuse in England and Wales: Prosecution and prevalence 1918–1970. *History and Policy*, 18 June 2015.

Jackson, R. H. (1995) The history of childhood accident and injury prevention in England: Background to the foundation of the Child Accident Prevention Trust. *Injury Prevention,* 1(1), 4–6.

Jackson, R. and Nesbitt, E. (1993) *Hindu Children in Britain*. Stoke-on-Trent: Trentham Books.

Jay, A. (2014) *Independent Inquiry into Child Sexual Exploitation in Rotherham 1997–2013*. London: Home Office.

Johnson, A. (2013) *This Boy*. London: Bantam Press.

Joseph Rowntree Foundation (2024) *Joseph Rowntree: The Essential Guide to Understanding Poverty*. York: Joseph Rowntree Foundation.

Joyce, R. and Ziliaki, J. (2019) Relative poverty in Great Britain and the United States 1979–2017. *Fiscal Studies*, 40(4), 485–518.

Kempe, C. H. (1978) Sexual abuse, another hidden pediatric problem. *Pediatrics*, 62(3), 382–9.

Kim, J. H., and Scialli, A. R. (2011) Thalidomide: The tragedy of birth defects and the effective treatment of disease. *Toxicological Sciences*, 122(1), 1–6.
King's College, London (2023) *World Values Survey. Parenting Priorities: International Attitudes Towards Raising Children*. London: The Policy Institute, King's College.
Kingdon, D. (2020) Why hasn't neuroscience delivered for psychiatry? *British Journal of Psychiatry Bulletin*, 44(3), 107–9.
Klaus, M. H., and Kennell, J. H. (1978) *Maternal-Infant Bonding*. St. Louis: C. V. Mosby.
Klein, M. (1998) *Love, Guilt and Reparation*. London: Vintage Classics.
Kynaston, D. (2009) *Family Britain 1951–1957*. London: Bloomsbury.
Laming, H. (2003) *The Victoria Climbie Inquiry: Report of an Inquiry by Lord Laming*. London: House of Commons Health Committee.
Lang, S., Loving, S., McCarthy, N., et al. (2019) Two centuries of immunisation in the UK, Part II. *Archives of Disease in Childhood*, 105, 216–22.
Law Commission (1988) *Review of Child Care Law: Guardianship and Custody*. London: Law Commission.
Lawton, D. (1968) *Social Class, Language and Education*. London: Routledge.
Leach, P. (1977) *Your Baby and Child: The Essential Guide for Every Parent*, 3rd Edition. London: Penguin Books.
Lee, E., Sheldon, S., and Macvarish, J. (2018) The 1967 Abortion Act 1967 fifty years on: Abortion, medical authority and the law revisited. *Social Science and Medicine*, 212, 26–32.
Lenton, S. (2016) *History of the British Association for Community Child Health (BACCH) Formerly the Community Paediatric Group (CPG)*. London: British Association for Community Child Health.
Levy, F., Hay, D., McStephen, M. et al. (1997) Attention-Deficit Hyperactivity Disorder: A category or a continuum? Genetic analysis of a large-scale twin study. *Journal of the American Academy of Child & Adolescent Psychiatry*, 36(6), 737–44.
London Borough of Brent (1985) *A Child in Trust: The Report of the Panel of Enquiry into the Circumstances Surrounding the Death of Jasmine Beckford*. London: London Borough of Brent.
Lotter, V. (1966) Epidemiology of autistic conditions in young people. I Prevalence. *Social Psychiatry*, 1, 124–37.
Major, L. E., Eyles, A., Lillywhite, E., and Machin, S. (2024) *A Generation at Risk: Rebalancing Education in the Post-pandemic Era*. London: Nuffield Foundation.
Marinho, V. C. C., Higgins, J., Logan, S., et al. (2025) Fluoride toothpastes for preventing dental caries in children and adolescents. *Cochrane Database of Systematic Reviews*, Issue 1. Art. No.: CD002278.
Marmot, M. (2010) *Fair Society, Healthy Lives*. London: The Health Foundation.
Mason, W. (2017) *Identifying and Understanding Inequalities in Child Welfare Intervention Rates: Comparative Studies in Four UK countries*. London: Nuffield Foundation.
Maughan, B., Collishaw, S., Meltzer, H., and Goodman, R. (2008) Recent trends in UK child and adolescent mental health. *Social Psychiatry and Psychiatric Epidemiology*, 43(4), 305–10.
McAleavy, T. and Elwick, A. (2016) *School Improvement in London: A Global Perspective*. London: Education Development Trust.

McAndrew, F., Thompson, J., Fellows, et al. (2010) *Infant Feeding Survey*. London: Information Centre for Health and Social Care.

McSmith, A. (2011) *No Such Thing as Society*. London: Constable.

Mercer, C. H., Tanton, C., Prah, P., et al. (2013) Changes in sexual attitudes and lifestyles in Britain through the life course and over time: Findings from the National Surveys of Sexual Attitudes and Lifestyles (NATSAL). *Lancet*, 382(9907), 1781–94.

Migration Observatory (2021) *Migrants in the UK*. Oxford: University of Oxford.

Migration Observatory (2022) *Children of Migrants in the UK*. Oxford: University of Oxford.

Miller, H., and Pomson, A. (2024) *Jewish Lives and Jewish Education in the UK*. Chicago: Open Books.

Mills, J. (1968) Child Guidance Clinics: (A review of their development, present structure and future trends). *The Journal of the Royal Institute of Public Health and Hygiene*, 31(2), 38–52.

Ministry of Education (1955) *The Underwood Report. Report of the Committee on Maladjusted Children*. London: HMSO.

Ministry of Health (1959) *Welfare of Sick Children in Hospital: The Platt Report*. London: Ministry of Health.

Montessori, M. (1912) *The Montessori Method*. London: Heinemann.

Mortimore, P. (2013) *Education Under Siege*. London: Policy Press.

Mrazek, P., Lynch, and Bentovim, M. (1983) Sexual abuse of children in the United Kingdom. *Child Abuse & Neglect*, 7(2), 147–53.

Mullan, K. (2022) *A Child's Day*. Bristol: Bristol University Press.

Mullen, J. (2005) History of water fluoridation. *British Dental Journal*, 199, 1–4.

Murray, J. J., Vernazza, C. R., and Holmes, R. D. (2015) Forty years of national surveys: An overview of children's dental health from 1973–2013. *British Dental Journal*, 219(6), 281–5.

National Food Strategy (2021) *Report of an Independent Review*. Chair: Henry Dimbleby.

Newell, P. (1989) *Children Are People Too*. London: Bedford Square Press.

Newlove-Delgado, T. and Creswell, C. (2025) *Impact of the Pandemic on the Mental Health of Children and Young People*. Expert Report for the UK Covid 19 Inquiry. London.

Newlove-Delgado, T., McManus, S., Sadler, K., et al. (2021) Mental health of children and young people. Child mental health in England before and during the COVID-19 lockdown. *Lancet Psychiatry*, 8(5), 353–4.

Newson, J., and Newson, E. (1963) *Patterns of Infant Care in an Urban Community*. London: Penguin Press.

NHS Digital (2018) *Mental Health of Children and Young People in England*. London: NHS Digital.

NHS England (2024a) *Integrated Screening Outcomes Surveillance Service (ISOSS) Report*. London: NHS England.

NHS England (Digital) (2024b) *Smoking, Drinking and Drug Use Among Young People in England, 2023*. London: NHS England.

NSPCC Learning (2024) *Neglect*. London: Statistics Briefing.

Oakley, G. (2019) The scientific basis for eliminating folic acid-preventable spina bifida: A modern miracle from epidemiology, *Annals of Epidemiology, 19*(4), 226–30.

Office of National Statistics (2021) *Child and Infant Mortality in England and Wales*. London: Office of National Statistics.

Office for National Statistics (2022a) *2021 Census*. London: Office for National Statistics.

Office of National Statistics (2022b) *Mortality in England and Wales: Past and Projected Trends in Average Lifespan*. London: Office of National Statistics.

Olweus, D. (1993) *Bullying at School: What We Know and What We Can Do*. Oxford: Blackwell.

Pape, H., Rossow, I., and Brunborg, G. (2019) Adolescents drink less: How, who and why? A review of the recent research literature. *Drug and Alcohol Review*, 37(51), 598.

Parton, N. (1996) The new politics of child protection. In Pilcher, J., and Wagg, S. (Eds), *Thatcher's Children* (pp. 43–60). London: Falmer Press.

Payne, S. (2021) *Broken Heartlands: A Journey Through Labour's Lost England*. London: Macmillan.

Piotrowski, C. C. (2020) Chapter 15: ACEs and trauma-informed care. In *Adverse Childhood Experiences* (pp. 307–28). New York: Academic Press.

Pitts, J. (2002) Youth crime in England and Wales. In Bateman, T., and Pitts, J. (Eds), *Youth Justice. Lyme Regis* (pp. 12–18). Russell House Publishing.

Platt, L. (2024) What has happened to child poverty in the UK in the last 30 years? *Inequality and Poverty. Economics Observatory*, 9 July 2024.

Platts-Mills, T. (2015) The allergy epidemics: 1870–2010. *Journal of Allergy and Clinical Immunology*, 136(1), 3–13.

Plumb, J. L., Bush, K. A., and Kersevich, S. E. (2016) Trauma-sensitive schools: An evidence based approach. *School Social Work Journal*, 40(2), 37–60.

Prince, J., and Gibbens, T. (1963) *Child Victims of Sexual Offences*. London: Institute for the Study and Treatment of Delinquency.

Public Health England (2023) *National Dental Epidemiology Programme, Report*. London: Public Health, England.

Purba, A., Henderson, Baxter, A., et al. (2025) The relationship between time spent on social media and adolescent cigarette, e-cigarette, and dual use: A longitudinal analysis of the UK millennium cohort study. *Nicotine & Tobacco Research*, 27(4), 693–704.

Radford, L., Corral, S., Bradley, C., et al. (2011) The prevalence and impact of child maltreatment and other types of victimization in the UK: Findings from a population survey of caregivers, children and young people and young adults. *Child Abuse & Neglect*, 37(10), 2013, 801–13.

Raine, P., and Diplock, G. (2001) Socio-economic analysis of UK home accidents. *Injury Control and Safety Promotion*, 8(2), 163–7.

Richman, N., Stevenson, J., and Graham, P. (1982) *Preschool to School: A Behavioural Study*. London: Academic Press.

Rodway, C., Tham, S. G., Richards, N., et al. (2023) Online harms? Suicide related online experience: A UK-wide case series study of young people who die by suicide. *Psychological Medicine*, 53, 4434–45.

Rolph, C., and Robertson, G. (1990) *The Trial of Lady Chatterley: Regina v Penguin Books, The Transcript of the Trial*. London: Penguin Books.

Rose, S., Lord, P., Ager, R., et al. (2024) *Impact of School Closures in Key Stage 1 on Attainment and Social Skills of Pupils in Year 4 and Year 5 in Academic Year 2023/2024*. National Foundation for Educational Research.

Royal College of Nursing (2023) *Once Upon a Time … A History of Children and Young People's Nursing*. London: Royal College of Nursing.
Royal College of Paediatrics and Child Health (2024) *Paediatric Sub-specialties*. London: Royal College of Paediatrics and Child Health.
Russell, G., et al. (1987) An evaluation of family therapy in anorexia nervosa and bulimia nervosa. *Archives of General Psychiatry*, 44, 1047–56.
Rutter, M. (1972) *Maternal Deprivation Reassessed*. London: Penguin.
Rutter, M., Cox, A., Tupling, C, Berger, M., and Yule, W. (1975) Attainment and adjustment in two geographical areas. 1. Prevalence of Psychiatric Disorders. *British Journal of Psychiatry*, 126, 493–509.
Rutter, M., Graham, P., and Yule, W. (1970) *A Neuropsychiatric Study in Childhood*. Clinics in developmental medicine, Nos. 35/36. Heinemanns: SIMP.
Rutter, M., Graham, P., Chadwick, O., et al. (1976) Adolescent turmoil: Fact or fiction? *Journal of Child Psychology And Psychiatry*, 17, 35–56.
Rutter, M., Maughan, B., Mortimore, P., and Ouston, J. (1979) *Fifteen Thousand Hours*. London: Open Books.
Rutter, M., Tizard, J., and Whitmore, K. (1970) *Education, Health and Behaviour*. London: Longmans.
Rutter, M., Yule, W., Berger, M. et al. (1974) Children of West Indian Immigrants-1. Rates of behavioural deviance and of psychiatric disorder. *Journal of Child Psychology and Psychiatry*, 15(4), 241–62.
Rutter, M., Yule, B., Quinton, D., Rowlands, O., Yule, W., and Berger, M. (1976). Attainment and adjustment in two geographical areas: III – Some factors accounting for area differences. *The British Journal of Psychiatry*, 1975, 120(6), 520–33.
Saigal, S., and Doyle, L. (2008) An overview of mortality and sequelae of preterm birth from infancy to adulthood. *Lancet*, 9608, 261–8.
Sayal, K., Prasad, V., Daley, D., et al. (2018) ADHD in children and young people: Prevalence, care pathways, and service provision. *Lancet Psychiatry, 5*(2), 175–186.
Shaw, K. (2022) Insulin: A tremendous transformation in diabetes care from the 1970s to the millennium. *British Journal of Diabetes*, 22, Supplement 1.
Shoard, M. (1980) *The Theft of the Countryside*. London: Temple Smith.
Shroff, R., Rees, L., Trompeter, R., et al. (2006) Long-term outcome of chronic dialysis in children. *Pediatric Nephrology*, 21, 257–64.
Siberry, G. K. (2014) Preventing and managing HIV infection in infants, children, and adolescents in the United States. *Pediatrics in Review*, 35(7), 268–86. https://doi.org/10.1542/pir.35-7-268.
Sideropoulos, V., Dukes, D., Hanley, M., et al. (2022) The impact of COVID-19 on anxiety and worries for families of individuals with special education needs and disabilities in the UK. *Journal of Autism and Developmental Disorders, 52*, 2656–69.
Singh, A., Shah, N., Mbeledogu, C., et al. (2021) Child wellbeing in the United Kingdom following the COVID-19 lockdowns. *Paediatrics and Child Health*, 31(12), 445–8.
Spencer, C. (2024) *A Very Private School*. London: William Collins.
Spitz, L. (2012) The history of paediatric surgery in the United Kingdom and the influence of National Health Service on its development. *Journal of Pediatric Surgery*, 47, 29–35.

Spock, B. (1960) *Baby and Child Care*, 9th Edition. London: Bodley Head.

Stamatakis, E. et al. (2005) Overweight and obesity trends from 1974 to 2003 in English children: What is the role of socioeconomic factors? *Archives of Disease in Childhood*, 90(10), 999–1004.

Stamatakis, E., et al. (2010) Time trends in childhood and adolescent obesity in England from 1995 to 2007 and projections of prevalence to 2015. *Journal of Epidemiology and Community Health*, 64(2), 167.

Stevenson, J. and Graham, P. (1988) Behavioural deviance in 13 year old twins: Genetic influences on items, scales and clusters. *Journal of the American Academy of Child and Adolescent Psychiatry*, 27, 791–7.

Stewart, J. (2013) *Child Guidance in Britain, 1918–1955*. London: Routledge.

Stewart-Brown, S., and Schrader-McMillan (2019) *Home and Community-Based Parenting Support Programmes and Interventions. Report of the Workpackage Two of the DataPrev Project*. Coventry: Warwick Medical School.

Tahir, I. (2022) *The UK Education System Preserves Inequality*. London: Institute of Fiscal Studies.

Tanner, J. M., and Whitehouse, R. H. (1967) Growth response of 26 children with short stature given human growth hormone. *British Medical Journal*, 2(5544), 69–75.

Thane, P. (2011) *The History of Early Years Childcare*. Based on a presentation at the Department for Education on 6 October 2011.

Thane, P., and Davidson, R. (2016) *The Child Poverty Action Group, 1965–2015*. London: CPAG.

Timmins, N. (1995) *The Five Wants: A Biography of the Welfare State*. London: Fontana Press.

Tizard, B., and Hodges, J. (1978) The effect of early institutional rearing on the development of eight year old children. *Journal of Child Psychology and Psychiatry*, 19(2), 99–118.

Tizard, B., and Hughes, M. (1984) *Young Children Learning*. London, Fontana.

Tizard, B., and Phoenix, A. (1989) Black identity and transracial adoption. *Journal of Ethnic and Migration Studies*, 15(3), 427–37. https://doi.org/10.1080/1369183X.1989.9976130

Towers, E., Gewirtz, S., Maguire, M. et al. (2022) A profession in crisis? Teachers' responses to England's high-stakes accountability reforms in secondary education. *Teaching and Teacher Education*, 117, 103778.

Trafford, A., Carr, M., Ashcroft, D., et al. (2023) Temporal trends in eating disorder and self-harm incidence rates among adolescents and young adults in the UK in the 2 years since onset of the COVID-19 pandemic: A population-based study. *Lancet Child and Adolescent Health*, 7, 544–54.

Trussell Trust (2024) *The Use of Food Banks*. London: Trussell Trust.

UNICEF (2014) *Why Businesses Should Invest in Digital Child Safety*. New York: UNICEF.

United Nations (1945) *Declaration of Human Rights*. New York: United Nations.

van der Horst, F. C. P., and van der Veer, R. (2009) Changing attitudes towards the care of children in hospital: A new assessment of the influence of the work of Bowlby and Robertson in the UK, 1940–1970. *Attachment & Human Development*, 11(2), 119–42.

Vernon, D., Foley, J., Sipowicz, R., and Schulman, J. (1965) *The Psychological Response of Children to Hospitalization and Illness*. Springfield, IL: Charles C. Thomas.

Viagni, G. (2024) *Parental Childcare and Family Time*. The Future of Families Policy Conference.

Wade, E., Stiebahl, S., and Wong, H. (2024) *Research Briefing, UK Disability Statistics: Prevalence and Life Experiences*. House of Commons Library.

Waite, P., Pearcey, S., Shum, A., et al. (2021) How did the mental health symptoms of children and adolescents change over early lockdown during the COVID-19 pandemic in the UK? *JCPP Advances*, e12009. https://doi.org/10.1111/jcv2.12009.

Wakefield, A. J., Murch, S. H., Anthony, A., et al. (1998) Ileal lymphoid nodular hyperplasia, non-specific colitis, and pervasive developmental disorder in children [retracted]. *Lancet*, 351, 637–41.

Ward, C. (1988) *The Child in the Country*. London: Robert Hale.

Warnock, M. (1994) *Imagination and Time*. Oxford: Blackwell.

Warnock, M. (2005) *Special Educational Needs: A New Look*. London: Philosophy of Education Society of Great Britain, Impact Series. No. 11.

Watson, J. B. (1928) *The Psychological Care of Infant and Child*. New York: W. W. Norton.

Webb, S. (2012) *A 1960s East End Childhood*. Stroud: The History Press.

Weidmann, B., Allen, R., Bibby, D., et al. (2022) *Covid-19 Disruptions Attainment Gaps and Primary School Responses*. London: Education Endowment Foundation.

Weidmann, B., Allen, R., Bibby, D., et al. (2023–2024) *Covid-19 Disruptions Attainment Gaps and Primary School Responses*. London: Education Endowment Foundation.

Wellings, K., and Mills, A. (1984) Contraceptive trends, *The British Medical Journal (Clinical Research Edition)*, 289, 939–40.

Wild, N. J. (1986) Child sexual abuse of children in Leeds. *British Medical Journal*, 292, 1113.

Williams, C. (2021) *Courage to Be: Organised Gay Youth in England, 1967–1990*. London: The Book Guild.

Wilson, D. S. (2006) A new look at the affluent worker: The good working mother in post-war Britain. *Twentieth Century British History*, 17(2), 206–29.

Wing L. (1981) Asperger's Syndrome: A clinical account. *Psychological Medicine*, 11(1), 115–29.

Wolff, S. (1969) *Children Under Stress: Understanding the Emotionally Disturbed Child*. London: Penguin Books.

Woodrow, N., and Moore, K. (2021) The liminal leisure of disadvantaged young people in the UK before and during the COVID-19 pandemic. *Journal of Applied Youth Studies*, 4, 475–91.

World Health Organisation (1977) *International Classification of Diseases, 10th Edition*. Geneva: WHO.

World Health Organisation (2019) *International Classification of Diseases, 11th Edition*. Geneva: WHO.

INDEX